SHAPE IT! 1

COMBO

STUDENT'S BOOK

WITH DIGITAL PACK

Claire Thacker

with Melissa Wilson and Daniel Vincent

CAMBRIDGE
UNIVERSITY PRESS

CONTENTS

STARTER

WELCOME!

VOCABULARY

Months

S.01 **1 Put the months in the correct order. Then listen, check, and repeat.**

April	☐	January	1	May	☐
August	☐	June	☐	November	☐
December	☐	July	☐	October	☐
February	☐	March	☐	September	☐

Get It Right!

In English, months and days of the week start with a capital letter. Is it the same in your language?

2 Complete the sentences. Compare with a partner.

1 This month is ______________.
2 My birthday is in ______________.

Cardinal and Ordinal Numbers

3 Write the numbers.

1 the number of letters in my name ______
2 the date today ______
3 the number of people in my house ______

LEARN TO LEARN

Learning Numbers Together

Learn and practice cardinal and ordinal numbers together.

23 – twenty-three, 23rd – twenty-third

S.02 **4 Listen. Circle the numbers you hear.**

1 a 17 b (70)
2 a 13 b 30
3 a 12th b 20th
4 a 51st b 61st

Use It!

5 Take turns saying a cardinal number. Your partner says the ordinal number.

S.03 **6 Listen and complete the sentences with the date.**

1 Laura's birthday is July 24.
2 Omar's birthday is ______________.
3 Bella's birthday is ______________.
4 Nico's birthday is ______________.

7 Complete the sentences. Then tell your partner.

1 My birthday is ______________.
2 Today is ______________.

Colors

S.04 **8 Add the colors and write the new color. Listen, check, and repeat.**

1 purple 2 ______ 3 ______ 4 ______

S.05 **9 Do the quiz with a partner. Circle the correct answer. Then listen and check.**

THE GREAT BIG NUMBER QUIZ

1 The number of countries in the world is … .
a 195 b 100 c 95

2 … million people speak English as their first language.
a 3 b 36 c 360

3 There are … seconds in a year.
a 36,536,000 b 31,536,000 c 35,636,000

4 … million people have the same birthday as you.
a 19 b 6 c 10

READING

An Online Profile

1 **Look at the photos. Where do you think Diana and Thiago are from? Read the profiles quickly and check your answers.**

2 **Read the profiles again. Are the sentences *T* (true) or *F* (false)?** S.06

1. Diana is from Granada. T
2. Miranda is Turkish. ___
3. Diana's favorite place is her bedroom. ___
4. Thiago is from São Paulo. ___
5. Thiago's favorite color is blue. ___
6. Thiago is good at soccer. ___

3 **Find nationalities in the profiles to match the countries.**

1. Spain Spanish
2. Mexico ___
3. Turkey ___
4. Brazil ___
5. the U.S.A. ___

Welcome to My Life!

Home | Profile | Photos | Events

Hi! My name's Diana.
I'm from Granada in Spain.
I'm 13 years old.

In this photo, I'm with Miranda and Suki. They're my best friends. They aren't Spanish. Miranda's Mexican and Suki's Turkish.

My birthday is March 9. When is your birthday?

My favorite color is blue.

My favorite place is my bedroom. Guess what color it is!

My dream is to be a singer like Rihanna. She's incredible! 🙂 Are you a good singer?

What's your name? How old are you? Let me know! 🙂

4 **Complete the chart with the countries and nationalities.**

Flag	Country	Nationality
	Australia	1 Australian
	2 ___	Canadian
	China	3 ___
	4 ___	German
	Poland	5 ___
	the UK	6 ___

Voice It!

5 **Complete the sentences with your ideas. Compare with a partner.**

1. Diana's bedroom is ___ because ___.
2. Thiago's favorite colors are yellow and green because ___.

Home | Profile | Photos | Events

Hello! My name's Thiago. I'm from Brasília. It's the capital of Brazil. I'm Brazilian. I'm 14. I'm with Bruno and Victor in this photo. They're my best friends. We're in the same grade in an American school, but I'm not in their class.

My favorite colors are yellow and green. Can you guess why?

My favorite number is 10.

My dream is to be a soccer player like Neymar Júnior. He's amazing! I'm good, too! 🙂 Are you a soccer fan?

What's your name? Where are you from? Write soon!

GRAMMAR IN ACTION

Subject Pronouns and Possessive Adjectives

Watch video S.1
Where is Isabella from?
What is Martine's dream?

Subject Pronouns	Possessive Adjectives	Subject Pronouns	Possessive Adjectives
I	1 ______	it	**its**
you	2 ______	we	**our**
he	**his**	they	**their**
she	**her**		

1 **Complete the examples in the chart above. Use the profiles on page 5 to help you.**

2 **Circle the correct words.**

1. Alana is (my) / *I* best friend.
2. *Our* / *We* aren't from Brazil. *Our* / *We* 're from Spain.
3. *Her* / *She* name is Luna. *Her* / *She* 's 13.
4. *Their* / *They* names are Kit and Bella. *Their* / *They* aren't British.

Verb *To Be*

Affirmative	I[1]'m (**am**) from Granada. She[2] ______ (**is**) incredible! He[3] ______ (**is**) amazing! We[4] ______ (**are**) in the same grade. They[5] ______ (**are**) my best friends.
Negative	They [6] ______ Spanish. Miranda **isn't** Turkish. I[7] ______ in their class.
Questions and short answers	How old [8] ______ you? [9] ______ you a soccer fan? Yes, I **am**. / No, I'**m not**. **Is** Thiago 12? Yes, he **is**. / No, he **isn't**. **Are** Bruno and Victor Brazilian? Yes, they **are**. / No, they **aren't**.

3 **Complete the examples in the chart above. Use the profiles on page 5 to help you.**

S.07 **4** **Complete the profile with the correct form of *to be*. Guess the person. Listen and check.**

His birthday [1] is (✓) March 1.
He [2] ______ (✗) American.
He [3] ______ (✓) Canadian. My favorite songs [4] ______ (✓) *Boyfriend* and *Sorry*.
[5] ______ (?) he your favorite singer?
______

5 **Write questions with the verb *to be*.**

1. you / 12? Are you 12?
2. you / from / Quito? ______
3. your best friends / in your class? ______
4. your teacher / American? ______
5. today / June 19? ______

Use It!

6 **Ask and answer the questions in Exercise 5.**

Question Words

7 **Match the question words with their functions.**

1 What — d
2 Where
3 When
4 How old
5 Who

a age
b people
c places
d things
e time and dates

8 **Complete the questions with *is* or *are*.**

1. Where are you from?
2. How old ______ you?
3. When ______ your birthday?
4. Who ______ your best friend?
5. What ______ your favorite color?

Use It!

9 **Ask and answer the questions in Exercise 8.**

VOCABULARY AND LISTENING

Classroom Objects

S.08 **1** **Match the words in the box with the objects 1–12 in the picture. Listen, check, and repeat.**

board	1	desk		notebook		poster	
calculator		dictionary		pen		ruler	
chair		door		pencil		window	

LEARN TO LEARN

Recording Vocabulary

Divide the pages in your notebook to record new vocabulary. Write a translation and draw a picture to help you remember the words.

Classroom Objects	Translation	Picture

2 **Organize your notebook and write new vocabulary from this unit.**

3 **Test a partner. Say a word in your language. Your partner says it in English. Can you remember all the new words?**

A Talk

S.09 **4** **Listen and circle the correct answer.**

Stefan is …

a a teacher. b a student.

S.09 **5** **Listen again. Circle the correct answer.**

1 Stefan is in *seventh* / *tenth* grade.

2 Stefan *is* / *isn't* a friendly person.

3 It's the students' *first* / *second* day at the school.

4 At the end, Luiza *is* / *isn't* in the classroom.

Use It!

6 **Answer the questions with a partner.**

1 What classroom objects are on your desk?

2 What is in your bag?

GRAMMAR IN ACTION

Whose + Possessive Pronouns

Watch video S.2
What color is Mia's pen?
What classroom objects are there?

Whose ... ?	**Possessive Pronouns**
Whose dictionary is this?	It's **mine**.
	It's **yours**.
	It's **his**.
	It's **hers**.
	It's **ours**.
	It's **theirs**.

This, That, These, Those	
 **This** is my pencil.	 **That** is my calculator.
 **These** are my notebooks.	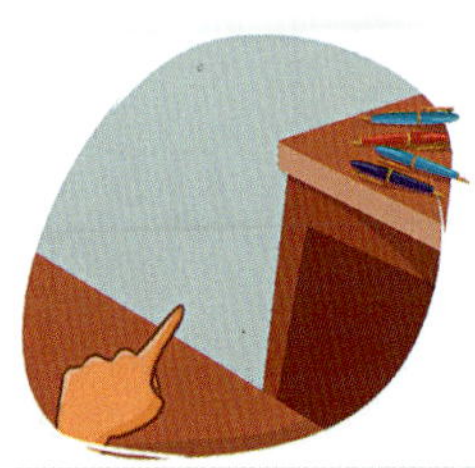 **Those** are my pens.

1 Look at the chart above. Complete the second sentence with a possessive pronoun.

1 It's your pencil. It's yours .
2 That's his notebook. That's ________ .
3 This desk is my desk. This desk is ________ .
4 Those are our chairs. Those are ________ .
5 Is this your calculator? Is this ________ ?
6 Are these her pens? Are these ________ ?

S.10 **2 Write the questions. Then listen and match the questions with the answers.**

1 book / whose / this / is
Whose book is this? [b]
2 posters / those / are / whose
________ [ ]
3 are / pens / whose / these
________ [ ]
4 that / ruler / whose / is
________ [ ]

a It's his.
b It's mine.
c They're hers.
d They're ours.

Imperatives

Close the door! [ ]	Don't be late! [ ]

3 Look at the chart above. Which sentence is positive (✓)?

S.11 **4 Complete the instructions with the verbs in the box. Listen and check.**

don't forget ~~don't write~~ listen to use write

1 Don't write on the desks!
2 ________ new words in your notebook!
3 ________ to bring your pen!
4 ________ your teacher!
5 ________ a dictionary!

S.12 **5 Listen and follow the instructions.**

Use It!

6 Take turns giving your partner instructions. Use classroom objects or your own ideas.

Pick up your pen!

Write your birthday!

WRITING
An Informal Letter

1 Read Gloria's letter. Who is Mrs. Weston?

1022 Conrad Street
San Francisco, CA 94131
September 16

Dear Mrs. Weston,

1 ☐ My name is Gloria Rodriguez **and** I'm 13. I'm from Ottowa in Canada. I'm Canadian.

2 ☐ I'm a student at the International School. It's my first day in this school. I'm happy! I'm in class 7A. That's your class!

3 ☐ The students here are from all over the world. My best friends are Marco **and** Leona. They're in my class. They aren't Canadian like me. Marco is Italian **and** Leona is German.

4 ☐ My favorite color is pink **and** my favorite place is my English classroom. My dream is to be a teacher – just like you!

Best wishes,

Gloria

2 Match topics a–d with paragraphs 1–4.

a information about your favorite things
b information about you
c information about your friends
d information about your school

3 Read Gloria's letter again. Which information isn't in the letter? ______

age birthday country dream
favorite color and place name
names of her best friends nationality

4 Look at the *Useful Language* box and complete the information with words from Gloria's letter.

Useful Language

To start: [1] ______ + *Mr.* (man) or *Mrs./Ms.* (woman) + person's surname
To end: *Sincerely,* or [2] ______
To join two ideas in one sentence: [3] ______

5 Join the sentences with *and*.

1 My name is Hugo. I'm 13 years old.
______
2 I'm Japanese. I'm from Tokyo.
______
3 My favorite number is 15. My favorite color is red.
______

PLAN

6 Write an informal letter. Decide what information to include in each paragraph. Use the information in Exercise 2 to help you.

WRITE

7 Write your letter. Remember to include four paragraphs, the address and date, and expressions from the *Useful Language* box.

CHECK

8 Do you …

- introduce yourself and give your name, age, and nationality?
- give information about your friends and your favorite things?
- use *and* to join ideas?

1 What is your family like?

LEARNING OUTCOMES

I can ...

- understand texts about families and a festival
- call a friend
- write an email
- understand how to use *to have*; possessive *'s*; questions with *How many ... ?*
- talk about families and describe people
- draw pictures to remember words and increase vocabulary; organize my notebook

Start It!

1 Look at the photo. What kind of family is this?

2 Before you watch, how are families different?

3 Where are Laura and Andrés from? Watch and check.

4 Which is your favorite family? Why?

Watch video 1.1

p13

Grammar in Action 1.2

p15

Grammar in Action 1.3

p16

Everyday English 1.4

p18

Globetrotters 1.5

VOCABULARY
Family Members

1.01 **1 Look at Beth's family tree. Match nine words in the box with the people a–i. Then listen and check.**

aunt	☐	grandma	☐	niece	☐
brother	☐	grandpa	a	sister	☐
cousin	☐	grandson	☐	son	☐
dad	☐	husband	☐	uncle	☐
daughter	☐	mom	☐	wife	☐
granddaughter	☐	nephew	☐		

1.02 **2 Look again at Beth's family tree. Complete the answers with words from Exercise 1. Then listen, check, and repeat.**

1. Andy + Sara = husband and *wife*
2. Lizzie + Olga = mom and ______
3. Amanda + Theo = grandma and ______
4. Ryan + Beth = ______ and ______
5. Lizzie + Theo = ______ and ______
6. Theo + Beth = ______ and ______

3 Complete the lists with the family words in Exercise 1.

Male: *brother* ______ ______ ______
______ ______ ______ ______

Female: ______ ______ ______ ______
______ ______ ______ ______

Both male and female: ______

LEARN TO LEARN

Making Connections (1)

Think of examples from your own life to help you remember new words.

4 Draw your family tree in your notebook. Use Beth's family tree to help you.

5 Don't show your family tree. Take turns saying the name of a person in your family. Can your partner guess who they are?

Carlos.

Is he your brother?

No, he isn't. Try again.

Use It!

6 Imagine you are a famous person. Write sentences to decribe your family. Tell your partner. Can they guess who you are?

I'm British. My brother is Harry. My wife is Kate. My children are George, Charlotte, and Louis.

Are you Prince William?

Yes, I am.

Explore It!

Guess the correct answer.

A Canadian woman, Vera Sommerfeld, is a great-great-great grandma. There are … generations in her family.

a two b four c six

Find another interesting family fact. Then write a question for your partner to answer.

READING
A Webpage

1 Tell your partner two things you know about the circus and two things you want to know about the topic.

1.03 2 Read the webpage. What is it about?

1 a visit to the circus
2 life in a circus family
3 a circus school

MEET THE *Flying* CORTES FAMILY

Ysabella Wallenda-Cortes isn't from a typical family. She's from a circus family. Ysabella is a trapeze artist like her parents. Her parents' names are Robinson and Alida. She has two brothers, Lukas and Tomas, but she doesn't have any sisters.

Ysabella's uncle and aunt are in the circus, too. Her uncle Alex is her dad's brother and he's an acrobat and a trapeze artist. Her aunt Aurelia is her mom's sister and she's one of Ysabella's teachers. Her grandparents, Olinka and Tino, are also part of the circus. Olinka isn't a performer anymore. Her job is to help the rest of the family. Tino is in his 60s, but he's still a tightrope walker. Lukas and Tomas don't have jobs in the circus ... yet!

Where is home? They have two homes – one in the U.S.A. and a mobile home. The mobile home is also a school during tours. Imagine a school on wheels!

3 Find words in the webpage to match the photos.

a *trapeze artist*

b ____________

c ____________

d ____________

4 Read the webpage again. Complete the sentences with the correct family words.

Ysabella's ...

1 *parents* are trapeze artists.
2 ____________ is an acrobat and a trapeze artist.
3 ____________ is a circus teacher.
4 ____________ aren't circus performers yet.

5 Correct the sentences.

1 Ysabella is a tightrope walker.
Ysabella isn't a tightrope walker.
She's a trapeze artist.
2 Robinson and Alida are brother and sister.
____
____
3 Lukas and Tomas are cousins.
____
____
4 Alida and Aurelia are friends.
____
____

Voice It!

6 Discuss the questions.

1 What do you think is a typical family?
2 Is family life in the circus like your family life? Why / Why not?
3 What are the good and bad things about life in the circus?

Finished? p118 Ex. 1

Watch video 1.2
True or false?
Tess has two brothers.
Marco has a big family.

GRAMMAR IN ACTION

To Have: Affirmative and Negative

	I/You/We/They	He/She/It
+	They **have** two homes.	Ysabella [2] ___has___ two brothers.
–	Lukas and Tomas **do not (don't)** [1] ______ jobs in the circus.	She **does** [3] ______ **(doesn't) have** any sisters.

1 **Complete the examples in the chart above. Use the webpage on page 12 to help you.**

1.04 **2** **Circle the correct form of *to have*. Then listen and check.**

This Week's Circus Stars!

Bibi and Bichu Tesfamariam are brothers, and they are incredible jugglers. They [1] *has / have* a circus school in Ethiopia. It [2] *has / have* 150 students. They [3] *has / have* their own circus, too! It's called Circus Abyssinia, and it [4] *has / have* some amazing Ethiopian acrobats. We think Bibi and Bichu [5] *has / have* a great future!

3 **Complete the sentences with the correct form of *to have*. Then check your answers in the webpage on page 12.**

1 Ysabella ___has___ a job in the circus.
2 Lukas and Tomas ______ a sister in the circus.
3 Alida and Robinson ______ three children.
4 Tino ______ a job in the circus.
5 Robinson doesn't ______ a sister in the circus.

Get It Right!

Use **have** after **don't** and **doesn't**.

He doesn't have a job. **NOT** ~~*He doesn't has a job.*~~

Possessive *'s*

Alex is her dad**'s** brother.	Her parents**'** names are Robinson and Alida.

4 **Look at the chart above. Complete the sentences. Use the words in parentheses with *'s* or *s'*.**

1 ___Aurelia's___ niece is Ysabella. (Aurelia)
2 Alida is ______ wife. (Robinson)
3 ______ names are Ysabella, Alex, Robinson, and Alida. (the trapeze artists)
4 ______ grandparents are Olinka and Tino. (Ysabella)
5 Aurelia is ______ sister. (Alida)

Use It!

5 **Write true and false sentences with *'s* or *s'* and the correct form of *to have*. Use the ideas below or your own ideas.**

My ______'s name ______.
______ has ______.
My ______s' house ______.
______ have ______.
My sister's classroom ______.
I don't have ______.

My grandparents' house is pink. They have a big backyard.

6 **Take turns saying your sentences. Can your partner guess the false sentences?**

My mom's name is Sandra. She has two sisters.

False! Your mom's name is Emma.

Finished? p118 Ex. 2

VOCABULARY AND LISTENING

Describing People

1.05 **1 Complete the chart with the words for describing people in the box. Listen, check, and repeat.**

beard	blond	brown (x2)	freckles
glasses	gray (x2)	long	mustache
red	short (x2)	tall	wavy

Eyes	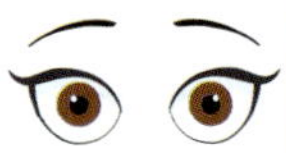	brown	________
Hair		________ ________	________
Hair Color		________ ________	________ ________
Height		________	________
Other Features		________ ________	________ ________

LEARN TO LEARN

Drawing Pictures

Drawing pictures can help you remember new words.

2 Draw pictures of the words in Exercise 1.

Describing People

brown eyes 

3 Cover the words and show your pictures to a partner. Can they guess the correct words?

Get It Right!

Adjectives go before nouns in English.

brown eyes **NOT** ~~*eyes brown*~~

Use It!

4 Describe the people. Use words from Exercise 1.

5 Work in pairs. Take turns describing members of your family. Can your partner guess who they are?

He's tall. He has short brown hair.

Is it your dad?

Yes, it is. / No, it isn't.

A Conversation

1.06 **6 Look at the photo and listen. Who is the actor?**

1.06 **7** EXAM **Listen again. Circle the correct answers.**

The actor …

1 is A American. (B) Australian. C Austrian.
2 has A green eyes. B blue eyes. C brown eyes.
3 has A one brother. B two brothers. C three brothers.
4 has A a Spanish wife. B a British wife. C A Polish wife.
5 has A two daughters. B two sons. C two children.

Watch video 1.3
Does Rafael have blue eyes?
Does he have short black hair?

GRAMMAR IN ACTION

To Have Questions

?	**Do** they [1] have any children?	Does he have blue eyes?
+	Yes, they [2] ________.	Yes, he **does**.
–	No, they **don't**.	No, he [4] ________.
?	How many pets **do** they [3] ________?	How many sisters [5] ________ he **have**?

Pronunciation p141

1 Complete the examples in the chart above.

1.10 2 Write the questions and answers about the famous people in the quiz below. Then circle the correct answer, a or b. Listen and check.

THIS WEEK'S star INTERVIEW

1 How many / brothers and sisters / Daniel Radcliffe?
How many brothers and sisters does Daniel Radcliffe have?
a one brother
He has one brother.
(b) (✗) brothers or sisters
He doesn't have any brothers or sisters.

2 Scarlett Johansson / a brother?
____
a yes – a twin brother
____
b no – a twin sister
____

3 Mila Kunis / green eyes?
____
a no – blue eyes
____
b no – one green eye and one brown eye
____
____

Get It Right!

Remember **Do** and **Does** in questions with **have**.
Does she have blue eyes? **NOT** ~~*Has she blue eyes?*~~

3 Work in pairs. Write three questions like the ones in Exercise 2 about famous people. Ask another pair. Can they guess the answer?
1 ________
2 ________
3 ________

Use It!

4 Write a class quiz. Write questions with the correct form of *to have*.
1 brown eyes
____
2 a twin brother or sister
____
3 a pet
____
4 a phone
____
5 a niece or nephew
____

5 Ask the people in your class your quiz questions. Write down their answers.

Do you have brown eyes?

Yes, I do.

No, I don't. I have gray eyes.

6 Compare your answers with your classmates. What is interesting or surprising?

Finished? p118 Ex. 3

SPEAKING
Calling a Friend

1.11 **1** **Listen to the conversation. Who is Jack?**

LILY	[1] Hey , Evan.
EVAN	Hi, Lily. Are you alright? [2] ____________?
LILY	OK, thanks. [3] ____________?
EVAN	[4] ____________, thanks. So, how's school?
LILY	It's good.
EVAN	Do you have any new friends?
LILY	Yes, I do. I have one new friend. His name's Jack.
EVAN	Cool! There's a new boy in my class. His name's Jack, too.
LILY	Does he have wavy black hair and blue eyes?
EVAN	Yes, he does. That's funny! Maybe it's the same boy. Imagine if it is!
LILY	That's so not funny, Evan!
EVAN	Gotta go! [5] ____________!
LILY	OK. [6] ____________.

1.11 **2** **Complete the conversation with the phrases from the *Useful Language* box. Then listen and check.**

Useful Language

Bye! Hey, (Evan). How's it going?
OK/Fine, thanks. You? See you later.

3 **Look at the *Everyday English* box. Find and <u>underline</u> the phrases in the conversation.**

Watch video 1.4
Everyday English

Are you alright? Cool! Gotta go!
That's funny! That's so not funny!

4 **Work with a partner. Practice the conversation.**

PLAN

5 **Write questions to ask your friend on the phone. Use the ideas below.**

School? ____________

____

New friends? ____________

____

Family? ____________

____

SPEAK

6 **Practice a phone conversation with your partner. Remember to use *to have*, the vocabulary from this unit, and phrases from the *Useful Language* and *Everyday English* boxes.**

CHECK

7 **Work with another pair. Listen to their phone conversation and complete the notes.**

School: ____________

New friends: ____________

Family: ____________

Javi's new school penpal is Martin, from England.

Hello Martin,

1 ☐ I'm Javi and I'm from Montijo, a small town in the west of Spain. I have a big house and a very big family!

2 ☐ I have six brothers and one sister. My brother Dani is my twin. He's tall. He has short straight brown hair and brown eyes, like me. He's my brother and my friend! My sister, Claudia, is ten. She has long brown hair, blue eyes, and lots of freckles! I have a pet rabbit. His name is Thumper! My best friend's name is Toni. She's funny!

3 ☐ Here's a photo of me with Dani (he has a red shirt) and Claudia. We're in my uncle's backyard.

4 ☐ Do you have a big family? Do you have any pets? Who's your best friend?

Write soon!

Javi

WRITING

An Informal Email

1 **Look at the photo. Which boy is Javi? Read his email and find the answer.**

2 **Match topics a–d with paragraphs 1–4.**

- a Javi's questions for Martin
- b family and friends
- c introduction
- d extra information

3 **Read the email again and answer the questions.**

1. How old is Javi's sister? ______
2. How many brothers and sisters does Javi have? ______
3. Who is Thumper? ______
4. Who is Javi's best friend? ______

4 **Complete the *Useful Language* box with examples from Javi's email.**

Useful Language

At the beginning: Hi, Hey, 1 ______

At the end: Email me soon, That's all for now, 2 ______ !

Contractions: I'm, 3 ______ , She's, 4 ______ , 5 ______ , Who's

Symbols: use emojis to help express your feelings

PLAN

5 **Plan an informal email to a new friend. Take notes about these things.**

Age: ______

Family: ______

Pets: ______

Friend(s): ______

Decide what information to include in each paragraph. Use the information in Exercise 2 to help you.

WRITE

6 **Write your email. Remember to include four paragraphs, the verbs *to be* and *to have*, and phrases from the *Useful Language* box.**

CHECK

7 **Do you …**

- use expressions to start and end your email?
- give information about you and your family in the second paragraph?
- ask questions in the last paragraph?

Finished? p118 Ex. 4

AROUND THE WORLD

READING
An Article

1.12 **1 Look at the photo below. Where are the children? What is special about them? Read the article to check your answers.**

2 Find words in the article that mean:

1 two children born at the same time ____________
2 three children born at the same time ____________
3 four children born at the same time ____________
4 very young children ____________

3 Read the article again. Circle the correct words.

1 The Festival of Twins is one *week* / *day* long.
2 Pleucadeuc isn't a *big* / *small* town.
3 The festival is for twins, triplets, and quadruplets from *France* / *all over the world*.
4 Oscar and Oliver *have some* / *don't have any* photos as babies at the Festival of Twins.

Globetrotters
Watch video 1.5
Children's Day

- What is Children's Day?
- When is Children's Day in Japan?
- Which city are the superheroes in?

Voice It!

4 Discuss the questions.

1 The Festival of Twins celebrates something unique. Why is it important to celebrate things that are unique?
2 How can it be difficult to be unique?
3 What is something unique about you?

Twins Day

France is the third-biggest country in Europe and it has a lot of different festivals. They have a film festival in Cannes, music festivals in Paris and in Lyon, and there's a festival of lights.

But perhaps one of the most unusual festivals of all is "Deux et Plus" or "Festival of Twins" on August 15 in the small town of Pleucadeuc in the northwest of France. More than 1,000 twins, triplets, and quadruplets from all over the world meet in one place. Some look the same and some look different. Some even speak their own language! Imagine that!

The festival has its own traditions. Each twin, triplet, or quadruplet is usually in the same clothes with the same hairstyle. There are also a lot of interesting activities to do, like face painting, watching live music, dancing, and playing fun games.

Oscar and Oliver have photos from their first visit to the Festival of Twins as babies. Now they are 13. "It's a great day! We have a lot of new friends this year." Their new friends have the same thing in common – they all have twin brothers or sisters!

LEARN TO LEARN

Increasing Your Vocabulary

When you learn an adjective, it's a good idea to learn the opposite adjective. Learning word pairs increases your vocabulary.

5 Write the opposite adjectives for words 1–4. Then find and underline them in the article.

1 big ______ small
2 last ______
3 normal ______
4 old ______

6 Close your books. Say an adjective from Exercise 5. Can your partner remember the opposite adjective?

Explore It!

Guess the correct answer.

Identical twins have the same DNA, but they don't have the same …

a eye color. b fingerprints. c hair color.

Find two more interesting facts about twins. Choose your favorite fact and write a question for your partner to answer.

SHAPE IT!

CULTURE PROJECT

A Poster

Oscar and Oliver go to the Festival of Twins in France. Choose another festival from around the world. In groups, design and present a poster about it.

Teacher's Resource Bank

1 REVIEW

VOCABULARY

1 Look at Ruben's family tree. Complete the sentences.

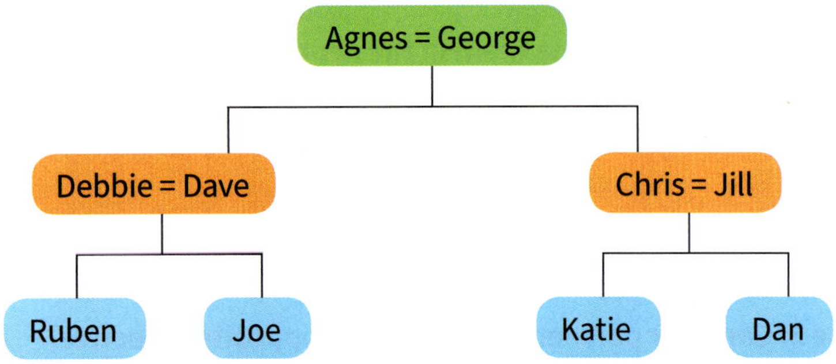

1 Joe: Agnes and George are my ______________.
2 Debbie and Dave: Ruben is our ______________.
3 Ruben: Katie and Dan are my ______________.
4 Jill: Ruben is my ______________.
5 Katie and Dan: Dave is our ______________.

2 Complete the descriptions with words from the box.

brown (x2) glasses gray long red short (x2) tall wavy

Kirsty is [1] ______________.
She has [2] ______________
______________ ______________ hair.
She has [3] ______________ eyes.

Jack is [4] ______________.
He has [5] ______________
______________ hair.
He has [6] ______________ eyes.
He has [7] ______________.

GRAMMAR IN ACTION

3 Rewrite the sentences. Replace the underlined words with the words in parentheses and *'s* or *s'*.

1 Their names are Jack and Sara. (My parents)
____
2 Is that her phone? (Anna)
____
3 They're their bags. (my friends)
____
4 That's his bike. (Danny)
____

4 Write the questions with *to have*. Then answer them with the information in parentheses.

1 how many / sisters / you (four)
____
____
2 Toby / any cousins (✗)
____
____
3 you / a big family (✓)
____
____
4 your best friend / a pet (✓) (two cats)
____
____
5 you / a phone / in your bag (✗)
____
____

Self-Assessment

I can talk about members of my family.
I can use adjectives to describe people.
I can use *to have* in affirmative and negative sentences.
I can use *to have* in questions.

LEARN TO ... ORGANIZE YOUR NOTEBOOK

It's important to organize your notebook to help you to find your notes and study for exams.

1 Ask and answer with a partner.

1. Do you have a notebook?
2. Is it for all your subjects or for English only?
3. Are your notes easy or difficult to read?

2 Look at Omar's notebook. Match 1–4 with a–d.

1. today's vocabulary *c*
2. today's date ___
3. today's homework ___
4. today's grammar ___

a September 23

b

To Have	
I / you / we / they	have / don't have ...
he / she / it	has / doesn't have ...

c

Family Members	
dad	mom
husband	wife
brother	sister
son	daughter
uncle	aunt
nephew	niece
grandpa	grandma
grandson	granddaughter
cousin	cousin

d Learn the family words from Unit 1.

3 Look at Azra's notebook. Is her notebook different from Omar's? How?

grammar | vocabulary | notes | homework

Verb To Be

Affirmative	Negative	Questions
I'm from Turkey.	I'm not from Turkey.	Am I Brazilian?
She's my sister.	She isn't my sister.	Is she Mexican?
He's my brother.	He isn't my brother.	Is he from Ecuador?
We're at school.	We aren't at school.	Are we 12?
They're my cousins.	They aren't my cousins.	Are they at school?

4 Ask and answer with a partner.

1. What is good about Omar's notebook? What is good about Azra's?
2. What are some other ways to organize a notebook?
3. Which is your favorite way? Why?

SHAPE IT!

5 Discuss with a partner. Decide how to organize your notebook.

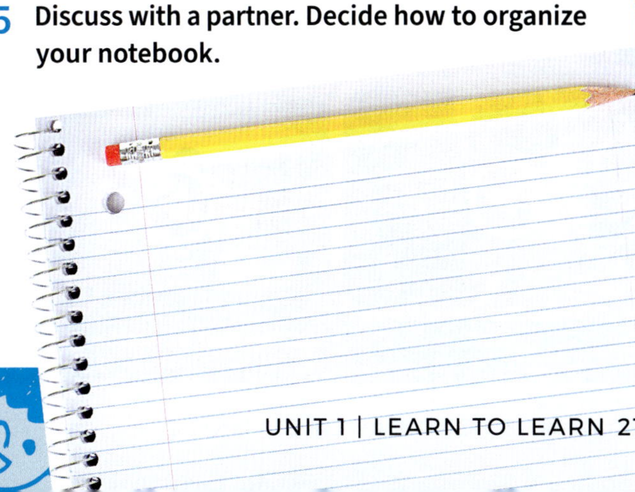

2 What's your day like?

LEARNING OUTCOMES

I can ...

- understand texts about daily routines
- ask and respond to interview questions
- write an article
- understand how to use the simple present and adverbs of frequency
- talk about daily routines and free-time activities
- identify word partners
- do a survey, present results, and work in pairs

Start It!

1 Is the girl in the photo happy? Why / Why not?
2 Before you watch, what time is it in India now?
3 Which countries are in the video? Watch and check.
4 Which is your favorite activity in the video? Why?

Watch video 2.1

p25

Grammar in Action 2.2

p27

Grammar in Action 2.3

p28

Everyday English 2.4

VOCABULARY
Daily Routines

2.01 **1** **Match eight of the activities in the box with the pictures a–h. Then listen, check, and repeat.**

brush your teeth		
check your phone		
do your homework		
get dressed	*a*	
get up		
go home		
go to bed		
go to school		
have breakfast		
pack your bag		
take a shower		
wake up		

2.02 **2** **Which activities in the box in Exercise 1 are not in the pictures? Write them in the correct order. Then listen, check, and repeat.**

wake up ______ ______
______ ______

2.03 **3** **Listen to Eduardo talking about his day. Put all the activities in the correct order. Write 1–13 in the boxes in Exercise 1. Write two numbers in one box.**

Get It Right!

Use **at** with times.

I get up at 7:00 a.m. on Mondays.

LEARN TO LEARN
Word Partners (1)
When you learn new words, think about the words that go with them. This will help you remember them.

4 **Complete the chart with activities from Exercise 1. Then think of one more activity for each verb.**

Go	*to school*		
Get			

Use It!

5 **Work in pairs. Take turns saying an activity from Exercise 1. Your partner guesses what time you do the activity.**

have breakfast *7 o'clock?* *No, try again.*

Explore It!

Guess the correct answer.

When you brush your teeth and leave the tap on, you use … liters of water every minute.

a two **b** five **c** ten

Find another interesting fact about another daily routine. Then write a question for your partner to answer.

READING

A Profile

A Day in the Life of ...

Amir is from the Bajau tribe in Borneo. His life is unusual. He lives with his family in a house – but it's in the water. Amir doesn't know his age or the date of his birthday. The Bajau don't count days and hours; they use the movement of the ocean to count time.

Every morning, Amir wakes up early, but he doesn't have breakfast. He and his father go out in their boat. They swim in the water to look for food for the day. Amir and the people in his tribe can see really well underwater. Amir catches a fish for breakfast and his father catches an octopus for dinner.

After breakfast, Amir usually meets his friends. They don't go to school and they don't study subjects like English. The older Bajau people teach them how to make nets and build boats.

In the afternoon, Amir and his friends dive into the water from bridges, and they play in the water, too. It's their favorite place!

In the evening, Amir's mother and sisters cook the octopus and then the family has dinner together. It's always delicious!

1 **Tell your partner three things you do after breakfast.**

2 **Read the profile. Say one surprising thing about Amir's routine.** 2.04

3 **Find words in the profile to match the photos.**

a

______

b

______

c

______

d

______

4 EXAM **Read the profile again. Circle the correct answers.**

1 Where is Amir from?
A Australia B Bajau (C) Borneo

2 Amir and his father wake up early and …
A play in the water.
B cook breakfast.
C catch fish.

3 The older Bajau people teach Amir …
A how to make nets and build boats.
B how to speak English.
C how to swim underwater.

4 When do Amir and his friends play in the water?
A every morning
B in the afternoon
C in the evening

5 What is Amir's family like?
A He has a father, a mother, and brothers.
B He has a father, a mother, and sisters.
C He has a mother, a brother, and sisters.

Voice It!

5 **Discuss the questions.**

1 How is Amir's life different from yours?
2 What do you like about Amir's day?

Finished? p119 Ex. 1

Watch video 2.2
Name three things he does in the morning. Is he always on time for school?

GRAMMAR IN ACTION

Simple Present: Affirmative and Negative

	I/You/We/They	He/She/It
+	Amir and his father **go** out in their boat.	Amir **lives** with his family.
+	They [1] ___swim___ in the water to look for food.	Amir [3] ______ a fish for breakfast.
–	Amir and his friends [2] ______ ______ to school.	He **doesn't know** his age.

Pronunciation p141

1 **Complete the examples in the chart above. Use the profile on page 24 to help you.**

2 **Correct the sentences. Check your answers in the profile on page 24.**

1 Amir knows the date of his birthday.
Amir doesn't know the date of his birthday.

2 He plays with his friends in the evening.
______

3 He and his friends study English.
______

4 He and his friends don't like the water.
______

5 He doesn't have dinner with his family in the evening.
______

2.08 **3** **Complete the text with the simple present form of the verbs in parentheses. Then listen and check.**

Nadia is 13 years old and she [1] ___comes___ (come) from Siberia. Her family is part of the Nenet tribe. They [2] ______ (not live) in the same place all year round. In the summer, Nadia [3] ______ (travel) more than 1,000 km to the north of the country. She [4] ______ (not have) a house. She [5] ______ (live) in a tent with her family. In the winter, they [6] ______ (move) to the south of the country and their tent [7] ______ (go), too! How cool is that?

Adverbs of Frequency

After breakfast, Amir [1] ______ meets his friends.
It's [2] ______ delicious.

4 **Complete the examples in the chart above. Use the profile on page 24 to help you.**

5 **Complete the timeline with the adverbs of frequency.**

often sometimes usually

0% — 100%

never [1] ______ [2] ______ [3] ______ always

Use It!

6 **Imagine you are a famous person. Write three positive and three negative sentences with adverbs of frequency about your daily routine. Use the ideas in the box.**

do exercise do interviews have breakfast sing travel watch TV all afternoon

I always have breakfast in bed.

7 **Swap your sentences with your partner. Guess who they are.**

Are you Taylor Swift?

Yes, I am.

Finished? p119 Ex. 2

VOCABULARY AND LISTENING

Free-Time Activities

2.09 **1 Match the activities in the box with the pictures. Listen, check, and repeat.**

chat online	☐	make videos	☐
download songs	☐	play an instrument	☐
go for a bike ride	☐	play video games	☐
go shopping	☐	read a book/magazine	☐
hang out with friends	☐	take photos	☐
listen to music	☐	watch TV	1

LEARN TO LEARN

Word Partners (2)

When you learn new words, learn them with the words that go with them. This will help you remember them.

2 Complete the chart with the activities in Exercise 1.

	Free-Time activities
Indoors	chat online
Outdoors	
Indoors and Outdoors	

3 Change the words in bold and write the correct sentences.

1 I usually **chat** music on my phone.
I usually listen to music on my phone.

2 We never **read** videos.

3 Victor **listens to** photos all the time!

4 Alex **downloads** online with his friends every evening.

5 Evie and Laura **take** the piano.

Street Interviews

2.10 **4 Listen. Which activities from Exercise 1 do you hear? Underline them in the list in Exercise 1.**

2.10 **5 Listen again. Circle the correct answers.**

1 Nina and her friends *like* / *don't like* the same music.
2 Nina *does* / *doesn't do* her homework before she chats online.
3 Anton *plays* / *doesn't play* video games on his own.
4 George *lives* / *doesn't live* near Anton.
5 Anton *has* / *doesn't have* a bike and a camera.

Use It!

6 Write five sentences in your notebook about your free-time activities. Use adverbs of frequency.

7 Work with a partner. Take turns saying your sentences. Are any the same?

I always chat online after school.

I never chat online after school. I often read a book.

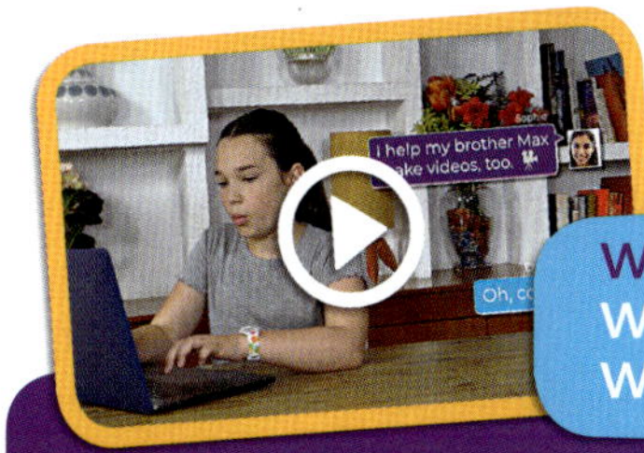

Watch video 2.3
Where does Sophie live?
What does Max make?

GRAMMAR IN ACTION

Simple Present: Questions

	I/You/We/They	He/She/It
Yes/No	**Do** they **like** the same music?	[4] *Does* your best friend **live** near you?
	Yes, they [1] ______ . / No, they **don't**.	Yes, he **does**. / No, he [5] ______ .
Wh-	**What** [2] ______ you **do**?	**Who does** Anton **play** with?
	How often [3] ______ you **chat** online?	**How often** [6] ______ she **do** that?

1 **Complete the examples in the chart above.**

2 **Put the words in the correct order to make questions. Then write the answers.**

1 Nina / hang out with friends / does ✓
Does Nina hang out with friends?
Yes, she does.

2 Nina and her friends / do / like / reading ✗
______
______

3 Nina / her homework / in the evening / does / do ✓
______
______

4 Anton / walk / to George's house / does ✗
______
______

3 **Use the ideas to write questions. Then ask and answer with a partner.**

1 play video games with friends (you)
Do you play video games with friends?
Yes, I do. / No, I don't.

2 live near you (your friends)
______
______

3 listen to music in the car (your parents)
______
______

4 get up early on the weekend (you)
______
______

Get It Right!

Remember to use the base verb form with **do** and **does**.
Where does your best friend live? **NOT** ~~*Where does your best friend lives?*~~

Wh- Questions

4 **Complete the questions with the words in the box.**

How often | What | What time | ~~When~~ | Where

1 *When* do you have breakfast?
2 ______ does your best friend live?
3 ______ do you get up on weekdays?
4 ______ do you do in your free time?
5 ______ does your English teacher give you homework?

Use It!

5 **Write questions. Then ask and answer with a partner.**

1 What video games / you and your friends / like?
What video games do you and your friends like?

2 Where / your best friend / live?
______

3 Who / you / meet / before school?
______

What video games do you and your friends like?

I like adventure games, but my friends usually play soccer games.

Finished? p119 Ex. 3

SPEAKING
An Interview

2.11 **1 Listen to the conversation. Who is Mr. Green?**

AMELIA	Hello, Mr. Green. [1] I have some questions to ask you for the school magazine. [2] ________?
MR. GREEN	Go ahead.
AMELIA	What time do you get up in the morning?
MR. GREEN	That's easy. I get up at 5:30 a.m.
AMELIA	Wow! How often do you get up at 5:30?
MR. GREEN	Almost every day.
AMELIA	[3] ________. What time do you go to work?
MR. GREEN	It depends. I usually arrive at 7:30 a.m.
AMELIA	You're a history teacher here. Do you like your job?
MR. GREEN	Good question! Yes, I do.
AMELIA	That's good. [4] ________.
MR. GREEN	Sure!
AMELIA	What's your favorite day of the week?
MR. GREEN	That's a difficult one! Saturday.
AMELIA	[5] ________.
MR. GREEN	You're welcome.

2.11 **2 Complete the conversation with the phrases from the *Useful Language* box. Then listen and check.**

Useful Language

I have some questions to ask you.
I just have one more question.
Is that OK?
Thank you very much for your time.
That's interesting.

3 Look at the *Everyday English* box. Find and underline the phrases in the conversation.

Watch video 2.4
Everyday English

Go ahead. It depends.
No problem. Sure! That's easy.

4 Work with a partner. Practice the conversation.

PLAN

5 Work with a partner and decide who you want to interview. Write four questions that you want to ask. Use the ideas below. Then decide on the person's answers.

1 What time / get up?
What time do you get up in the morning?
____

2 What time / go to work?
____
____

3 Like job?
____
____

4 Favorite day?
____
____

SPEAK

6 Practice the interview with your partner. Remember to use verbs in the present, the vocabulary from this unit, and phrases from the *Useful Language* and *Everyday English* boxes.

CHECK

7 Work with another pair. Listen to their interview and complete the notes.

Who do they interview? ________
Favorite day: ________
Something interesting: ________
____

WRITING

An Article

1 **Read the article. Discuss the best title. Write it in the space at the top of the article.**

1 What do you do all day?
2 What's your daily routine?
3 What does a vlogger do all day?

2 **Match topics a–c with paragraphs 1–3.**

a description of Amy's evening routine
b description of her morning routine
c description of her afternoon routine

3 **Read the article again. What does Amy do at these times?**

1 7:00 a.m. *She wakes up.*
2 11:00 a.m. ______
3 1:00 p.m. ______
4 9:00 p.m. ______

4 **Look at the *Useful Language* box. Then write the punctuation used in 1–6.**

1 I read a book. *period*
2 Close the door! ______
3 Do you chat online? ______
4 Canadian Amy Ritchie ______
5 chair, table, notebook ______
6 I'm they're don't ______

Useful Language

apostrophe ' capital letter **A, B, C**
comma **,** exclamation point **!**
period **.** question mark **?**

5 **Find and circle examples of the punctuation in the *Useful Language* box in the article and title.**

Get It Right!

Use **from** ... **to** ... to give a start and end time.
I study from 4:00 to 5:30. **NOT** ~~*I study 4:00 to 5:30.*~~

______

Amy Ritchie is a Canadian vlogger. She vlogs about her life.

1 ☐ She always wakes up at 7:00, has breakfast, and checks her phone. She plans her vlog, but she doesn't make it. She usually goes for a bike ride at 11:00.

2 ☐ She has lunch at 1:00 and listens to music. From 2:00 to 3:00, she practices her vlog. She takes some photos and posts them.

3 ☐ Amy doesn't have much free time. She sometimes watches TV before dinner. She always uploads her vlog at 9:00 p.m. and she goes to bed at 11:00.

One day I want to be a vlogger like Amy!

PLAN

6 **Plan an article about daily routines. Choose a famous person. Think about their daily activities. Decide what information to include in each paragraph. Use the information in Exercise 2 to help you.**

WRITE

7 **Write your article. Remember to include the information in the correct order, the simple present, adverbs of frequency, and correct punctuation from the *Useful Language* box.**

CHECK

8 **Do you ...**

- include an interesting title with a question?
- introduce the person, their nationality, and what they do?
- end the article with a sentence about you and your ambition?

Finished? p119 Ex. 4

MATH PROJECT

A Class Survey

1 Circle the correct answer.

A survey is a …

a test to check your knowledge.

b list of questions to find out information.

2 (2.12) **Look at the bar chart and complete the results of a class survey a–g. Then listen and check.**

3 Read the survey results again. Answer the questions.

1 How many people are in the class? ___30___

2 What question do the students want to ask?

____

3 How do the students present the results?

____

4 What is the class's favorite free-time activity?

____

4 (2.13) **Complete the summary of the survey results on page 31 with the words in the box. Then listen and check.**

class ~~free-time~~ girls question results students surprising

5 (2.13) **Read the *How To* box and listen again. Answer the questions.**

1 Do the students complete each stage from the *How To* box?

____

2 What is the students' conclusion after the survey?

____

3 Do you think it is a good summary? Why / Why not?

____

How to Present Survey Results

a Say what question you ask in your survey.

b Say why you want to do the survey.

c Give information about the people in the survey.

d Present the results.

e Give your opinion on the results.

f Comment on any surprising results.

g Summarize the survey results.

OUR CLASS SURVEY

SURVEY OF CLASS 7B: STUDENTS' FREE TIME

What do you do on Saturday morning?

Total number of students: 30

a	hang out with friends	9
b	play video games	
c	go shopping	
d	watch TV	
e	listen to music	
f	sleep in	
g	clean your bedroom	

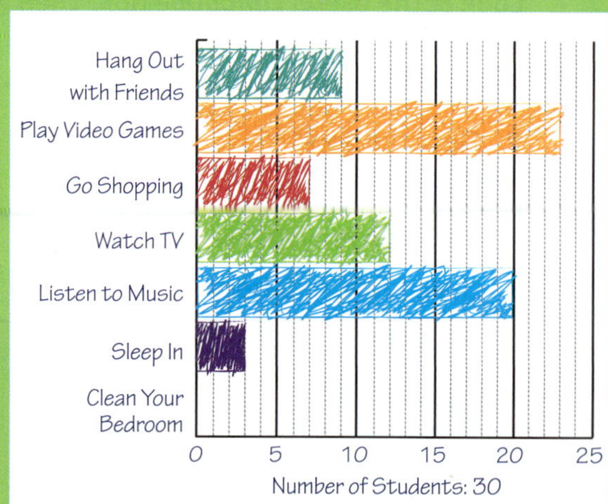

SHAPE IT!

Our survey is about [1]free-time activities on Saturday morning. The purpose of our survey is to understand the free-time activities people do because we want to plan an end-of-school party. It is good to know what people like!

Here are the results.

- There are 30 [2]______________ in our class. They are all between 12 and 13 years old. Sixteen are [3]______________ and 14 are boys.
- For answers to the [4]______________ "What do you do on Saturday morning?" please look at the information in the chart.

- In our opinion, the [5]______________ are interesting. Students do a variety of different activities.
- Only three students sleep in on Saturday morning. We think this is [6]______________, because we know we're all tired after a week at school, and we all like to sleep. Teenagers need between nine and ten hours of sleep a night, but we know free time is important for us, too.
- Most of the students in our [7]______________ play video games, and no one cleans their bedroom on Saturday morning!

PLAN

6 Work in groups. Choose one of these topics for a class survey. Then complete the steps below.

morning routines during the week
after-school activities
evening activities
weekend activities

- Decide on your question and the activities you want to include.
- Ask students your question and write down their answers.
- Add up the results.
- Draw a bar chart to show your results.

PRESENT

7 Present your results to the class. Remember to include carefully recorded information, an accurate bar chart, and the tips in *How to Present Survey Results*.

CHECK

8 Listen to your classmates' presentations. Complete the notes about one presentation. Then discuss in your group.

What question do they ask?

____

What is their conclusion after the survey?

____

Write down two interesting or surprising facts.

____

____

2 REVIEW

VOCABULARY

1 Match the verbs with the activities.

1 brush
2 get
3 check
4 take
5 pack
6 go

a your bag
b home
c a shower
d dressed
e your teeth
f your phone

2 Circle the correct verb.

1 *play / go / chat* video games
2 *read / watch / make* a book
3 hang out with *music / friends / photos*
4 *listen to / go / chat* music
5 *chat / go / make* videos
6 *watch / take / listen to* photos

GRAMMAR IN ACTION

3 Complete the blog post with the simple present form of the verbs in parentheses.

WELCOME TO

My Morning Routine!

My day 1 __________ (start) at 7:00 a.m. on weekdays. I 2 __________ (wake up), but I 3 __________ (not get up). I 4 __________ (check) my phone. My best friend, Yusuf, always 5 __________ (send) me a photo in the morning. He's funny!

Breakfast is at 7:30. Then my sister and I 6 __________ (pack) our bags for school. I 7 __________ (not meet) Yusuf in the morning because he 8 __________ (not go) to my school.

What's your morning routine like?

4 Write questions. Then answer the questions for you.

1 your best friend / play an instrument?

____

____

2 how often / you / watch / TV?

____

____

3 what / your friends / do / on the weekend?

____

____

4 what time / school / start / in the morning?

____

____

5 where / you / hang out / with friends?

____

____

6 how often / you / go / for a bike ride?

____

____

5 Put the words in the correct order to make sentences.

1 watch / never / we / before school / TV

____

2 chats / sometimes / she / online

____

3 shopping / they / on the weekend / go / often

____

4 music / bedroom / I / my / listen to / usually / in

____

Self-Assessment

I can talk about my daily routine.

I can talk about my free-time activities.

I can use the simple present in affirmative and negative sentences.

I can use the simple present to ask questions.

LEARN TO ... WORK IN PAIRS

When you work in pairs, you learn from your partner.

1 **Complete the advice 1–6 with *Always* or *Never*.**

Let's work well together!

1 Always listen to your partner.

2 ________ answer your partner's questions.

3 ________ speak at the same time as your partner.

4 ________ help your partner with words they don't know.

5 ________ laugh at your partner's mistakes.

6 ________ ask questions to get more information.

SHAPE IT!

2 **Ask and answer questions with a partner. Then complete sentences 1–4. Practice the advice in Exercise 1.**

1 We both like ________.
2 My partner likes ________, but I don't.
3 I like ________, but my partner doesn't.
4 We don't like ________.

Do you like hanging out with friends?

Yes, I do.

Me, too. Let's write "hanging out with friends" in sentence 1.

3 **Complete the sentences about how you work in pairs with *always*, *sometimes*, or *never*.**

When I work in pairs, ...

1 I always listen to my partner.
2 I ________ answer my partner's questions.
3 I ________ speak at the same time as my partner.
4 I ________ help my partner with words they don't know.
5 I ________ laugh at my partner's mistakes.
6 I ________ ask questions to get more information.

4 **Tell your partner your sentences from Exercise 3. Do they agree? Why / Why not?**

I always listen to my partner.

Hmm. You sometimes listen to your partner.

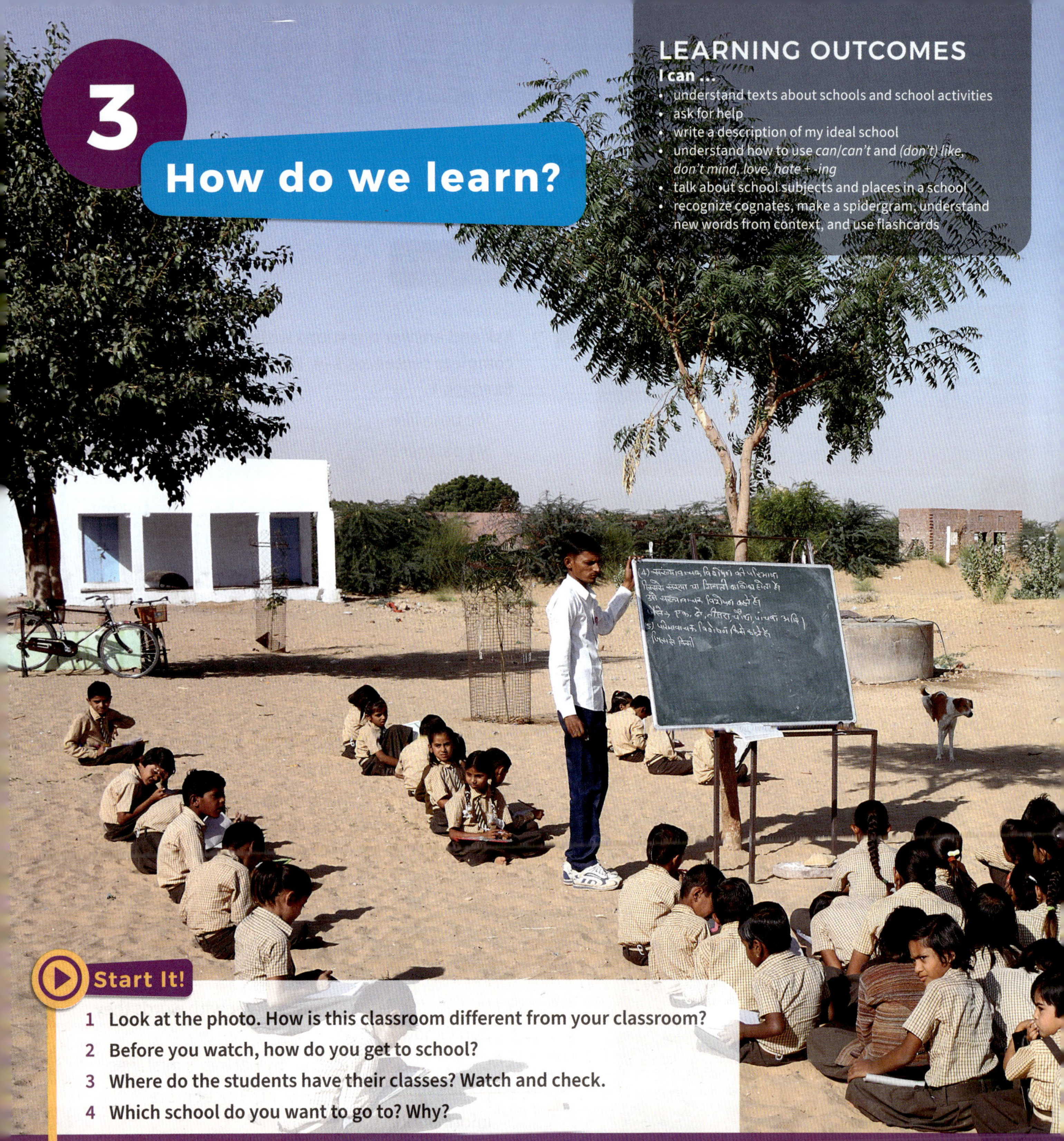

3 How do we learn?

LEARNING OUTCOMES

I can ...

- understand texts about schools and school activities
- ask for help
- write a description of my ideal school
- understand how to use *can/can't* and *(don't) like, don't mind, love, hate* + *-ing*
- talk about school subjects and places in a school
- recognize cognates, make a spidergram, understand new words from context, and use flashcards

Start It!

1 Look at the photo. How is this classroom different from your classroom?

2 Before you watch, how do you get to school?

3 Where do the students have their classes? Watch and check.

4 Which school do you want to go to? Why?

Watch video 3.1

p37

Grammar in Action 3.2

p39

Grammar in Action 3.3

p40

Everyday English 3.4

p42

Globetrotters 3.5

VOCABULARY

School Subjects

3.01 **1 Match the school subjects with the pictures. Then listen, check, and repeat.**

art	☐	music	☐
drama	☐	nutrition	☐
English	☐	physical education (PE)	☐
geography	☐	science	☐
history	☐	Spanish	☐
information technology (IT)	☐	vocational education	☐
math	*a*		

2 Circle the correct subjects.

1. *Math* / *Art* is my favorite subject. I love difficult problems.
2. I don't like *PE* / *nutrition* when we go outside. I prefer it inside.
3. This year I want to study Shakespeare in *science* / *English*.
4. I never remember all the dates in *history* / *IT*.
5. *Geography* / *English* isn't just about countries. It's also about populations and people.
6. *Music* / *Spanish* is great this year. My word of the week is *gracias*.

3 Work with a partner. Ask and answer about your schedules. Talk about:

subjects you're good at — your favorite subjects
subjects you're not good at — good/bad days

I'm good at PE. I'm not good at art. What about you?

LEARN TO LEARN

Recognizing Cognates

Some English words are similar to words in your language, but we don't always use them in the same way.

4 Write the subjects from Exercise 1 under the headings. Can you add any more subjects?

Similar to the Names of Subjects in My Language	Very Different from the Names of Subjects in My Language

Use It!

5 Write five definitions for school subjects. Can your partner guess the subjects?

You draw and paint in this subject. — *Art!*

Explore It!

Guess the correct answer.

In Australia, students have a six-week *summer* / *winter* break from mid-December to the end of January.

Find another interesting fact about schools. Then write a question for your partner to answer.

READING
A Webpage

Ballet School

Rumba, mambo, and salsa are just some of the dance styles that come from Cuba, and dancers are big stars in Cuba. The Cuban National Ballet School in Havana **trains** boys and girls to do **ballet**, and many of the students become the world's **top** ballet dancers.

Children usually start at the school when they are ten years old, for five years of training. Then, they sometimes train for three and a half more years at a professional level.

The school day starts at 7:00 a.m. and ends at 7:00 p.m. That's a 12-hour day! And some students go to school before classes start to do exercises! In the morning, students study subjects like history, math, languages, science, and music. At lunchtime, they can take a break, but they can't go home. In the afternoon, they dance.

Oscar is a student there. "It's **tough** and I practice a lot. I can dance and read music pretty well, but I can't play the piano very well. My best friend Carlos can dance very well. He can sing well, too, but I can't – I can't sing at all! One day, I want to be a dancer like my **hero**, Javier Rojas."

Learning to be a top ballet dancer is really hard work! Are you strong enough?

1 **Look at the photo and read the title. What do you want to know about the webpage?**

3.02 **2** **Read the webpage. Close your book. Write two things you remember about it.**

3 **Find the words in bold in the webpage and then (circle) the correct words in sentences 1–5.**

1. To "train" is to *prepare yourself for* / *think about* an activity.
2. "Ballet" *isn't* / *is* a type of dance.
3. To be "top" is to be number *one* / *two*.
4. Something "tough" is *easy* / *difficult*.
5. A "hero" is a person you think is *great* / *not very good*.

4 **Read the webpage again and complete the sentences.**

1. The Cuban National Ballet School is in ___Havana___.
2. A lot of the students become world-famous ______.
3. Most students start training at the ballet school when they are ______.
4. Some students ______ in the morning before classes start.
5. The students can take a break at ______.
6. In the afternoon, the students ______.

Voice It!

5 **Discuss the questions.**

1. Does your country have schools like Oscar's school? What are they like?
2. What are the similarities and the differences between your school and Oscar's?
3. Do you want to go to a ballet school like Oscar's? Why / Why not?

Finished? p120 Ex. 1

GRAMMAR IN ACTION

Can for Ability and Permission

Watch video 3.2
Can he speak another language?
Can anyone become a vlogger?

	I/You/He/She/It/We/They	
	Ability	**Permission**
+	I [1] *can* dance.	At lunchtime, they [3] ________ take a break.
–	Oscar **can't** play the piano.	Students [4] ________ go home at lunchtime.
?	[2] ________ Oscar sing well? Yes, he **can**. / No, he **can't**.	**Can** they dance here? Yes, they **can**. / No, they **can't**.

Pronunciation p141

1 **Complete the examples in the chart above. Use the webpage on page 36 to help you.**

2 **Circle the correct word. Then check your answers in the webpage on page 36.**

1 Oscar *can* / *can't* read music.
2 Oscar *can* / *can't* sing.
3 Carlos *can* / *can't* dance very well.

3.06 **3** **Complete the text with the correct form of *can*. Then listen and check.**

Get It Right!

After **can**, we use the verb without **to**.

Vicki can sing. **NOT** ~~*Vicki can to sing.*~~

A Day in Huaho School

Huaho school in Finland is different. Can you guess why?

Students [1] *can choose* (choose) the subjects they want to study. Teachers [2] ________ (tell) them what to do. Students [3] ________ (use) their phones in class to do research.

[4] ________ (you / do) that in your school?

Students and teachers [5] ________ (take) a break after every class. They [6] ________ (chat) with friends or go outside.

Students [7] ________ (do) homework. Why? Because the teachers don't give them any!

[8] ________ (you / imagine) a school like this?

4 **Remember the information from the webpage on page 36 and complete the sentences.**

very well | pretty well | (not) very well | (not) at all

1 Oscar can read music ________.
2 He can't play the piano ________.
3 Carlos can dance ________.
4 Oscar can't sing ________.

Use It!

5 **Write sentences about things you can or can't do and how well you do them in your notebook. Use the ideas below or your own ideas.**

count to ten in a different language | do ballet
sing a song in Russian | write music

I can't do ballet at all, but I can dance pretty well.

6 **Ask and answer questions. Find one thing you and your partner can both do well and one thing you can't do at all.**

Can you count to ten in a different language?

Yes, I can. I can count to ten in English very well.

Finished? p120 Ex. 2

VOCABULARY AND LISTENING

Places in a School

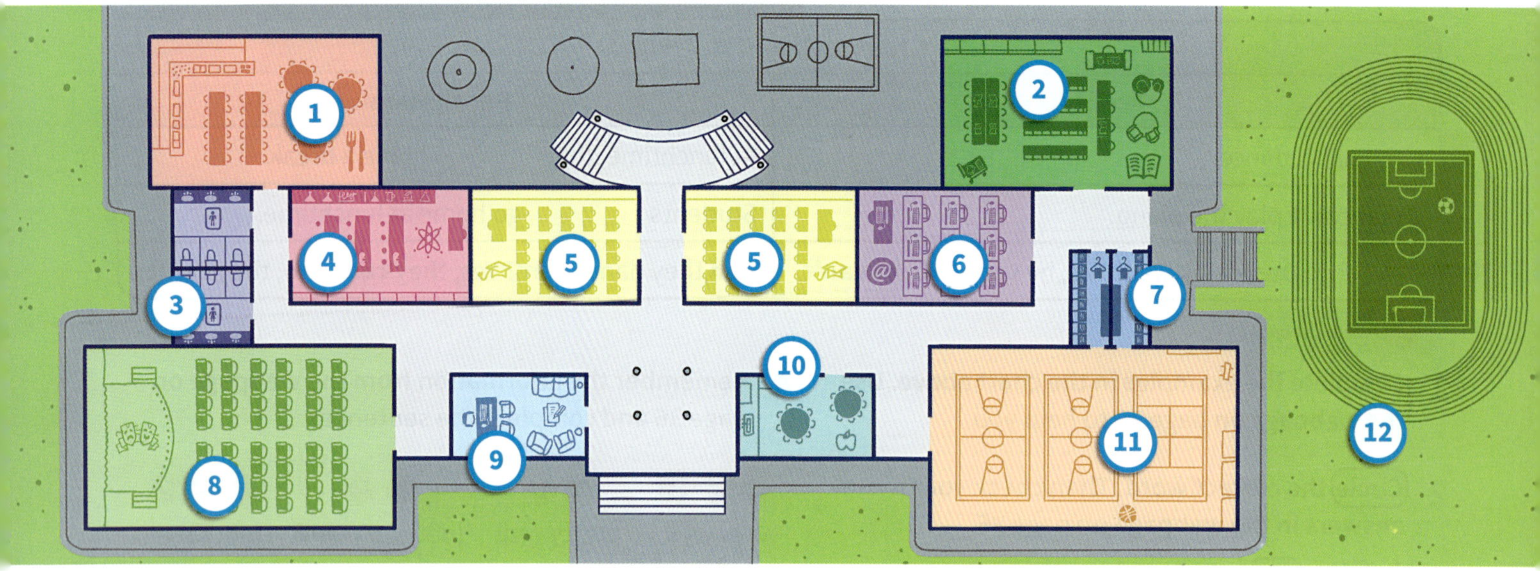

1 (3.07) **Match the words with places 1–12 in the plan. Listen, check, and repeat.**

athletic field	☐	gymnasium	☐	science lab	☐
auditorium	☐	library	☐	teacher's lounge	☐
cafeteria	1	locker room	☐		
classroom	☐	office	☐		
computer lab	☐	restrooms	☐		

2 (3.08) **Listen and write the seven places you hear.**

1 ....
2 ....
3 ....
4 ....
5 ....
6 ....
7 ....

LEARN TO LEARN

Making a Spidergram

Try to think of other words related to new words and make spidergrams to increase your vocabulary.

3 Choose places in your school from Exercise 1. Write down other words related to them.

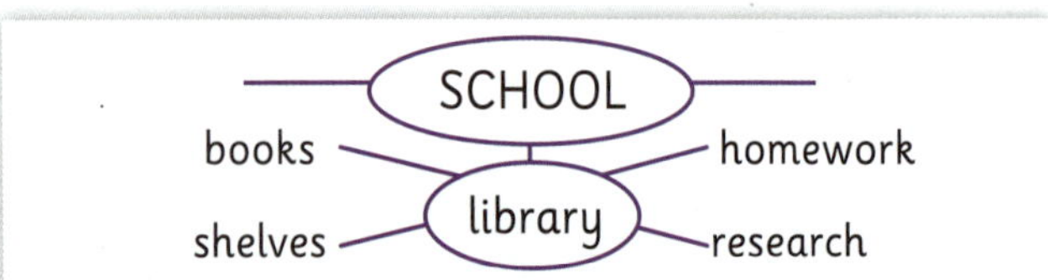

Use It!

4 Ask and answer about the places in your school.

Where do you do homework?

I do my homework in the library. What about you?

A Radio Show

5 (3.09) **Listen. What is the radio show about?**

6 (3.09) EXAM **Listen again. Circle the correct answers.**

1 The club usually meets in the …
A auditorium. (B) library. C cafeteria.

2 The club meets …
A every day B once a week.
C once a month.

3 The club starts at …
A 2:00. B 2:45. C 3:15.

4 Mrs. McKenzie is Lidia's …
A English teacher. B drama teacher.
C science teacher.

5 Max likes learning about new …
A clubs. B books. C friends.

Voice It!

7 Discuss the questions.

1 What kinds of books do you like?
2 Do you have a book club at your school?

Watch video 3.3
What's her favorite subject?
What does she love doing?

GRAMMAR IN ACTION

Verb Forms: (*Don't*) *Like*, *Don't Mind*, *Love*, *Hate* + *-ing*

We all **love reading** books. ☺☺☺	I **don't mind staying** for the book club. 😐
We **like** [1]**talk**ing ______ about them, too. ☺	I [3] ______ **like going** to after-school clubs. ☹
Some of my friends **hate** [2]**read** ______ . ☹☹☹	

1 **Complete the examples in the chart above.**

2 **Complete the sentences. Which ones are correct (✓)?**

1. Lidia loves reading (read) books. ☺☺☺ ✓
2. The students at the book club ______ (talk) about books. ☹ ☐
3. Max usually ______ (go) to after-school clubs. ☹☹☹ ☐
4. Max ______ (stay) for this club. 😐 ☐
5. All of Max's friends ______ (read). ☺ ☐

3 **Write true sentences in your notebook. Use the ideas in the box or your own ideas.**

do homework with friends get up early hang out with friends learn new vocabulary listen to rap music read a book study for exams take photos

I like doing homework with friends.

4 **Ask and answer. Find three things you have in common.**

Do you like getting up early?

No! I hate getting up early. What about you?

I don't mind getting up early on weekdays.

Object Pronouns

We use object pronouns (*me, you, him, her, it, us, them*) after a verb or preposition to replace nouns and to avoid repeating the same word.

5 **Match the object pronouns with the people or things.**

1. Lidia's here with **me**. — b
2. We like talking about **them**, too!
3. We have English class with **her**.
4. What's **it** about?

a books
b the radio show host
c Lidia's book
d Mrs. McKenzie

6 **Complete the sentences.**

1. Is Logan in this class? I want to talk to him.
2. Our teacher always gives ______ a lot of homework.
3. Where are Jess and Marco? Let's call ______ now.
4. The seat next to Ava is free. You can sit next to ______.
5. Is this your dictionary? Can I borrow ______, please?

Use It!

7 **Think about things you like and don't like at your school. Compare your ideas with a partner. Agree on changes you want to make.**

I don't like eating in the cafeteria. The food isn't very good.

I agree. Let's change our routine on Mondays. We can cook lunch at home on the weekend and bring it to school.

8 **Present your favorite idea to the class with your partner. The class chooses the best idea.**

Finished? p120 Ex. 3

SPEAKING
Asking for Help

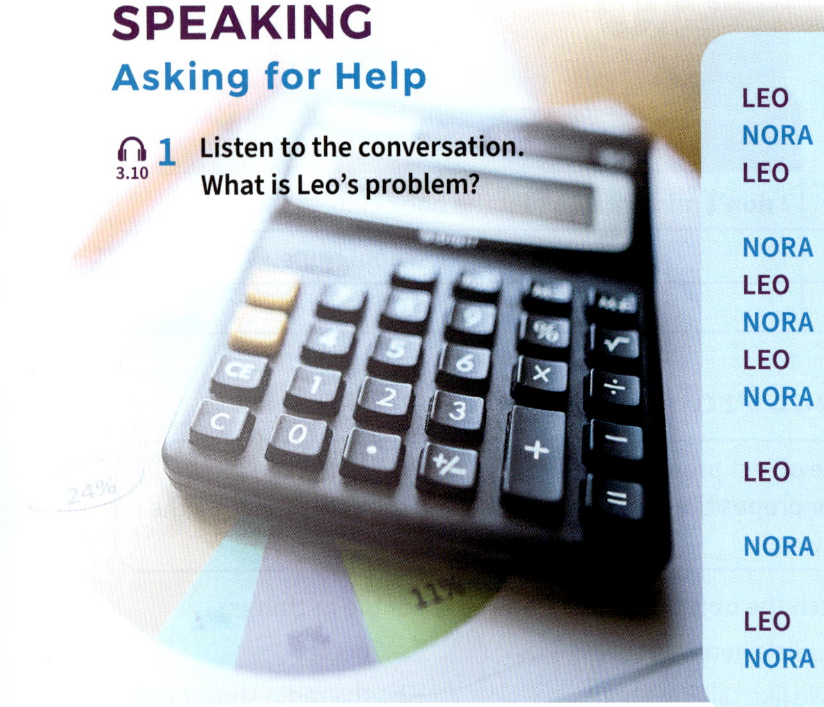

3.10 **1 Listen to the conversation. What is Leo's problem?**

LEO Hi, Nora. How's it going?
NORA Not bad, thanks. You?
LEO Not great. I can't do my math project. I'm stuck!
NORA Oh, dear! Not again!
LEO [1] Can you help me, please?
NORA What's the problem?
LEO I hate calculating survey results. I can't do it.
NORA Don't be silly! Of course you can. [2] ______ the results?
LEO [3] ______? I don't mind drawing the bar chart. I can do that!
NORA Of course I'm sure. Let's work on it after school. Can you do [4] ______ now?
LEO Sure.
NORA Stop talking about math and let's go get lunch!

3.10 **2 Complete the conversation with the phrases from the *Useful Language* box. Then listen and check.**

Useful Language

Are you sure?
Can you do me a favor?
Can you help me, please?
Do you need a hand with … ?

3 Look at the *Everyday English* box. Find and underline the phrases in the conversation.

Watch video 3.4
Everyday English

Don't be silly! I'm stuck.
Not again! Not great. Oh, dear!

4 Work with a partner. Practice the conversation.

PLAN

5 Work with a partner. Decide what the problem is and what help you need to solve it. Use the ideas below or your own ideas.

a school project a science experiment
your (math/drama, etc.) homework

SPEAK

6 Practice a conversation asking for help with your partner. Remember to use *can/can't* and *(don't) like, don't mind, love, hate + -ing*. Also use the vocabulary from this unit and phrases from the *Useful Language* and *Everyday English* boxes.

CHECK

7 Work with another pair. Listen to their conversation and complete the notes.

What is the problem? ______
______

What help do they need? ______
______

What is the solution to the problem? ______
______

WRITING
A Description

1 **Read Azra's description. Do you think *Dream Academy* is a real school? Why / Why not?**

Dream Academy

I'm a student at Dream Academy.

1 ☐
Students can study traditional subjects like math and English. They can also study "how to" subjects, such as how to make videos, record and produce music, be a photographer, or be a DJ. My favorite subject is how to be a DJ!

2 ☐
Students choose their own teachers. They interview them and decide together. For example, the music teacher is a famous pop star.

3 ☐
Students never have more than four classes a day. Students can choose when classes start and end.

4 ☐
Students don't have classes in classrooms – they are in learning pods. My favorite space is the music pod. I love listening to music in it.

I love studying at Dream Academy.

Azra

2 **Match headings a–d with paragraphs 1–4.**

- **a** Only Four Classes
- **b** Creative Spaces
- **c** Amazing Subjects
- **d** Star Teachers

3 **Read the *Useful Language* box. Find and underline sentences with these words in Azra's description.**

Useful Language

for example like such as

PLAN

4 **Plan a description of your ideal school. Make a spidergram to organize your ideas.**

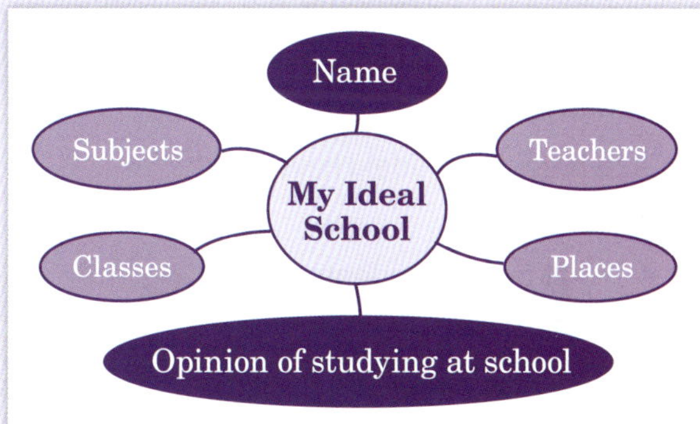

Decide what information to include in each paragraph of your description. Use your spidergram and the information in Exercise 2 to help you.

WRITE

5 **Write your description. Remember to include four paragraphs, *can/can't*, and phrases from the *Useful Language* box.**

CHECK

6 **Do you ...**

- give the name of the school in the opening sentence?
- include all of the information from your spidergram?
- give your opinion about studying at the school in your closing sentence?

Finished? p120 Ex. 4

AROUND THE WORLD

READING

A Blog Post

Globetrotters

Watch video 3.5
The School of the Air

- Where is Jamie and Paul's school?
- What subjects do they study?
- What do Jamie and Paul love doing?

3.11 **1** **Write three things you want to know about student life in Japan. Compare with a partner. Then read the blog. Does it answer your questions?**

2 **Read the blog again and answer the questions.**

1. What does Hideki do when he gets to school?
   He takes off his shoes and puts them in his locker.
2. How often do the students have an assembly?
   ______
3. Where does Hideki have lunch?
   ______
4. What do the students do at 3:30 p.m.?
   ______
5. How many hours does Hideki spend at school on Tuesdays and Fridays?
   ______

3 **Find and <u>underline</u> words in the blog to match the definitions.**

1. paragraph 1: (adj) for wearing or doing outside; not inside a building
2. paragraph 5: (n) letters or numbers you use when you write
3. paragraph 6: (n) something you play with small pieces, for example, chess

Voice It!

4 **Discuss the questions.**

1. Who takes responsibility for the cleaning in Hideki's school?
2. Why is it important to accept responsibilities?
3. What responsibilities do you have?

Welcome to My School Day!

Hi, I'm Hideki!

My school day starts at 8:30 a.m. When I arrive, I take off my shoes and I put them in my locker. We can't wear outdoor shoes at school, so we put on special **indoor** shoes.

We have an assembly with the principal in the auditorium on Monday mornings, and we have six 50-minute classes every day. My best subjects are Japanese, science, and art.

Lunchtime starts at 12:30 p.m. We don't eat lunch in a cafeteria – we stay in our classroom. Different students **serve** the meal every day and a teacher eats with us.

When classes end at 3:30 p.m., we all stay to clean up and take out the **trash**. I don't mind doing these jobs. It's important to keep our school clean and I like having the responsibility.

Almost everyone belongs to an after-school club. One of my clubs meets on Mondays and Thursdays to learn about traditional Japanese arts like *shodo* and *haiku*. *Haiku* is a type of Japanese poetry. *Shodo* is writing Japanese characters (*kanji*). I can write some characters pretty well now.

My other club is the *Go* club. It's on Tuesdays and Fridays. *Go* is a Chinese board game and it's more than 2,500 years old. I love playing it, but when I leave school after a long, busy day at 5:30 p.m., I'm usually **exhausted**.

LEARN TO LEARN

Understanding New Words from Context

When you read a text, don't look up every word. Find other words you know in the same sentence. Then try to guess the meaning of the new word.

5 **Look at the words in bold in the blog. What do they mean? Which other words in the sentences do you know?**

6 **Find and circle these phrasal verbs in the text. What do they mean?**

clean up   put on   take off   take out

7 **Complete the sentences with the phrasal verbs from Exercise 6.**

1 It's hot in here. ______ your coat!
2 Now it's cold. Can I ______ my coat again?
3 This room is messy. Please ______ before you leave.
4 We can all help to ______ the trash.

Explore It!

Is the sentence *T* (true) or *F* (false)?

Japanese teachers and students work even during breaks! ☐

Find three more interesting facts about school life in Japan. Choose your favorite fact and write a question for your partner to answer.

SHAPE IT!

CULTURE PROJECT

A Haiku

A haiku is a type of Japanese poetry. In groups, choose a topic and write a haiku.

Teacher's Resource Bank

3 REVIEW

VOCABULARY

1 Write the school subjects.

1 

2 

3 

4 

5 

6 

7 

8 

9 

2 Read the sentences and write the places.

1 Teachers have lunch here. ______
2 We do experiments here. ______
3 We can choose books here. ______
4 We always have lunch here. ______
5 We go here for an assembly. ______

GRAMMAR IN ACTION

3 Answer the questions. Write sentences that are true for you.

How well can you …

1 speak English?
______
2 use a computer?
______
3 do difficult math problems?
______
4 cook?
______
5 dance?
______

4 Write questions and short answers. Use *can*.

1 Jack / ride a bike? (✓)
______
______
2 Layla / sing well? (✗)
______
______
3 your grandma and grandpa / use a computer (✓)
______
______
4 we / drive a car? (✗)
______
______

5 Complete the sentences with the correct object pronouns.

1 We can't do this. Can you help ______?
2 Is that James? I'm not sure it's ______.
3 Where's my phone? Do you have ______?
4 Liz is stuck. Can you give ______ a hand?

6 Write the sentences.

1 She / love / do / math every day
______
2 We / not mind / get up / early for school
______
3 They / hate / play / soccer
______
4 He / not like / study / for exams
______

Self-Assessment

I can talk about my school subjects.
I can talk about the places in my school.
I can use *can* and *can't* to talk about ability and permission.
I can use verbs to talk about what I like and don't like doing.

LEARN TO ... USE FLASHCARDS

Flashcards can help you remember new vocabulary.

1 **Match the front and back of the flashcards.**

1 ________ technology (IT)

2 

3 hang ________ with friends

4 a place where you do experiments

5 

a science lab

b glasses

c mustache

d information

e out

2 **Mark the types of flashcard you can see in Exercise 1.**

1 ☑ picture + word
2 ☐ phrase with one word missing
3 ☐ word in English + word in your language
4 ☐ word + meaning
5 ☐ word + example sentence

3 **Choose five words or phrases from Unit 3. Use the words or phrases to make the five different types of flashcards in Exercise 2.**

SHAPE IT!

4 **Show the front of your flashcards from Exercise 3 to your partner. Can they guess what is on the back of each flashcard?**

physical ________

Physical ... Oh, I don't know!

It's a school subject.

Physical education!

Yes! That's right!

5 **Discuss with your partner. Which is your favorite type of flashcard from Exercise 2? Why?**

4 What do you like to eat?

LEARNING OUTCOMES

I can …

- understand texts about food
- order food and drink in a snack bar
- write a description of my favorite food
- understand how to use countable and uncountable nouns and *there is/are*
- talk about and describe food
- personalize vocabulary, answer true/false questions, and play vocabulary games
- design a food truck and evaluate a design project

Start It!

1 Look at the picture. What can you see?
2 Before you watch, name three types of food.
3 How can you learn to cook? Watch and check.
4 Do you like cooking?

Watch video 4.1

p49

Grammar in Action 4.2

p51

Grammar in Action 4.3

p52

Everyday English 4.4

a

b

c

d

e

f

g

h

i

VOCABULARY
Food and Drink

1 Write all the food and drink words you know in English. Compare with a partner.

2 Match the words in the box with the photos. Then listen, check, and repeat. 4.01

apples	☐	chicken	☐	meat	☐
bananas	☐	chocolate	*a*	rice	☐
beans	☐	eggs	☐	soda	☐
carrots	☐	fish	☐	water	☐
cheese	☐	juice	☐		

j

k

l

m

n

LEARN TO LEARN
Personalizing Vocabulary

Think about your own routines and habits when you learn new vocabulary.

3 When do you have the food and drinks in Exercise 2? Write the words in the chart.

Breakfast	Lunch	Dinner

4 Compare with a partner. Write sentences about your partner's meals. Use adverbs of frequency.

Eva always has an egg and juice for breakfast.

Get It Right!

We say *I don't like apples.* **NOT** ~~*I don't like the apples.*~~

Use It!

5 Discuss the questions.

1 Which food do you love/hate?
2 Which food do you eat when the weather is hot? What about when it's cold?

Explore It!

Guess the correct answer.

One hundred grams of ants have …

a less protein than an egg.
b more protein than an egg.
c the same protein as an egg.

Find another interesting fact about food. Then write a question for your partner to answer.

Time for a Snack

a

Leakena is from Cambodia. She doesn't have a banana for a snack today, she has a spider. She usually buys one tarantula from a food stall on the way home from school. "You cook them in **oil** and then add some **salt** and some sugar. They're like chicken or fish. The legs are my favorite!"

b

Kgosi is from Botswana in southern Africa. He doesn't have any apples today, but he has some Mopane worms. "I like sharing them with friends at school. They're great with some **peanut butter** or some rice, and they have more protein than meat. I don't have any rice today, just 50 worms!"

c

Jorge is from Oaxaca, Mexico. He has some chocolate today, but he also has a grasshopper taco. "My mom cooks grasshoppers in some oil, and she always adds some **garlic**. They're my favorite snack, and I sometimes buy them at the market."

Bugs such as grasshoppers, spiders, and worms are good for you and the planet. They give us protein and they aren't expensive to feed. Which bug do you want to try?

READING
An Article

1 **Look at the photos of food in the article. Where do you think people eat this food? Do they enjoy it?**

4.02 2 **Read the article and check your answers to Exercise 1.**

3 **Check the meaning of the words in bold in the article.**

4 EXAM **Circle the correct answers.**

Which person ...

	Leakena	Kgosi	Jorge
1 enjoys sharing snacks with friends?	A	(B)	C
2 usually buys a snack after school?	A	B	C
3 enjoys the snack with garlic and oil?	A	B	C
4 likes eating the snack with rice?	A	B	C
5 has two types of snack today?	A	B	C
6 likes eating a bug's legs?	A	B	C

Voice It!

5 **Discuss the questions.**

1 Do people in your country eat bugs?
2 Which of these bugs do you want to try?
3 How is eating bugs good for the planet?

Finished? p121 Ex. 1

Watch video 4.2
What food is there at the market today?
What's her favorite food?

GRAMMAR IN ACTION

Countable and Uncountable Nouns

Countable Nouns	Uncountable Nouns
Some nouns are countable: you can count them. *one tarantula, 50 worms, a taco, an apple*	Other nouns are uncountable: you can't count them. *chocolate, salt, sugar, meat, garlic*

1 **Complete the chart with the food words in the box.**

~~beans~~ bread carrots cheese eggs fish juice meat milk rice tomatoes

Countable	Uncountable
beans	

2 **Work with a partner. Add more food words to the chart in Exercise 1. How many do you have?**

A/An, Some/Any

	Singular Countable	Plural Countable	Uncountable
+	Leakena has [1] *a* spider.	Kgosi has [3] ____ worms.	Jorge has [5] ____ chocolate today.
–	She doesn't have [2] ____ banana.	He doesn't have [4] ____ apples.	Kgosi doesn't have [6] ____ rice today.
?	Do you have **a** spider?	Do you have **any** worms?	Do you have **any** chocolate?

3 **Complete the examples in the chart above. Use the article on page 48 to help you.**

4.03 **4** **Complete the conversation with *a*, *an*, *some*, or *any*. Then listen and check.**

CELIA Do we have [1] *any* food for the party?
OSCAR Let's take a look. Alright, we have [2] ____ cheese.
CELIA OK. Do we have [3] ____ bread?
OSCAR Sorry. We don't have [4] ____ bread, but we have [5] ____ pasta.
CELIA Do we have [6] ____ fruit or vegetables?
OSCAR We have [7] ____ apple and [8] ____ carrot.
CELIA What about drinks?
OSCAR We have [9] ____ water.
CELIA Great. What a party! I can't wait.

Use It!

5 **Work with a partner. Change the food and drink words in Exercise 4 and write your own conversation. Practice your conversation.**

Alright, we have a carrot.

OK. Do we have any apples?

Sorry. We don't have any apples, but we have some bananas.

6 **Listen carefully to other conversations. Which party do you want to go to?**

Finished? p121 Ex. 2

VOCABULARY AND LISTENING

Adjectives

4.04 **1 Complete the sentences with the adjectives in the box. Listen and check.**

cold	delicious	disgusting	fresh	healthy
hot	salty	spicy	sweet	~~unhealthy~~

1 

Soda isn't good for you, but I sometimes drink it. I know it's unhealthy.

2 

Careful! The soup is ________.

3 

Peanuts usually have salt on them. They're ________, *but they aren't bad for you.*

4 

Yuck! I really hate cheese. I think it's ________.

5 

These beetles taste great! They're ________.

6 

In my family we often use chili pepper to make the food taste ________.

7 

Dark chocolate doesn't have much sugar in it. It isn't ________, *but I love it!*

8 

I never eat ice cream in the winter. The weather is ________ *and so is ice cream!*

9 

The vegetables and fruit in our garden are always ________, *and they're a* ________ *snack.*

4.05 **2 Listen and repeat the words in Exercise 1. Which words have a negative meaning?**

Pronunciation p141

Use It!

3 Write four sentences to describe a type of food. Use adjectives.

4 Work with a partner. Take turns saying your sentences. Can your partner guess the type of food?

They're disgusting and salty.

Are they spiders?

A Quiz

LEARN TO LEARN

True or False Sentences

With true or false sentences, you have a 50 percent chance of being correct! Before you listen, read the sentences and try to predict if they are true or false.

5 Read the sentences in Exercise 6 and predict if they are *T* (true) or *F* (false).

4.08 **6 Listen to the quiz and check. How many of your predictions are correct?**

1 There are 1,000 peanuts in a jar of peanut butter. ___

2 You can't eat durians on public transportation. ___

3 White chocolate isn't really chocolate. ___

4 Carmine is an orange powder from beetles. ___

durian

cocoa

carmine

GRAMMAR IN ACTION

There Is/Isn't, There Are/Aren't

Watch video 4.3
What is in her juice?
How many hours does she sleep?

	Countable Singular	Uncountable	Countable Plural
+	**There's** a quiz in this magazine.	**There's** some water in the fridge.	**There are** 540 peanuts in a jar.
–	**There isn't** a quiz in the magazine.	**There** [1] isn't any water.	**There aren't** any oranges in this drink.
?	**Is there** a quiz in the magazine?	**Is** [2] ______ any water?	[5] ______ **there** any oranges?
	Yes, **there is.** / No, **there isn't**.	Yes, [3] ______ ______. / No, [4] ______ ______.	Yes, **there are**. / No, [6] ______ ______.

1 **Complete the examples in the chart above.**

4.09 **2** **Circle the correct words. Listen and check.**

ALI I'm hungry! Let's make some chicken and rice.
BEN We can't! There [1]*is* / (*isn't*) any rice.
ALI OK. What about an omelet? [2]*There are* / *Are there* any eggs?
BEN [3]*There's* / *There are* only one!
ALI Oh, no! [4]*There is* / *Is there* any pasta?
BEN No, there [5]*is* / *isn't*.
ALI Let's make fries! [6]*Is* / *Are* there any potatoes?
BEN No, there [7]*are* / *aren't*. There [8]*isn't* / *aren't* any food in the house!
ALI [9]*There's* / *There are* a farmers' market today. Let's go!
BEN OK. No, wait! I don't have any money!

3 **Write questions about the picture.**

1 any fruit? Is there any fruit?
2 any eggs?
______
3 any juice?
______
4 a sandwich?
______

4 **Ask and answer the questions in Exercise 3.**

Is there any fruit? *Yes, there is.*

Much/Many, A Lot Of

	Countable Plural	Uncountable
+	There are **a lot of** peanuts.	I have **a** [2] ______ **of** homework.
–	There aren't **many** eggs.	I don't have **much** time.
?	**How** [1] ______ eggs are there?	**How** [3] ______ time do you have?

5 **Complete the examples in the chart above.**

Use It!

6 **Write questions with *how much* / *how many*.**

1 fruit / do you eat / every day?
How much fruit do you eat every day?
2 people / are there / in your family?
______
3 books / do you read / in a year?
______
4 time / spend / with friends on the weekend?
______

7 **Ask and answer the questions in Exercise 6.**

How much fruit do you eat every day?

I eat an apple and an orange.

Finished? p121 Ex. 3

SPEAKING

Ordering Food and Drink

1 4.10 **Listen to the conversation. What does Julia choose from The Juice Stop?**

JUST JUICES: $6.00

THE JUICE STOP

Fresh and Natural

Sunshine Start
Start your day with a delicious mix of fruit and vegetables.

Green Goodness
Gives you energy with fresh green vegetables, and there's an apple, too!

Re-Fresh Zing
3 oranges, 2 limes, some mineral water, and our secret ingredient.

WATER STOP: $1.50
mineral water

SNACK STATION: $0.75
apple, banana, carrot

SERVER Hi. [1] *Can I help you* ?
JULIA [2] ____________ juice, please.
SERVER No problem. [3] ____________ ?
JULIA I'm not sure. [4] ____________ Sunshine Start?
SERVER There are two oranges, a carrot, and three tomatoes in that one. It's really healthy.
JULIA Hmm. What about the Green Goodness? That sounds delicious.
SERVER There are some green beans and a green apple in that.
JULIA Thanks. [5] ____________ some mineral water and an apple?
SERVER No worries. [6] ____________ ?
JULIA Yes, it is. Thank you. [7] ____________ ?
SERVER [8] ____________ $2.25, ____________ .
JULIA Here you go.
SERVER Thanks. Enjoy!
JULIA Thank you. Bye!

2 4.10 **Complete the conversation with the phrases from the *Useful Language* box. Then listen and check.**

Useful Language

Can I have … ?	Can I help you?
How much is that?	I'd like a/an/some …
Is that everything?	That's … , please.
What kind?	What's in the …?

3 **Look at the *Everyday English* box. Find and underline the phrases in the conversation.**

Watch video 4.4
Everyday English

Enjoy! Here you go.
No problem. No worries.

4 **Work with a partner. Practice the conversation.**

PLAN

5 **Work with a partner. Plan a conversation about ordering food and drink. Decide on these things.**

Where you are: ____________

What's on the menu: ____________

____

How much money the customer has:

____

What to choose from the menu: ____________

____

SPEAK

6 **Practice the conversation. Remember to use *there is(n't) / there are(n't)* and *how much / many*. Also use the vocabulary from this unit and phrases from the *Useful Language* and *Everyday English* boxes.**

CHECK

7 **Work with another pair. Listen to their conversation and complete the notes.**

Where are they? ____________

What does the customer choose from the menu? ____________

WRITING
A Description

My Favorite Food

by João Pereira

1 ☐ My name's João and I'm from Recife in Brazil. Here are some photos of my favorite types of food. I often have these on the weekend.

2 ☐ My dad makes cheese bread for breakfast. There's a lot of cheese in it. It's excellent and I eat it when it's hot!

3 ☐ I usually buy lunch from a food stand. There are a lot of them in my part of town, so it isn't difficult to find delicious food! We often have chicken *xim xim*. It's very healthy. It's chicken with rice and there are a lot of peanuts. They're salty, but they're great.

4 ☐ I love chocolate balls. I always buy them after lunch from Thiago's stand. They're very sweet. I love eating them with my hands, but I can't eat more than two or three. They're definitely my favorite dessert!

1 **Look at the photos. What do you think the food is? Read the description and check.**

2 **Match topics a–d with paragraphs 1–4.**

a dessert

b introduction: who you are, what the description is about

c breakfast

d lunch

3 **Find and underline examples of *and*, *but*, and *or* in João's description. Complete the information in the *Useful Language* box.**

Useful Language

We use [1]_____ to add similar information.

We use [2]_____ to contrast different information.

We use [3]_____ when there is a choice (usually between two things).

PLAN

4 **Plan a description of your favorite types of food. Take notes about where you get it from, what's in it, and what it's like. Decide what information to include in each paragraph. Use the information in Exercise 2 to help you.**

WRITE

5 **Write your description. Remember to include four paragraphs, *there is/are*, countable and uncountable nouns, and phrases from the *Useful Language* box.**

CHECK

6 **Do you ...**

- introduce yourself and say when / how often you eat your favorite foods?
- use adjectives to describe food?
- say why you like each type of food?

Finished? p121 Ex. 4

ART PROJECT

Design a Food Truck

1 Discuss the questions.

1 What food do you buy in the street or from food trucks?
2 When do people buy food from a food truck?
3 Are there any food trucks near where you live?

2 Look at the design for a food truck and answer the questions.

1 What kind of food do you think it sells? Caribbean food
2 What kind of soup is there? ____________
3 How much does today's special cost? ____________
4 What sweet food can you buy? ____________
5 What is the special offer? ____________

3 Work with a partner. Choose the food you want to order from the food truck. Compare with another pair.

How to Evaluate a Design

4.11

4 What do you think are the most important things in a design project? Circle the things in the list. Then listen and check.

a design
b content
c punctuation
d grammar
e paragraphs
f spelling

5 How well do you think the *Caribbean Sunshine* project presents the things in the chart? Use the key to evaluate them.

Key
Excellent ✓✓✓✓ Very Good ✓✓✓ Good ✓✓ Developing ✓

Information		Design	
Name		Menu Presentation	
Type of Food		Pictures	
Food and Drinks		Colors	
Prices			

PLAN

6 Work in groups. Choose the theme for your food truck. Then complete the steps below.

- Choose a name for your food truck.
- Decide on the design and illustrations for it.
- Decide and agree on the food you want to sell.
- Decide and agree on the prices.
- Plan and design the menu.
- Draw and illustrate your food truck.

PRESENT

7 Display your food truck design on your classroom wall. Remember to include an interesting menu with well-organized information, an attractive design, and the tips in *How to Evaluate a Design*.

CHECK

8 Look at your classmates' designs and complete the notes. Then discuss in your group.

What is the theme of each food truck? ______________________

____

Which food truck has the best design? ______________________

Which food truck would you like to eat from? Why? ______________________

____

____

4 REVIEW

VOCABULARY

1 Complete the food words with the missing vowels.

1 w __ t __ r
2 __ p p l __
3 r __ c __
4 b __ __ n s
5 j __ __ c __
6 c h __ __ s __

2 Complete the sentences with the correct adjectives.

1 I have a h__________ lunch today: an egg, an apple, and some water.
2 I hate beans. I think they taste d__________.
3 This burrito is very s__________. It has chili peppers in it.
4 The tomatoes in this sandwich are f__________. We get them from the garden every morning.
5 I love eating spiders. They're d__________.
6 Soda has a lot of sugar in it. It's u__________.

GRAMMAR IN ACTION

3 Are the words countable (*C*) or uncountable (*U*)?

1 beans __
2 chocolate __
3 worms __
4 meat __
5 rice __
6 vegetable __
7 tomato __
8 milk __

4 Complete the sentences. Use *a*, *an*, *some*, or *any* and the correct food word.

1 Do you have ______ ______  ?
2 Sam always eats ______ ______  at break time.
3 Sorry. We don't have ______ ______  .
4 I always have ______ ______  and ______ ______  for a snack.

5 Circle the correct words.

1 How *much* / *many* money do you have?
2 There *is* / *are* some rice and some chicken for dinner.
3 There's *much* / *a lot of* sugar in this drink. It's very unhealthy.
4 There *isn't* / *aren't* any carrots in the soup.
5 I don't eat *many* / *much* vegetables, but I eat *many* / *a lot of* fruit.
6 How *much* / *many* students *is* / *are* there in your class?
7 There *is* / *are* a lot of cheese in the fridge.
8 How *much* / *many* free time do you have on the weekend?
9 *Is there* / *Are there* any eggs? I want to make an omelet!
10 Why aren't there *much* / *many* books in the library?

Self-Assessment

I can name 14 food and drinks words in English.

I can use adjectives to describe food.

I can use countable and uncountable nouns with *a*/*an* and *some*/*any*.

I can use *there is*/*isn't* and *there are*/*aren't*.

LEARN TO … PLAY VOCABULARY GAMES

Games can help you practice and remember new language.

1 Ask and answer with a partner.

1 What games do you like to play?
2 What is your favorite game?
3 Do you play any games to practice English?

SHAPE IT!

2 Work in pairs. Play Word Wizard.

1 Your partner chooses a letter of the alphabet. *a*

2 Write all the food or drink words you know beginning with the letter in one minute. Don't show your partner.
apples

3 Compare your lists. You get 5 points for a word on both lists. You get 10 points for a word only on your list.

4 Play the game again. This time you choose the letter of the alphabet.

5 The person with the most points is the **Word Wizard**.

3 Work in pairs. Play Three Clues.

Player A: Think of a food or drink. Don't say it! Give Player B three clues.

Player B: After each clue, guess Player A's word. Start with 3 points. Lose 1 point for each wrong guess.

Take turns being **Player A** and **Player B**. The player with the most points at the end of the game is the winner.

Clue 1. They're healthy.
Vegetables.
No! Clue 2. They're sweet.
Bananas!
No. Last clue. Sometimes they're green and sometimes they're red.
Apples!
Yes, apples! You get 1 point!

4 Answer the questions. Write *TC* (Three Clues) or *WW* (Word Wizard).

1 Which game practices food nouns? ______
2 Which game practices food adjectives and food nouns? ______

5 Discuss with a partner. Think of word games you play in your language. Can you play them in English?

5 What's your style?

LEARNING OUTCOMES

I can ...

- understand texts about fashion and a Hindu wedding
- buy clothes and accessories
- write a description of a photo
- understand how to use present tenses
- talk about clothes and accessories
- make a picture dictionary, practice vocabulary by making connections, listen for the general idea, and guess the meaning of words

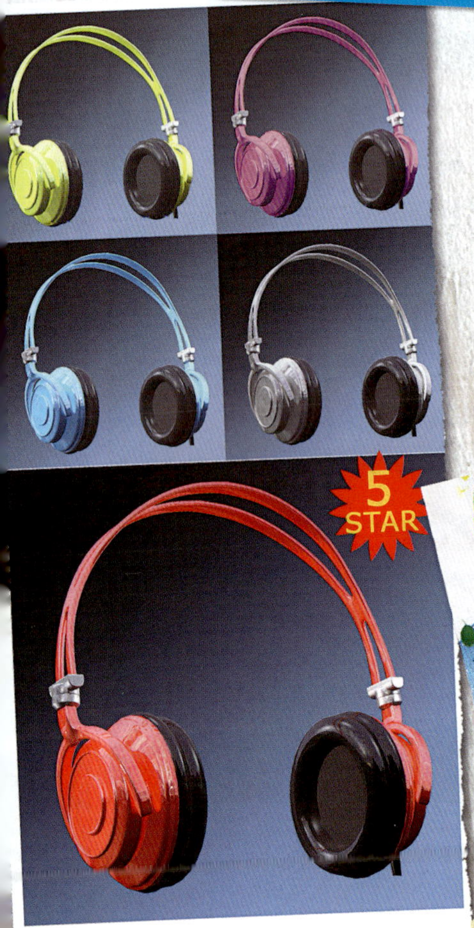

Headphones
available in five stunning colors

897-65trb
Pure cotton T-shirts
25 great new designs this year

Start It!

1. What is your style? Look at the photos. What do you like wearing?
2. Before you watch, which people wear uniforms?
3. Do all schools have uniforms? Watch and check.
4. Do you think uniforms are a good idea?

Watch video 5.1

p61
Grammar in Action 5.2

p63
Grammar in Action 5.3

p64
Everyday English 5.4

p66
Globetrotters 5.5

VOCABULARY
Clothes

5.01 **1 Match the words in the box with the pictures. Then listen, check, and repeat.**

boots	☐	shirt	☐
cap	☐	shorts	a
flip-flops	☐	skirt	☐
hoodie	☐	sneakers	☐
jacket	☐	sweatpants	☐
jeans	☐	T-shirt	☐

2 Which look do you prefer? Why? Compare with a partner.

3 Circle the one that doesn't fit.

1 skirt / jeans / sweatpants / shorts
2 flip-flops / sneakers / shirt / boots
3 shorts / jacket / hoodie
4 shirt / hoodie / jeans / T-shirt
5 jacket / cap / shirt / hoodie

LEARN TO LEARN

Making a Picture Dictionary

Drawing and labeling pictures helps you remember new words.

4 Make a picture dictionary for the clothes in Exercise 1. Compare with a partner.

5 Add more pictures to your dictionary. Cover the labels and show the pictures to a partner. Can they guess the words?

6 EXAM **Ask and answer the questions with a partner.**

Student A:
What do you usually wear to school?
What is your favorite outfit? Why do you like it?

Student B:
What do you usually wear after school?
Do you have a favorite clothing item? Why do you like it?

Explore It!

Guess the correct answer.

Flip-flops have a lot of different names around the world. What do people in New Zealand call them?

a slops b jandals c chinelos

What do you call them?

Find another interesting clothes fact. Then write a question for your partner to answer.

READING

An Online Diary

1 Look at the photos and describe the clothes you see. Where do you think the people are from?

5.02 2 Read the online diary and check your answer to Exercise 1.

3 Choose the correct answer. Which person …

Akiko	Michiko	Sofia

1 has a pet? Michiko

2 has a math test? ______

3 wants to go outside? ______

4 is Michiko's friend? ______

5 is wearing boots? ______

6 is wearing sandals? ______

4 Find adjectives in the online diary for the headings. Then think of two more adjectives for each heading.

Color: black ______

Size: ______

Style: ______

Voice It!

5 Discuss the questions.

1 Do you dress like your friends? Why / Why not?

2 How do the people you like influence the clothes you wear?

3 How does the place you live in influence the clothes you wear?

Michiko'sMix.com

Saturday, 8 a.m.

HAPPY WEEKEND!

I'm writing this post in my bedroom. My cat, Candy, is sleeping right here beside me.

What are you doing this morning? It's so hot outside!

Comments:

10 replies ❤ 12 likes

Sofia: Hi, Michiko. I'm studying for a math test! ☹ It's really hot and I want to be outside!

Michiko: Poor you! Good luck! My friend is calling me. See you later!

10 a.m. (and back online!)

We ❤ Harajuku – the Fashion District

I'm sitting in a café with my best friend, Akiko. We're mixing old-fashioned clothes with our own clothes to create a unique style today. Look! We have an umbrella for the sun, and we're wearing summer dresses and sunglasses. I'm wearing big black boots, but Akiko isn't wearing the same boots. She's wearing *zori* (they're Japanese sandals).

We're also people-watching from the café! There are a lot of different looks. There's a boy outside the café. He's wearing a black and white striped T-shirt, a red shirt, tight jeans, a green jacket, and sneakers. What a cool retro look! What do you think?

Comments:

Kyle from London: I love it!

1 p.m. Lunchtime

I'm not having ramen today. I'm having sushi and sashimi. It's definitely a sashimi kind of day. Delicious! Are you having ramen for lunch?

Comments:

Lily: No, I'm not. I'm making pizza for ten friends!

Finished? p122 Ex. 1

GRAMMAR IN ACTION
Present Continuous

Watch video 5.2
What is he wearing?
Is Hiro wearing a uniform?

	I	He/She/It	We/You/They
+	I [1]'m writing this post in my bedroom.	Akiko **is wearing** Japanese sandals.	We [5] ______ ______ summer dresses.
–	I [2] ______ ______ ______ ramen today.	Akiko [4] ______ ______ black boots.	Michiko and Akiko **aren't wearing** the same boots.
?	[3] ______ I ______ this post in my bedroom?	**Is** Sofia **studying** this morning?	What **are** you **doing** this morning? [6] ______ you ______ ramen?
	Yes, I **am**. / No, **I'm not**.	Yes, **she is**. / No, **she isn't**.	Yes, I **am**. / No, I [7] ______ ______.

Pronunciation p142

1 **Complete the examples in the chart above. Use the online diary on page 60 to help you.**

2 **Complete the posts with the present continuous form of the verbs in parentheses.**

What [1] are you doing (do)?

I [2] ______ (draw) my own design on my T-shirt. I [3] ______ (create) my own style. 🙂 *Emy*

I [4] ______ (not sit) on the beach today because it [5] ______ (rain), but I [6] ______ (wear) flip-flops. *Felipe*

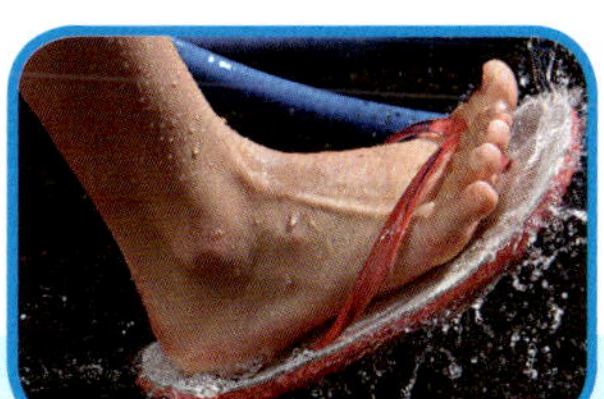

I [7] ______ (not wear) flip-flops, but that's a good idea! *Sergio*

3 **Remember the information from the online diary. Write sentences in the present continuous in your notebook. Check with a partner. How many sentences do you have?**

Get It Right!

We say: *Are you wearing a cap?* **NOT** ~~*You are wearing a cap?*~~

4 **Choose a classmate but don't tell your partner. Then ask questions to guess your partner's classmate. Ask ten questions. Your partner can only answer *Yes* or *No*!**

Is this person sitting near me?

No.

Use It!

5 **Write present continuous questions. Then ask and answer with a partner.**

1. what / you / wear / today?
   What are you wearing today?
2. which TV series / you / watch / this month? ______
3. where / your best friend / sit? ______
4. what / you / think about / right now? ______

What are you wearing today?

I'm wearing my favorite jeans, but I'm not wearing flip-flops.

Finished? p122 Ex. 2

VOCABULARY AND LISTENING

Accessories

1

2

3

4

5

6

7

8

9

10

11

12

5.05 **1 Match the words with the photos. Listen, check, and repeat.**

belt	☐	necklace	☐	sunglasses	☐
bracelet	☐	purse	1	umbrella	☐
earrings	☐	ring	☐	wallet	☐
gloves	☐	scarf	☐	watch	☐

2 Write the correct verb, *carry* or *wear*, for the accessories in Exercise 1. Complete the chart.

Carry	purse		
Wear	belt		

Use It!

3 Work with a partner. Ask and answer.

Which of the accessories in Exercise 1 …

1 are you wearing/carrying today?
2 do you have at home?
3 do you wear/carry every day?

An Interview

4 Look at the photos. Work with a partner. What are the people wearing? Do you like the clothes?

LEARN TO LEARN

Listening for the General Idea

When you listen for the first time, don't worry if you don't understand every word. Listen for the general idea.

5.06 **5 Listen to the interview. What is Tom talking about?**

a his family b his job c his clothes

5.06 **6 Listen again. Are the sentences *T* (true) or *F* (false)? Correct the false sentences.**

Tom …

1 designs clothes for musicians. ____
____
2 usually starts work at 7 a.m. ____
____
3 never works late. ____
____
4 is good at drawing. ____
____
5 makes the clothes. ____
____

GRAMMAR IN ACTION

Simple Present and Present Continuous

Watch video 5.3
Which clothes and accessories does she mention? Which three tips does she give?

	Simple Present (Facts, Habits, and Routines)	Present Continuous (Things Happening Now)
+	I **design** clothes for TV actors.	Today I [3] ________ **finishing** the designs.
–	I **don't make** the clothes.	Emily **isn't making** a shirt.
?	What [1] __do__ you **do**?	What [4] ________ she **making** now?
	I [2] ________ a costume designer.	She [5] ________ **making** a skirt and a belt.
	Time expressions: adverbs of frequency, days of the week, every day	Time expressions: now, just now, right now, today, this morning/week/month/year, at the moment

1 **Complete the examples in the chart above.**

2 **Match 1–5 with a–e. Compare with a partner.**

1 Tom is working on a TV series
2 Tom starts work
3 Tom is designing
4 Emily makes
5 Emily is making

a all the clothes.
b a skirt and a belt today.
c the girls' outfits today.
d at 7 a.m. every day.
e at the moment.

5.07 **3** **Complete the blog post with the simple present or present continuous form of the verbs in parentheses. Then listen and check.**

[1] __Do__ you __want__ (want) to know more about my life?

What [2] ________ we ________ (do) this week?
We [3] ________ (study) the history of fashion in art. It's really interesting and I [4] ________ (learn) a lot of cool new stuff.

We [5] ________ (prepare) our class fashion show this week, too. Take a look at the photo. Joe and I [6] ________ (wear) clothes from the 1980s. We [7] ________ usually ________ (not wear) clothes like this. We [8] ________ (not smile) in the photo, but we like the look! I ❤ [9] ________ (love) the 1980s.

What [10] ________ you ________ (do) right now?

Post a comment:

Use It!

4 **Write questions with the simple present or present continuous. Then ask and answer.**

What …

1 you / always / wear / on the weekend?
What do you always wear on the weekend?

2 music / you / listen to / at the moment?

____

Who …

3 you / sit next to / right now?

____

4 you / usually sit next to / at lunchtime?

____

What do you always wear on the weekend?

I always wear sweatpants on Saturday and jeans on Sunday.

Finished? p122 Ex. 3

SPEAKING

Buying Clothes or Accessories

1 **Look at the photo. What do you think Salif wants to buy?**

5.08 **2** **Listen to the conversation. Does Salif find what he's looking for?**

SALIF

SALES ASSISTANT

SALES ASSISTANT Good afternoon. [1] Can I help you?

SALIF Yes, please. [2] ______ a scarf for my grandma.

SA Sure. Let's take a look. [3] ______

SALIF My grandma doesn't wear pink. [4] ______ a different color?

SA Yes, I do. You're in luck! [5] ______ blue or purple.

SALIF [6] ______ the purple one, please?

SA Here you go. What do you think?

SALIF It's perfect. How much is it?

SA It's $15 but there's a special sale today. Buy two for $25.

SALIF No, thanks. I'm fine with just one.

SA Are you sure? It's a bargain.

SALIF No, honestly. One is fine.

5.08 **3** **Complete the conversation with phrases from the *Useful Language* box. Then listen and check.**

Useful Language

Can I help you?
Can I see the … one, please?
Do you have it in a different (size/color/style)?
How about this one / these?
I'm looking for …
It comes in …

4 **Look at the *Everyday English* box. Find and underline the phrases in the conversation.**

5 **Work with a partner. Practice the conversation.**

Watch video 5.4
Everyday English

It's a bargain. It's perfect.
No, honestly. You're in luck!

PLAN

6 **Work in pairs. Decide who is the customer and who is the sales assistant.**

CUSTOMER Decide what you are buying and who it is for. Use the ideas below or your own ideas.

something new to wear to a party
new earrings for your friend's birthday
some new sneakers for yourself

ASSISTANT Think about different colors and sizes, prices, and sales.

SPEAK

7 **Practice a conversation about buying something with your partner. Remember to use the simple present and present continuous, the vocabulary from this unit, and phrases from the *Useful Language* and *Everyday English* boxes.**

CHECK

8 **Work with another pair. Listen to their conversation and complete the notes.**

What does the customer buy?

______

How much is it?

______

Was it a special sale?

______

WRITING
A Description of a Photo

1 **Look at the photo. Which person is Eric? Read the description and find the answer.**

My Favorite Photo By Eric

1 ☐ This is a photo of my friends and me. We're all sitting on the beach. We're celebrating my friend Isabel's 13th birthday.

2 ☐ Isabel and I are in the middle. She's wearing a white T-shirt and a wool jacket. She's laughing. My friend Greg is on the left. Greg's wearing a red checked shirt. He usually wears a cap, but he isn't wearing it in this photo. He's holding some food, but he isn't eating. Sophie is next to Greg. She's wearing her new jeans. My brother Antonio is on the right. He's wearing his favorite checked shirt and his new sneakers. He's smiling. There isn't anyone in the back in this photo. I'm next to Antonio. I'm wearing khaki pants and a gray hoodie with a light gray T-shirt under it because it's cold.

3 ☐ This is my favorite photo because I'm with my friends and we're all having a great time.

2 **Read the description again and answer the questions.**

1 What are they celebrating?

______

2 Where are they?

______

3 What is Isabel wearing?

______

4 What does Greg usually wear?

______

5 Why does Eric like this photo?

______

______

3 **Match topics a–c with paragraphs 1–3.**

a description of the people in the photo
b brief description of who is in the photo
c opinion on why it is your favorite photo

4 **Complete the expressions in the *Useful Language* box.**

Useful Language

[1] __in__ the back
[2] ______ the middle
on [3] ______ left
[4] ______ the right
next [5] ______ (someone)

PLAN

5 **Plan your own description of a photo. Look at the photo below and take notes. Decide what information to include in each paragraph. Use the information in Exercise 3 to help you.**

WRITE

6 **Write your description. Remember to include the information in the correct order, the simple present and present continuous, and phrases from the *Useful Language* box.**

CHECK

7 **Do you …**

- describe people in the photo, including the clothes and accessories they are wearing?
- describe the people's positions in the photo?
- say why you like the photo?

Finished? p122 Ex. 4

AROUND THE WORLD

READING

A Magazine Article Interview

1 Look at the photo of the people. Discuss the questions.

1 Where do you think they are from?

2 What do you think they are celebrating?

2 5.09 **Read the interview and check your answers to Exercise 1.**

3 Read again and answer the questions.

1 How long does a Hindu wedding last?

2 What is a *lehenga*?

3 What does red symbolize?

4 What accessories is Mishal wearing?

5 What is a *sherwani*?

4 Complete the chart with adjectives ending in *-ful* from the interview. Check the meanings in a dictionary.

Noun	Adjective
1 wonder	*wonderful*
2 color	
3 beauty	
4 power	

Voice It!

5 Answer the questions.

1 At Hindu weddings, people use clothes to express their culture. What clothes can you wear to express your culture?

2 How do you use clothes and accessories to express your personality?

3 Why is it important to express yourself?

Globetrotters

Watch video 5.5 Culture and Fashion

- Where do the "blue people" live?
- What do the Sami make?
- Which color is important for the Maasai?

Special Days

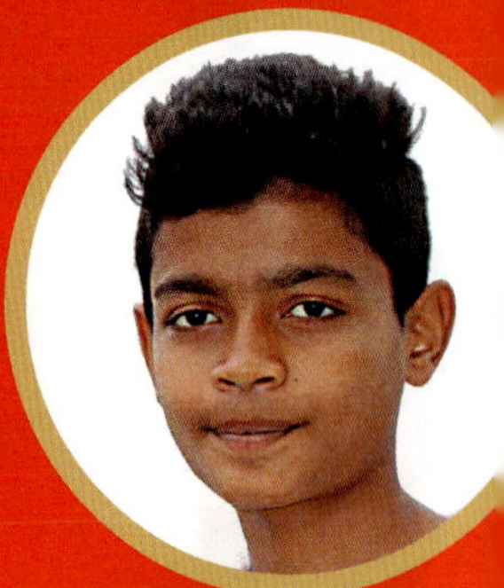

Weddings are a wonderful time for families and friends to celebrate together and to wear special clothes. This week, Amrit is talking about his cousin's Hindu wedding in India and some of their traditions.

Q: What are Hindu weddings like?

A: They're incredible! There's a lot of amazing food, music, and dancing. They're always very colorful events because everyone wears beautiful clothes. They last for three days.

Q: What does the bride wear?

A: The bride usually wears a *lehenga* (a long skirt with a top) and a long scarf. Red is very popular at Hindu weddings. It's a powerful color because in India it symbolizes love and new life. In this photo, my cousin Mishal is wearing a red and gold *lehenga*. She's also wearing special wedding accessories: a gold necklace, earrings, rings on her fingers and toes, and a lot of red and gold bracelets.

Q: What does the groom wear?

A: The groom usually wears a *sherwani* (a long jacket with gold designs on it), a pair of pants, and special wedding shoes. My cousin's new husband, Ranjit, is also wearing a red turban.

Q: Are there are any other special wedding traditions?

A: There are lots, but my favorite is *joota chupai* – a member of the bride's family steals the groom's wedding shoes and hides them. It's so much fun! In this photo, my aunt Jaz is holding Ranjit's shoes and everyone is laughing.

People around the world celebrate special days like weddings and birthdays in different ways. How do you celebrate special days in your country?

LEARN TO LEARN

Making Connections (2)

When you read an article, try to make connections with your own life and experiences. This can help you understand the article more easily.

6 **Think about a special celebration in your life and answer the questions.**

1 Is there a part of this article that reminds you of that special celebration?

2 Who and what does it remind you of: people, food, clothes, traditions?

7 **Explain your connections to your partner. Are your partner's connections the same or different?**

Explore It!

Guess the correct answer.

A Hindu bride has special paint on her hands. What does the design include?

a her age b her husband's name c the date

Find out about other interesting Hindu wedding traditions. Choose your favorite tradition and write a question for your partner to answer.

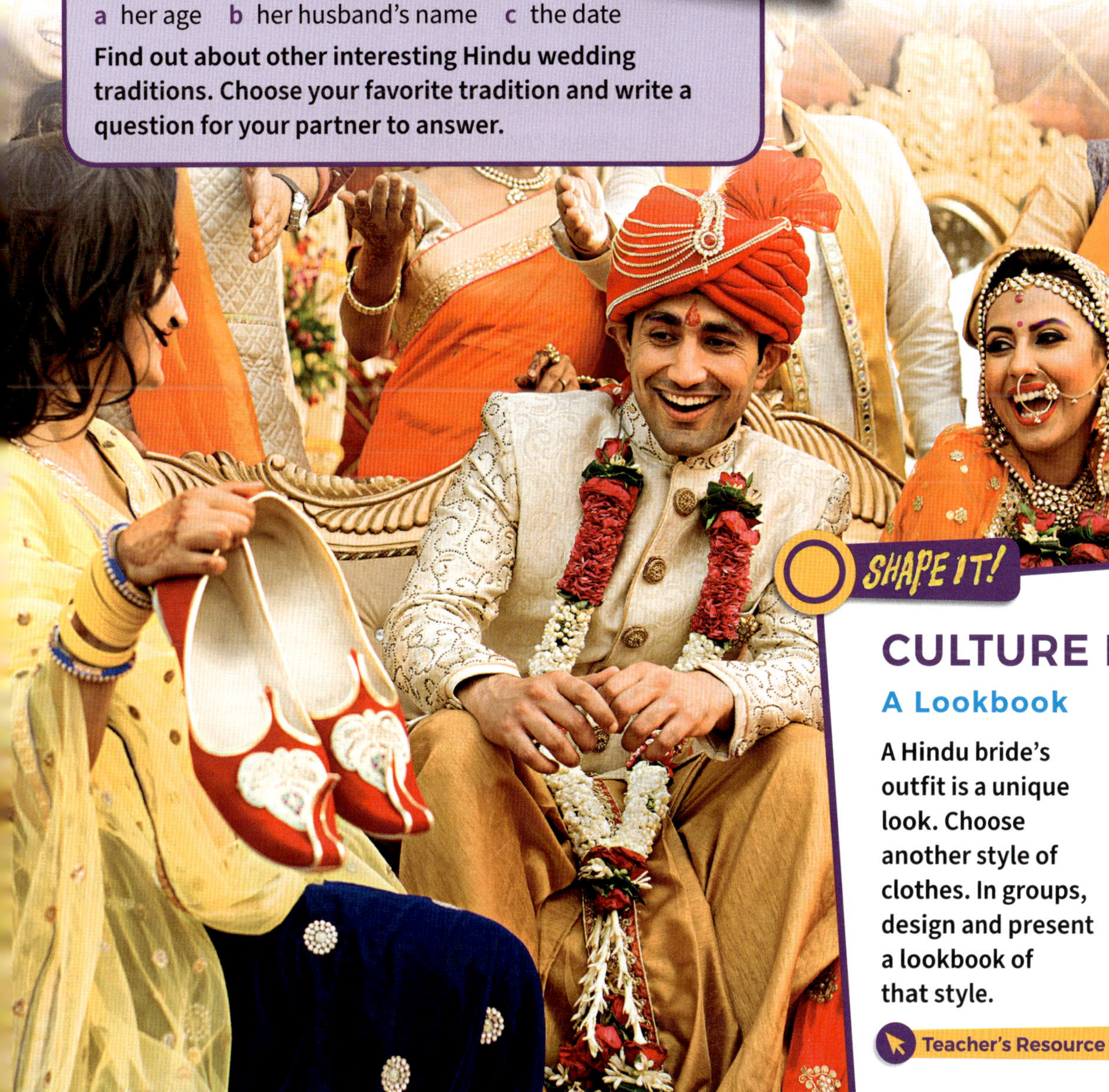

SHAPE IT!

CULTURE PROJECT

A Lookbook

A Hindu bride's outfit is a unique look. Choose another style of clothes. In groups, design and present a lookbook of that style.

Teacher's Resource Bank

5 REVIEW

VOCABULARY

1 Complete the names of clothes with the missing vowels.

1 j___ ___ns
2 sn___ ___k___rs
3 sh___rt
4 b___ ___ts
5 h___ ___d___ ___
6 sh___rts
7 c___p
8 sw___ ___tp___nts

2 Write the accessories.

1 two things you can wear on your wrist
_____________ _____________

2 two things you can put your money in
_____________ _____________

3 something you can use when it's raining
____

4 things you can wear in your ears
____

5 things you can wear on your hands when it's cold
____

3 Look at the pictures. What are they wearing? Write the clothes and accessories.

1 _____________
2 _____________
3 _____________
4 _____________
5 _____________
6 _____________
7 _____________
8 _____________

GRAMMAR IN ACTION

4 Complete the conversations. Use the correct form of the present continuous.

1 you / watch / TV right now?
✗ do / my homework
____
____

2 Lucia / wear / a red T-shirt today?
✗ wear / a blue shirt
____
____

3 Mike / chat / with his friends at the moment?
✗ take / a photo
____
____

5 Complete the posts with the simple present or present continuous form of the verbs in parentheses.

What [1] _____________ you usually _____________ (wear) at school?

I usually [2] _____________ (wear) jeans and a T-shirt. It [3] _____________ (rain) today, so I [4] _____________ (carry) an umbrella.

[5] _____________ your dad _____________ (work) today?

No, he [6] _____________ (not work) on Saturdays. He often [7] _____________ (play) soccer, but today he [8] _____________ (not do) that. He and Mom [9] _____________ (shop) downtown.

Self-Assessment

I can name 12 clothes words in English.

I can name 12 accessories in English.

I can use the present continuous to talk about what is happening now.

I can use the simple present and the present continuous together.

LEARN TO LEARN

LEARN TO ... GUESS THE MEANING OF WORDS

When you don't know a word, you can guess the meaning. This helps you read and listen in English.

1 Circle the answer that is true for you. Then compare and discuss your answer with a partner.

When I see a word I don't know, I usually ...

1. guess the meaning.
2. ask the teacher what it means.
3. look in a dictionary.
4. write it in my notebook.

2 Read the text. Then discuss the questions about each of the words in bold with a partner.

I don't like tight jeans. I prefer **baggy** jeans because they're comfortable. I have lots of T-shirts, T-shirts with long **sleeves**, T-shirts with short **sleeves**, but I don't like T-shirts with **logos** – I don't like pictures or writing on my clothes. I love sneakers. I have big feet, so it can be difficult to find my size, but my new sneakers **fit** really well. They're the perfect size!

1. Are they nouns, verbs, or adjectives?

   I think "baggy" is an adjective.

2. What clues about the meaning can you find in the text?

   Baggy jeans are not tight.
   Baggy jeans are comfortable.

3. What do you think each of the words in **bold** means?

   I think "baggy" means not tight.

SHAPE IT!

3 Read the text. Then answer the questions in Exercise 2 about each of the words in bold.

I never wear rings, bracelets, or earrings because I don't like **jewelry**, but I have lots of hats, gloves, and scarves. Why? Well, my grandma loves to make me clothes – she especially loves to **knit** me clothes. I'm happy about that, because I like to be **warm** on cold winter days, and wool clothes are great for that!

jewelry

1 noun
2 ____________________
3 ____________________

knit

1 ____________________
2 ____________________
3 ____________________

warm

1 ____________________
2 ____________________
3 ____________________

6 How can we be athletic?

LEARNING OUTCOMES

I can …

- understand texts about sports
- buy tickets
- write a profile of an athlete
- understand how to use comparatives and superlatives
- talk about sports
- say collocations out loud, remember vocabulary sets together, and write example sentences
- make an information pamphlet

Start It!

1 Look at the photo. What do you think these people are doing?
2 Before you watch, guess three sports from the video.
3 Which other sports do you see in the video? Watch and check.
4 Which sport do you want to try? Why?

Watch video 6.1

p73

Grammar in Action 6.2

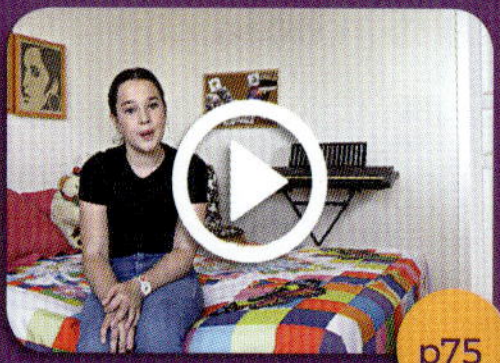

p75

Grammar in Action 6.3

p76

Everyday English 6.4

VOCABULARY

Sports

1 6.01 **Match the words in the box with the photos. Then listen, check, and repeat.**

basketball	☐	swimming	☐
gymnastics	☐	table tennis	a
hockey	☐	track and field	☐
rock climbing	☐	volleyball	☐
rugby	☐	windsurfing	☐
running	☐	yoga	☐
sailing	☐		

2 6.02 **Listen. Which six sports do you hear?**

1 *table tennis* ______ 4 ______
2 ______ 5 ______
3 ______ 6 ______

LEARN TO LEARN

Saying Collocations Out Loud

When you learn new collocations, say the words out loud. There are three main verbs we use with sports.

go	sports that end in *-ing*
play	sports with balls and other objects
do	other sports

3 Write the sports from Exercise 1 in the spidergram. Say them out loud as you write them. How many more sports can you add?

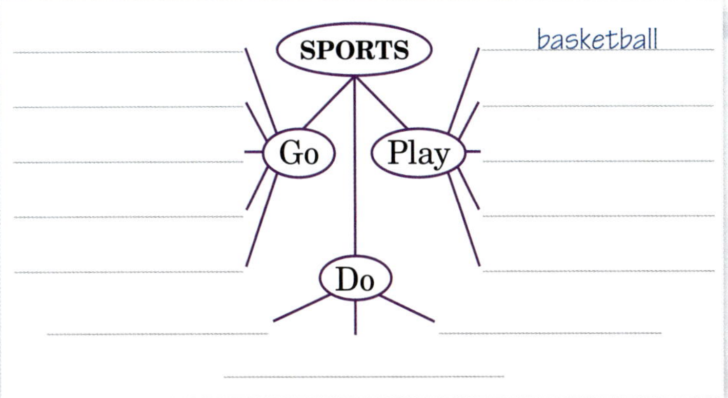

4 Work in pairs. Say a sport out loud and your partner says the verb.

5 EXAM **Ask and answer the questions with a partner.**

Student A:
What is your favorite sport?
Do you prefer to watch sports or play sports? Why?

Student B:
What sports are popular in your country?
Do you prefer to watch sports on TV or go to the game? Why?

Explore It!

Guess the correct answer.

Tennis star Serena Williams wears … every day during a tennis tournament.

a a lucky necklace
b different sneakers
c the same socks

Find another interesting fact about a sport and write a question for your partner to answer.

READING
Online FAQs

1 **What do you think the people in the photo are doing? Tell your partner.**

6.03 **2** **Read the article. Match the questions with the answers in the FAQs.**

3 **Read the article again. Are the sentences *T* (true) or *F* (false)?**

1. A bossaball team has a maximum of five people. T
2. Players can't use their feet. ____
3. A bossaball ball is the same size as a soccer ball. ____
4. You can play bossaball when it's raining. ____
5. The inventor of bossaball isn't a DJ. ____

4 **Find the meaning of the underlined words in the FAQs. Are they positive or negative? Can you add any more adjectives?**

Positive	Negative
amazing	

Voice It!

5 **Discuss the questions.**

1. Can you play bossaball in your town?
2. Do you think bossaball looks interesting or boring? Why?
3. Do you want to try it?

Finished? p123 Ex. 1

Bossaball

Do you need some help? You can't decide? What do you play: volleyball or soccer or maybe gymnastics? Don't worry! We have the answer – you can do all of them. Bossaball is the answer!

FAQs

Q1: What is it?
Q2: Is it a team game?
Q3: Where can I play it?
Q4: How big is a bossaball?
Q5: Can players touch the ball?
Q6: Is there an age limit?

Answers

A1: It's almost the same size as a volleyball and smaller than a soccer ball.
A2: No, there isn't. People of all ages can play it.
A3: Yes, it is. There are two teams and each team has three, four, or five players.
A4: Yes, they can. Players can use their hands and arms or their feet.
A5: It's a mixture of soccer, volleyball, and gymnastics with music. It's more <u>entertaining</u> than other ball sports, and in some places it's becoming more <u>popular</u> than beach volleyball.
A6: You can play it indoors if the weather's <u>bad</u>, but people usually play outdoors in a park or on a beach.

Bossaball players think it's better than volleyball and it's more <u>exciting</u> than soccer. It definitely isn't <u>boring</u> to watch, and it's even more <u>amazing</u> to play. What are you waiting for?

The inventor of Bossaball is Filip Eyckmans – he's Belgian. His favorite sports are tennis and soccer, and he also loves music and dancing. In fact, he's a DJ. Bossaball is a combination of his favorite things, and it's a lot of fun!

GRAMMAR IN ACTION
Comparatives

Watch video 6.2 Which sports does she talk about? Which sports are her favorites?

Comparative Adjectives		
Short Adjectives	**Long Adjectives**	**Irregular Adjectives**
A bossaball is [1] smaller than a soccer ball.	It's **more exciting** than soccer.	It's [3] ______ than volleyball.
A soccer ball is **bigger** than a bossaball.	Bossaball is becoming [2] ______ ______ than volleyball.	The weather is **worse** today than yesterday.

Pronunciation p142

1 **Complete the examples in the chart above. Use the article on page 72 to help you.**

2 **Write the comparative form of the adjectives.**

1 bad worse
2 big ______
3 boring ______
4 fast ______
5 good ______
6 tall ______

3 **Complete the sentences with the comparative form of the adjectives. Check your answers in the article on page 72.**

big ~~entertaining~~ exciting good

1 Bossaball is more entertaining than other ball sports.
2 Bossaball is ______ soccer.
3 A soccer ball is ______ a bossaball or a volleyball.
4 Do you think bossaball is ______ other sports you know?

4 **Write sentences with the comparative form of the adjectives in parentheses.**

1 windsurfing (exciting) swimming
Windsurfing is more exciting than swimming.
2 table tennis (interesting) yoga
______
3 climbing (difficult) volleyball
______
4 basketball players (tall) soccer players
______

Use It!

5 **Write sentences in your notebook to compare the things below or use your own ideas. Use adjectives from the box or your own. Discuss with a partner. Do you agree?**

boring comfortable difficult easy exciting good healthy interesting smart tasty

table tennis / tennis
hanging out with friends / going shopping
Italian food / Indian food
sweatpants / jeans

I think table tennis is more interesting than tennis. What do you think?

I don't agree. I think tennis is more interesting.

Finished? p123 Ex. 2

1 throw / (dive) / pass

2 kick / hit / jump

3 catch / lift / bounce

4 climb / run / score

VOCABULARY AND LISTENING

Sports Verbs

6.06 **1 Circle the correct verb to describe the photos. Then listen, check, and repeat. Can you guess the meaning of the other verbs?**

Get It Right!

You **win** or **lose** a game, match, race, or competition.

When you win, you **beat** the person or people you are competing with.

I want to win the race. **NOT** ~~*I want to beat the race.*~~

I think we can beat this team. **NOT** ~~*I think we can win this team.*~~

6.07 **2 Circle the correct verbs. Can you guess the sports? Listen and check.**

This is a popular team sport in Asia. It's a combination of volleyball and soccer. One player [1]*dives* / (*passes*) the ball to another player to start. Then players [2]*run* / *kick* the ball over the net – they can't use their hands. The first team to [3]*throw* / *score* 21 points in two games wins.

a capoeira
b underwater hockey
c sepak takraw

This is a team game with six soft balls. It's popular in PE classes around the world. Players [4]*lift* / *run* fast to pick up balls from the middle of the court. Then they [5]*dive* / *throw* their balls at the other team. If a ball [6]*hits* / *jumps* someone, that person is "out." Players can [7]*catch* / *score* a ball, but if it [8]*climbs* / *bounces* off another player, they can't use it.

a basketball
b dodgeball
c volleyball

LEARN TO LEARN

Remembering Vocabulary Sets

Think about which verbs you can use for each sport.

3 Work with a partner and add other verbs to the spidergram.

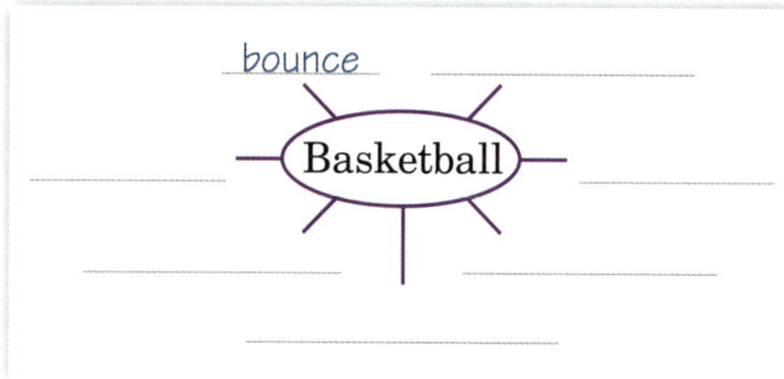

Use It!

4 Choose a sport and describe it in three sentences. Use verbs from Exercise 1. Can your partner guess the sport?

A Conversation

6.08 **5 Look at the photos. Why do you think these people are famous? Listen and check.**

Johanna Quaas

Sun Ming Ming

6.08 **6 Listen again. Circle the correct answers.**

1 Johanna Quaas trains for an hour every …
a week. b day. c morning.

2 She doesn't eat much …
a meat. b fruit. c meat or fruit.

3 Sun Ming Ming's sneakers are size …
a 41. b 55. c 37.

4 Sun Ming Ming and his wife are both very …
a popular. b tall. c old.

Watch video 6.3
Who is the most amazing painter? Who can play the piano?

GRAMMAR IN ACTION

Superlatives

Superlative Adjectives		
Short Adjectives	**Long Adjectives**	**Irregular Adjectives**
Does Sun Ming Ming have the **biggest** feet in the world?	The article is about some of the **most amazing** athletes in the world.	Fruit and vegetables are the **best** things to eat.

1 **Look at the chart above. Complete the sentences with the superlative form of the adjectives in parentheses.**

Johanna Quaas is [1] *the oldest* (old) active gymnast in the world. She's probably [2] __________ (fit) and [3] __________ (healthy) person of her age in the world.

Sun Ming Ming is [4] __________ (tall) basketball player in the world. Does the article say he is [5] __________ (good) player on his team?

2 **Complete the sports quiz with the superlative form of the adjectives. Then predict and circle the answers to the questions. Discuss with a partner.**

3 **Listen and check your answers to Exercise 2.**

6.09

THE BEST SPORTS QUIZ IN THE WORLD!

1. Fauja Singh is over 100 and he's very active. He's *the oldest* (old) person to *run a marathon* / *climb Mount Everest*.
2. Juju Noda doesn't have a car, but she can drive. She is __________ (young) person to drive a *Formula 1* / *Formula 4* racecar.
3. Many people say that *basketball* / *soccer* is __________ (easy) sport to learn to play.
4. __________ (fast) time for the men's 100 m race at the Olympic Games is *9.58* / *9.8* seconds.
5. *Volleyball* / *Table tennis* is __________ (popular) indoor sport. People of all ages play it. You only need a net, a ball, and a paddle.
6. __________ (good) food to eat before you play sports or exercise is a *carrot* / *banana*.

Use It!

4 **Write four sentences with your opinions about sports in your notebook. Use the words in boxes A and B. Then compare with a partner. Do you agree?**

A
easiest most boring
most difficult
most interesting

B
do learn play watch

I think rugby is the most boring game to watch.

5 **Write sentences with superlative adjectives about you in your notebook. Use the topics in the box or choose your own topics. Then ask and answer with a partner.**

athlete (amazing)
day of the week (good)
food (delicious)
person (happy)

Which is the best day of the week?

I think Friday is the best day of the week because school always ends early. What about you?

Finished? p123 Ex. 3

SPEAKING

Buying Tickets Online

6.10 **1 Listen to the conversation. How much do they pay for the tickets?**

6.10 **2 Complete the conversation with the phrases from the *Useful Language* box. Then listen and check.**

Useful Language

Do you want to go?
How much are the tickets?
Let's buy them.
Let's go.
They're ($145).
What's the (quickest/best/cheapest) way to get there?

3 Look at the *Everyday English* box. Find and underline the phrases in the conversation.

Watch video 6.4 Everyday English

Got them! Look! That's crazy!
What are we waiting for? Why not?

4 Work with a partner. Practice the conversation.

RUBEN Look! Our two favorite baseball teams are playing this afternoon. [1]Do you want to go?
OMAR Why not? [2]____________________?
RUBEN The best seats are the most expensive. [3]____________________.
OMAR That's crazy! Are there any cheaper tickets?
RUBEN Yes, there are. The cheapest tickets are $25, but they're the worst seats.
OMAR That's OK. I don't mind if you don't. [4]____________________.
RUBEN Got them! The game starts in an hour.
OMAR What are we waiting for? [5]____________________!
RUBEN [6]____________________?
OMAR If we hurry, the bus!
RUBEN Wait for me!

PLAN

5 Work with a partner. Plan a conversation about buying tickets online for a sports event. Decide on these things.

What event you want to see:

____

How much the tickets cost:

____

How you are going to get there:

____

a basketball game   a tennis match   a track meet

SPEAK

6 Practice the conversation with your partner. Remember to use comparatives and superlatives, the vocabulary from this unit, and phrases from the *Useful Language* and *Everyday English* boxes.

CHECK

7 Work with another pair. Listen to their conversation and complete the notes.

What event do they want to see?

____

How much are the tickets?

____

How are they going to get there?

____

WRITING

A Profile of an Athlete

1 **Look at the photo. What do you think Ashima's sport is? Read Kelly's profile and check.**

2 **Match topics a–c with paragraphs 1–3.**

a achievements
b basic information and description
c training and other interests

3 **Read the profile again and write two pieces of information for each topic in Exercise 2 in your notebook.**

Achievements: first woman to climb the Horizon rock

4 **Read the *Useful Language* box and circle the correct words.**

Useful Language

We use **also** and **too** to give extra information.
We use ***also*** [1]*before / after* the verb *to be*.
We use ***also*** [2]*before / after* other verbs.
We use ***too*** at the [3]*beginning / end* of a sentence.
We use a comma before **too**.

5 **Rewrite the second sentence with the word in parentheses.**

1 I like playing soccer. I enjoy hanging out with friends. (also)

______

2 Table tennis is easy to play. It's fun. (too)

______

3 She's running. She's jumping. (also)

______

4 He's wearing new sneakers. He's wearing a new T-shirt. (too)

______

My Favorite Athlete

By Kelly Nammour

1 ☐ My favorite athlete is Ashima Shiraishi. She's an American rock climber. She's 154 cm tall, she weighs 40 kg, and she's smaller and lighter than most climbers. She lives in New York.

2 ☐ She trains five days a week after school with her father, Hisatoshi. He's also her coach. Ashima goes rock climbing whenever she can and she practices on climbing walls in the gym, too. She loves climbing, but she also enjoys watching basketball on TV, listening to music, and watching movies.

3 ☐ I think she's amazing because she is the first woman and the youngest person to climb the Horizon rock in Japan. It's one of the most difficult rocks in the world to climb. She is one of the world's strongest climbers and one of the most successful young athletes in the world, too.

PLAN

6 **Choose an athlete to write about. Take notes about this person, and decide what information to include in each paragraph. Use the information in Exercise 2 to help you.**

WRITE

7 **Write your profile. Remember to include three paragraphs, comparatives and superlatives, and phrases from the *Useful Language* box.**

CHECK

8 **Do you …**

- give basic information and a description of your athlete?
- describe their sport using sports verbs?
- talk about their achievements and why you like them?

Finished? p123 Ex. 4

PE PROJECT

An Information Pamphlet

1 Look quickly at the pamphlet. Circle its purpose.

1 to give directions to basketball court
2 to give information about a sport
3 to give transportation times

2 Read the pamphlet and take notes on the ideas in the box.

What? When? Where? Who?
Equipment One of the rules One of the benefits

3 Read the pamphlet again. Are the sentences *T* (true) or *F* (false)?

1 You need some special equipment to play streetball. ___
2 There are sometimes ten players in a game of streetball. ___
3 You can't touch the ball with your hands in streetball. ___
4 Some sports are more expensive than streetball. ___

How to Design a Pamphlet

4 Read the tips about designing a pamphlet. Circle the ones you think are good pieces of advice.

a Use dark colors, not bright ones.
b Use photos and a map.
c Make sure the people are not smiling in the photos.
d Include contact details.
e Choose a clear font (if you're using a computer) or write neatly.
f Include everything you know about the sport.

6.11 **5 Listen to the advice and check your answers to Exercise 4.**

STREETBALL

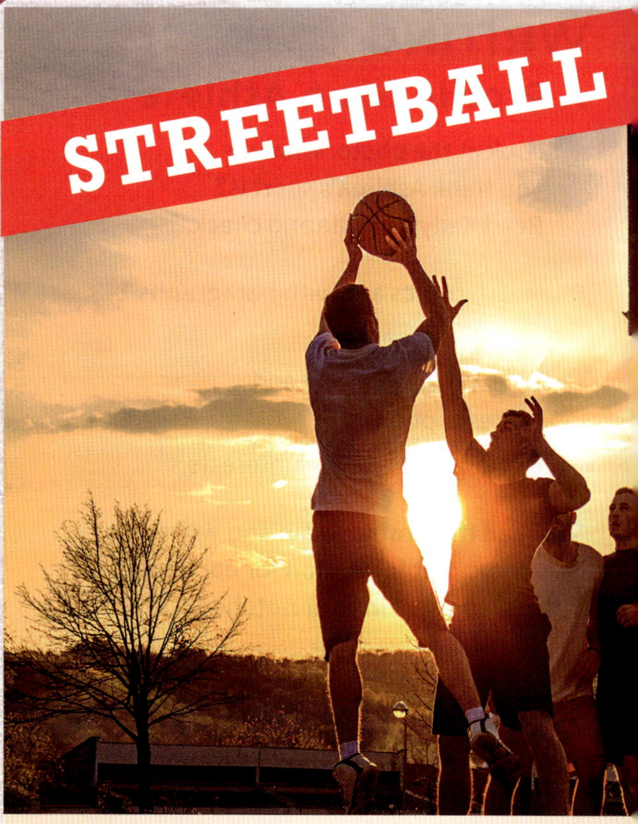

WHAT IS IT?

It's outdoor basketball in your local area.

WHERE AND WHEN?

We meet every Tuesday at 5:30 p.m. at the West Avenue basketball court. Come along and join us.

Find us here:

WHO?

Everyone is welcome! You don't need to belong to a team and you don't need special training.

WHY NOT JOIN US AND MAKE NEW FRIENDS?

EQUIPMENT

Equipment

We have a basketball and nets. Just bring yourself and your sneakers!

Teams

- A team can play with only two players, but there are never more than five.

Rules

Different streetball games have different rules, but these are ours:

- Players can bounce, throw, and catch the ball.
- When you score, your team gets one point.
- After you score, your team keeps the ball.
- A team wins when they score 7 points.

BENEFITS

- It's free!
- It's a great way to get fitter and healthier!
- The games are faster and more exciting than normal basketball.
- It's a lot of fun!

Any questions?
Contact Greg at gregscott@jmail.com.

SHAPE IT!

FACT

Bucharest is the unofficial streetball capital of the world! Every year, more than 1,000 streetball players travel to the Romanian capital city and play in a streetball competition.

PLAN

6 **Work in groups. Choose a street sport or another sport and find out information about it. Then complete the steps below.**

- Decide on the information you want to include.
- Choose the photos and illustrations to include.
- Draw a rough plan of the layout of the pamphlet.
- Make a first draft of your pamphlet.
- Discuss how you can improve your first draft.

PRESENT

7 **Prepare your final pamphlet and present it to the class. Remember to include facts about your sport, photos, illustrations and maps, and the tips in *How to Design a Pamphlet*.**

CHECK

8 **Look at your classmates' pamphlets and complete the notes. Then discuss in your group.**

Which sport is the most interesting?

____

Which pamphlet has the best design?

____

Which sport do you want to try? Why?

____

____

6 REVIEW

VOCABULARY

1 Complete the sentences with the sports in the box.

rock climbing rugby
sailing table tennis volleyball
windsurfing yoga

1 You need a net to play ________________ and ________________.
2 ________________ is a ball game that people always play outdoors.
3 People usually do ________________ indoors.
4 You need to be on the water to go ________________ or ________________.
5 ________________ can be dangerous, so you need very good equipment.

2 Circle the correct verbs.

1 We're playing soccer so we can *kick* / *score* the ball.
2 That looks heavy. Can you *climb* / *lift* it?
3 I want to *run* / *dive* a marathon one day.
4 *Catch* / *Throw* me that ball, please.
5 How do you *jump* / *score* in hockey?
6 It's important to *pass* / *hit* the ball in rugby.

GRAMMAR IN ACTION

3 Write the comparative form of the adjectives.

1 bad ________________
2 big ________________
3 easy ________________
4 exciting ________________
5 good ________________
6 interesting ________________

4 Look at the information and write sentences. Use comparative and superlative adjectives.

	Jack's Opinion		
	Table Tennis	Rugby	Hockey

Easy	★★★★	★★	★
Exciting	★	★★★★	★★
Good	★★	★★★★	★

1 table tennis / easy
____
2 rugby / easy / hockey
____
3 hockey / exciting / table tennis
____
4 table tennis / good / hockey
____
5 rugby / good
____
6 rugby / exciting
____

Self-Assessment

I can name 13 sports in English.
I can use 12 sports verbs to talk about sports.
I can use comparative adjectives to compare two things.
I can use superlative adjectives to compare three or more things.

LEARN TO ... WRITE EXAMPLE SENTENCES

Example sentences help you understand and remember vocabulary.

1 **Read Peiyu's blog. How does she remember new words? Why?**

https:\\peiyusenglishlearningblog.com

Today's Tip

Peiyu's English Learning Blog

Remembering New Words

When I learn new words, I use them in example sentences. I think it's better than writing them in my language. When I write sentences, I think about what the word means, and that helps me remember it.

Also, when you write example sentences, the meaning is easier to remember later because the other words in the sentence can help you. I try to write funny sentences or sentences about me and my friends because it's easier to remember the sentences.

Look at my notebook! What do you think?

My parents **do yoga** in the yard.

I **run** to school when I'm late.

2 **Circle the example sentences you prefer, a or b. Then compare your answers with a partner and say why.**

1 bananas
- a Bananas are nice.
- (b) Bananas are a long, yellow fruit.

I prefer example sentence b because the words "long," "yellow," and "fruit" help you remember what bananas are.

2 kick
- a In soccer, players kick a ball.
- b They kick it.

3 rugby
- a Rugby is my grandma's favorite sport.
- b Rugby is boring.

4 throw
- a Throw it!
- b My baby sister throws her food at me.

SHAPE IT!

3 **Write an example sentence for each of the words in the box.**

beat catch rock climbing score volleyball

1 ____________________
2 ____________________
3 ____________________
4 ____________________
5 ____________________

4 **Tell your partner your sentences from Exercise 3. Who has the best example sentence for each word?**

I prefer your sentence for "beat" because it's funny.

7 Why are animals important?

LEARNING OUTCOMES

I can …

- understand texts about animals
- ask for and respond to information
- write an article
- understand how to use different past tense forms
- talk about and describe animals
- categorize vocabulary, identify word forms, and use mind maps

Start It!

1. What's happening in the big photo?
2. What do you know about this animal?
3. Guess three animals in the video. Watch and check.
4. How many animals can you remember from the video?

Watch video 7.1

p85

Grammar in Action 7.2

p87

Grammar in Action 7.3

p88

Everyday English 7.4

p90

Globetrotters 7.5

VOCABULARY
Animals

7.01 **1** **Match ten animals with the photos. Then listen, check, and repeat. Which four animals are not in the photos?**

bear	☐	giraffe	a	mouse	☐
crocodile	☐	hippo	☐	parrot	☐
donkey	☐	horse	☐	snake	☐
duck	☐	lion	☐	whale	☐
eagle	☐	monkey	☐		

1 ____________ 3 ____________
2 ____________ 4 ____________

7.02 **2** **Listen to the noises. Which animals do you hear from Exercise 1?**

1 ____________ 4 ____________
2 ____________ 5 ____________
3 ____________ 6 ____________

3 **Work in pairs. Which of the animals have:**

1 a tail? 2 feathers? 3 fur?

LEARN TO LEARN

Word Categories

When you learn new words, put them into categories. This helps you remember the meaning.

4 **Complete the categories with animals from Exercise 1. Then write two more animals for each category.**

Mammals	Birds	Reptiles
giraffe	*parrot*	*snake*

Use It!

5 **Work in pairs. Guess the extra animals in each of your partner's categories.**

6 **Write new categories for the animals. Tell your partner the animals but NOT the categories! Can your partner guess your new categories?**

Mouse, parrot, snake

Is your category "pets"?

Explore It!

Guess the correct answer.

A blue whale's tongue weighs the same as …

a a crocodile. b an elephant. c a giraffe.

Find another interesting animal fact. Then write a question for your partner to answer.

Animals with a Difference

Snowflake

From 1964 to 2003, there was a special gorilla in the Barcelona Zoo. His name was Snowflake, and he was born in Africa. Snowflake was a celebrity in the zoo. He wasn't the same as the other gorillas because he was white. He was the world's only white gorilla.

Nómade

In the 1990s, in Mozambique, southern Africa, a baby elephant was born without tusks. Her name was Nómade. Her eleven sisters were born without them, too. In the 1930s, there weren't many African elephants without tusks, only 1 percent. But in some areas of Africa today, 98 percent of female elephants are born like this.

Artico

In 2004, a Bengal tiger named Artico was born in a wildlife center in Alicante, Spain. But Artico wasn't like his parents. He was white with no stripes, but his parents weren't. They were orange with black stripes. Today, there are only about 20 Bengal tigers without stripes in the world.

GORILLA FACT FILE

WEIGHT Up to 270 kg
HABITAT African forests and mountains
FOOD Fruit, leaves, and plants
FACT Gorillas are the largest mammals to build nests. They make a new nest every night.

AFRICAN ELEPHANT FACT FILE

WEIGHT Up to 6,000 kg
HABITAT African savannah and forests
FOOD Grass, leaves, trees, fruit, and plants
FACT Elephants use their feet to listen.

BENGAL TIGER FACT FILE

WEIGHT Up to 230 kg
HABITAT Forests and mountains in Southeast Asia
FOOD Deer, buffalo, antelopes, and other animals
FACT There aren't two tigers with the same stripes.

READING

Fact Files

1 **Tell your partner two things you know about gorillas, elephants, and tigers.**

2 **Look at the photos. What is different about Snowflake, Nómade, and Artico?**

3 7.03 **Read the text and the fact files. Check your answers to Exercise 2. Find out two more things about each animal.**

4 EXAM **Circle the correct answers.**

	Snowflake	Nómade	Artico
1 Who was born in Spain?	A	B	(C)
2 Who was female?	A	B	C
3 Who was very famous?	A	B	C
4 Who was similar to her sisters?	A	B	C
5 Who was not white?	A	B	C
6 Whose parents had stripes?	A	B	C
7 Who lived in a zoo?	A	B	C

5 **Find words in the fact files for each of these categories. Think of two more words for each category.**

Animals: *gorilla* ______
Things animals eat: ______
Habitats: ______

Voice It!

6 **Why do you think …**

1 tigers have stripes?
2 gorillas build a nest every night?
3 some elephants are born without tusks?

Finished? p124 Ex. 1

Watch video 7.2
What color was the flamingo when it was a baby?
What animals were there?

GRAMMAR IN ACTION

Simple Past: *To Be, There Was/Were*

	Singular	Plural
+	His name [1] was Snowflake.	They [6] ______ orange with black stripes.
	There [2] ______ a special gorilla in the zoo.	**There were** other gorillas in the zoo.
–	Artico [3] ______ like his parents.	His parents [7] ______ white tigers.
	There wasn't a white elephant.	**There** [8] ______ many elephants without tusks.
?	**Was** Artico completely white? Yes, he [4] ______. / No, he **wasn't**.	**Were** they tigers? Yes, they [9] ______. / No, they **weren't**.
	Was there a gorilla? Yes, **there was**. / No, **there** [5] ______.	**Were there** any elephants? Yes, **there were**. / No, **there** [10] ______.

1 **Complete the examples in the chart above. Use the text on page 84 to help you.**

2 **Find information in the text on page 84 to correct the sentences.**

1. Artico was a lion.
   He wasn't a lion. He was a tiger.
2. Snowflake was born in Barcelona.
   He ______
3. Nómade was an Indian elephant.
   She ______
4. Snowflake and Artico were black.
   They ______

3 **Complete the text with *was(n't)/were(n't)* or *there was(n't) / there were(n't)*.**

GIANT DRAGONS!

In the past, on the Island of Flores, [1] there were animals like elephants. But [2] ______ one difference: they [3] ______ very small. [4] ______ also Komodo dragons and huge rats on the island. [5] ______ people on Flores? Yes, [6] ______, but they [7] ______ very tall. They [8] ______ only about one meter tall. That's the size of a three-year-old! And their brain [9] ______ the size of an orange!

Use It!

4 **Write questions with *was/were*. Then ask and answer with a partner.**

1. Where / born?
   Where were you born?
2. What / favorite subject in elementary school?
3. What / favorite animal / when / you / six?
4. Who / best friend / when / you / eight?
5. Where / you / at six o'clock on Sunday evening?
6. When / your last vacation?

Finished? p124 Ex. 2

VOCABULARY AND LISTENING

Adjectives

7.04 **1 Circle the correct adjective to describe photos 1–6. Then listen, check, and repeat.**

2 Write opposite adjectives from Exercise 1 for the words below.

1. short ___long___
2. light ______
3. huge ______
4. quiet ______
5. safe ______

Use It!

3 Think of three animals. Write two sentences to describe each one in your notebook. Tell your partner. Can they guess the animal?

It's quiet and fast. It sometimes lives in houses.

Is it a mouse?

A Podcast

4 Discuss the questions with a partner.

1. What can parrots do?
2. Are parrots good pets? Why / Why not?

7.05 **5 Listen to the podcast and circle what it's about.**

a. a hungry parrot
b. an intelligent parrot
c. a dangerous parrot

LEARN TO LEARN

Preparing to Listen

Thinking about the questions before you listen can help you hear the correct answers.

6 Underline the question words in Exercise 7.

7.05 **7 Listen again and answer the questions.**

1. How old was Hannah? ___two years old___
2. Who was really noisy? ______
3. Who wasn't at home on the day of the story? ______
4. What was on the table? ______
5. Where was Meagan when Hannah ate the toast? ______

8 Work in pairs. Take turns telling the story.

There was a little girl named Hannah …

and there was a parrot named Willie.

GRAMMAR IN ACTION

Simple Past: Regular and Irregular Verbs

Watch video 7.3
Which animals ran away?
Who touched a snake?

	Regular Verbs	Irregular Verbs
+	They [1] lived in Denver.	Meagan **had** a pet parrot.
–	Hannah **did not** ([2] ________) **want** to wait.	Meagan **didn't** [4] ________ any children.
Past Time Expressions	It **happened** more than ten years [3] ________. You **shared** some great stories with us **last week**.	We **heard** this amazing story **yesterday**. They **wrote** to us **last year**.

> Irregular verbs p143   > Pronunciation p142

1 **Complete the examples in the table above.**

2 **Circle the correct words to complete the sentences. Mark the sentences that have irregular verbs.**

1. Meagan *made* / *didn't make* toast for Hannah. ☑
2. She *left* / *didn't leave* the toast on the table. ☐
3. The parrot *followed* / *didn't follow* Meagan. ☐
4. Hannah *ate* / *didn't eat* the toast. ☐
5. Meagan *heard* / *didn't hear* a lot of noise. ☐
6. Willie *stopped* / *didn't stop* saying the words. ☐
7. Meagan *ran* / *didn't run* into the kitchen. ☐
8. The parrot *saved* / *didn't save* Hannah's life. ☐

Get It Right!

Use the base form of the verb after **didn't**.

She didn't go to class. **NOT** ~~She didn't went to class.~~

7.09 **3** **Complete the text. Then listen and check.**

A Croc's Best Friend

Gilberto "Chito" Shedden was a fisherman in Costa Rica. One day, he [1] saw (see) a crocodile in the river. It [2] ________ (have) an eye problem, so Chito [3] ________ (decide) to take the crocodile home. He [4] ________ (feed) the crocodile and [5] ________ (give) it medicine. He named it Pocho. Chito [6] ________ (not leave) Pocho, and at night they [7] ________ (sleep) in the same room. When Pocho was healthy again, Chito [8] ________ (take) him to the river. But Pocho [9] ________ (not want) to stay in the river, so he [10] ________ (follow) Chito home! Pocho and Chito [11] ________ (become) best friends until Pocho [12] ________ (die) a few years ago.

Use It!

4 **Write sentences with *ago*. Change the words in bold so that the sentences are true for you. Then work with a partner and say your sentences. Are any the same?**

1. This class / start / **thirty minutes**
   This class started forty-five minutes ago.
2. I / get up / **four hours**
   ____
3. I / have / breakfast / **three hours**
   ____
4. I / meet / my English teacher / **six months**
   ____

5 **Write three true and three false sentences about yourself in your notebook. Use the simple past and past time expressions.**

6 **Take turns saying your sentences. Can your partner guess which are true and which are false?**

I went to Brazil on vacation last week.

False! You were at school last week.

Finished? p124 Ex. 3

SPEAKING

Talk About a Field Trip

7.10 **1 Listen to the conversation. Where was Martha yesterday?**

DANIEL Hey, Martha. [1] How was the field trip yesterday?
MARTHA [2] __________ really cool! We went to a safari park.
DANIEL Really? [3] __________?
MARTHA It was amazing!
DANIEL Were there any elephants?
MARTHA Yeah, there were, but I didn't see them.
DANIEL I can't believe you didn't see any elephants. [4] __________ lions?
MARTHA Yeah, there was a family of lions. One of them looked inside our car.
DANIEL Wow! No way!
MARTHA Yup. It did. Then it climbed in the window and ate my lunch.
DANIEL You're joking!
MARTHA Of course I'm joking!

7.10 **2 Complete the conversation with the phrases from the *Useful Language* box. Then listen and check.**

Useful Language

How was (the field trip)?	It was (really cool).
What about (lions)?	What was (it) like?

3 Look at the *Everyday English* box. Find and underline the phrases in the conversation.

Watch video 7.4 Everyday English

No way!	Really?
Wow!	You're joking!

4 Work with a partner. Practice the conversation.

PLAN

5 Work with a partner. Plan a conversation about a field trip. Decide on these things.

Where you went: __________

What you saw: __________

What you didn't see: __________

What happened: __________

____

SPEAK

6 Practice the conversation with your partner. Remember to use verbs in the past and phrases from the *Useful Language* and *Everyday English* boxes.

CHECK

7 Work with another pair. Listen to their conversation and complete the notes.

Place: __________

What they saw: __________

What they didn't see: __________

What happened: __________

____

WRITING
An Article

Skateboarding Dog
By Lidia Watson

1 ☐ Can you skateboard? Tillman, a dog from California in the U.S.A., could. He could skateboard 100 meters in 20 seconds!

2 ☐ In 2007, millions of people watched a video of him skateboarding. Soon, he became an international star. Tillman also liked other sports. He could snowboard and surf. Several years ago, he won first place in a surfing competition. On October 27, 2015, Tillman died. He was 10 years old.

3 ☐ Now there are many skateboarding, snowboarding, and surfing dogs. Some even have their own websites! Do you know any animals with amazing abilities?

1 **Look at the photo. Why do you think this dog is different? Read the article and check your ideas.**

2 **Match topics a–c with paragraphs 1–3.**

a description of things Tillman did
b introduction to the subject
c conclusion that asks a question

3 **Read the article again and complete the notes.**

Skateboarding Dog

Who Tillman
What ______
Where ______

4 **Look at the *Useful Language* box. Find and underline the time expressions in the article.**

Useful Language

In 2007 On October 27, 2015 Several years ago

Get It Right!

We use **on** for days and dates.
On Friday / On October 27
We use **in** for months and years.
In October / In 2007

PLAN

5 **Read the notes about a dog named Betsy. Use the notes to plan an article or make your own notes about a famous animal.**

Most Intelligent Dog

Who Betsy
What understands more than 340 words
Where Vienna, Austria

Decide what information to include in each paragraph. Use the information in Exercises 2 and 3 to help you.

WRITE

6 **Write your article. Remember to include three paragraphs, the simple past, and time expressions.**

CHECK

7 **Do you ...**

- introduce the animal in the first paragraph?
- describe what the animal did?
- use time expressions?

Finished? p124 Ex. 4

AROUND THE WORLD

READING

An Article

7.11 **1** **Look at the photo. Where do you think the girl is from? Why is she special? Read the article to check your answers.**

2 **Read the article again and answer the questions.**

1 How old are boys when they learn to hunt with eagles? ____13____
2 How fast can eagles fly? ________
3 Where was Aisholpan's baby eagle when she found it? ________
4 Who was Aisholpan's trainer? ________
5 Who was the youngest person in the 2016 Golden Eagle Festival competition? ________

Globetrotters
Watch video 7.5
Helpers with Hooves

- Where can you find camels?
- How much water can camels drink in ten minutes?
- What temperatures can camels survive in?

Voice It!

3 **Discuss the questions.**

1 Aisholpan was determined to succeed. How did she show determination?
2 Why is determination important?
3 Can you give an example of when you showed determination?

The Girl and the Golden Eagle

Can you imagine riding a horse in temperatures of –50 °C with a huge eagle on your arm?

The ancient tradition of eagle hunting started thousands of years ago in Mongolia. Traditionally, it was only for boys in Mongolia, and this tradition continues today. Boys learn to hunt when they are only 13. They use eagles because they can fly up to 320 kph and can see animals from more than four kilometers away. There are about 400 male eagle hunters today. But no 13-year-old girls … until now.

The 2016 film *The Eagle Huntress* tells the story of Aisholpan. When she was young, Aisholpan took care of her father's eagle, but she really wanted to be an eagle hunter like her father. So she went to the high Altai Mountains with her father to find a baby eagle to train. It wasn't easy. The climb to the eagle nest was difficult and dangerous. But Aisholpan did it. She found her baby eagle!

Aisholpan's father became her trainer. But was Aisholpan strong enough to hunt with the huge bird in freezing temperatures? Yes, because she was determined to succeed.

In 2016, Aisholpan competed in the Golden Eagle Festival. She was the first Mongolian girl to enter the competition. There were 70 competitors. She was the youngest and the only girl. And guess what? Her eagle won. What an amazing achievement!

LEARN TO LEARN

Noun and Verb Forms

When you learn a new word, try to learn some other forms of the word. This will help you understand reading texts. We can add different endings to verbs to make nouns, for example, *-er*, *-ing*, *-or*, *-tion*, etc.

4 Complete the chart with words from the text.

Verb	Noun (person)	Noun (thing)
1 compete	competitor	6 ______
hunt	4 ______	7 ______
train	5 ______	training
2 ______	climber	climb
3 ______	learner	learning

5 Write sentences with words from the chart in Exercise 4. Take turns saying sentences, but do NOT say the word you chose. Can your partner guess your word?

They … a mountain every year.

Is the word "climb"?

Explore It!

Guess the correct answer.

Eagle hunters use *male* / *female* eagles because they grow bigger and are more powerful.

Find three interesting facts about eagle hunters. Choose your favorite fact and write a question for your partner to answer.

SHAPE IT!

CULTURE PROJECT

A Scrapbook

Aisholpan is from the Altai Mountains. Choose a place with mountains in your country that you remember visiting.

In groups, make a paper or digital scrapbook about this place.

Teacher's Resource Bank

7 REVIEW

VOCABULARY

1 Write the animals.

1 

parrot

4 

______

2 

______

5 

______

3 

______

6 

______

2 Complete the adjectives with the missing vowels.

1 w i ld
2 t _ ny
3 n _ _ sy
4 b _ _ _ t _ f _ l
5 q _ _ _ t
6 l _ zy
7 d _ ng _ r _ _ s
8 h _ _ vy
9 c _ t _
10 l _ rg _
11 l _ ng
12 sm _ rt

GRAMMAR IN ACTION

3 Joe and Sylvie went to a wildlife park last week. Write sentences with the correct form of *there was/were*.

1 Were there many animals? (?)
2 ______ two lions. (✓)
3 ______ an elephant with no tusks. (✗)
4 ______ a tiger with no stripes. (✓)
5 ______ any donkeys. (✗)
6 ______ a white gorilla? (?)

4 Complete the text with the simple past of the verbs in parentheses.

Mammoths 1 lived (live) many, many years ago in Asia, Europe, and North America. They 2 ______ (die) because the weather 3 ______ (get) warmer and they 4 ______ (not can) find any food. They 5 ______ (be) about 3.5 m tall and 6 ______ (weigh) about 6,000 kg. Their tusks 7 ______ (be) very, very long – about five meters! They 8 ______ (be) herbivores, so they 9 ______ (not eat) other animals. They 10 ______ (eat) grass, plants, and flowers.

Self-Assessment

I can name 14 animals in English.

I can use adjectives to describe animals.

I can use *was* and *were* to describe the past.

I can use regular and irregular verbs to talk about the past.

LEARN TO ... USE MIND MAPS

Mind maps can help you think of ideas and plan how to organize them.

1 Discuss the questions.

1 What is a mind map?
2 Why do people make mind maps?
3 Do you use mind maps?

2 Look at the mind map below. What is the topic?

____

3 Complete the mind map with the words and phrases below.

1 Soccer
2 Where?
3 magazines
4 on the weekend

SHAPE IT!

4 Make a mind map about your favorite animal. Follow the instructions.

1 Write the topic in the middle.
2 Add three main ideas about the topic.
3 Write one or two questions about each main idea.
4 Write notes about your answers to each question.

5 Use your mind map to talk to your partner about your favorite animal.

6 Circle how you feel. Then compare and discuss your answers with a partner.

The mind map helped me ...	Agree → Disagree				
1 think of ideas.	5	4	3	2	1
2 organize my ideas.	5	4	3	2	1
3 remember to say all my ideas.	5	4	3	2	1
I enjoyed ...					
4 making the mind map.	5	4	3	2	1
5 using the mind map.	5	4	3	2	1

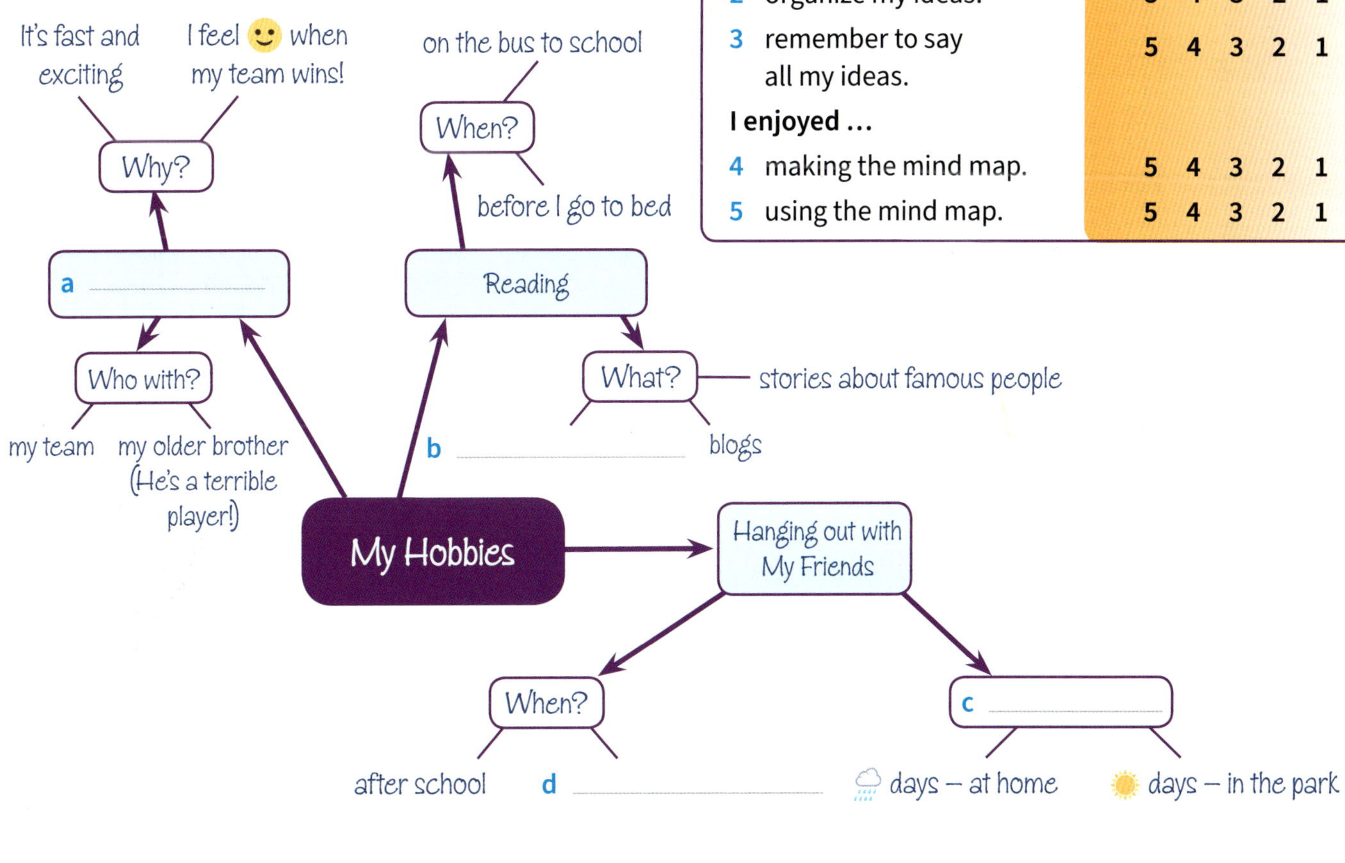

8 What did you find?

LEARNING OUTCOMES

I can ...

- understand texts about an unusual town and finding treasure
- help a friend
- write a blog post
- understand how to ask simple past questions
- talk about places in town and personal possessions
- use compound nouns, photos to predict content, and improve my writing
- do an interview

Start It!

1 Describe the photo. Where do you think this is?

2 Before you watch, where do you look when you lose something?

3 What do archaeologists want to know? Watch and check.

4 What's your favorite treasure? Why?

Watch video 8.1

p97 Grammar in Action 8.2

p99 Grammar in Action 8.3

p100 Everyday English 8.4

VOCABULARY
Places in Town

8.01 **1 Match the places in the box with the photos. Then listen, check, and repeat.**

aquarium	☐	parking lot	☐
bowling alley	a	post office	☐
gym	☐	shopping mall	☐
hospital	☐	skate park	☐
ice rink	☐	swimming pool	☐
movie theater	☐		

2 Which places in Exercise 1 are in your town? Which ones do you sometimes or often go to? Compare with a partner.

LEARN TO LEARN

Compound Nouns

There are lots of compound nouns in English. The two words together usually have a different meaning from the separate words.

3 Look at the places in Exercise 1. Which words are compound nouns? Can you think of any more compound nouns?

Use It!

4 Answer the questions. Then write two more questions about the places in Exercise 1 for your partner to answer.

Where do you go to …

1 buy clothes and accessories? ____________

2 see fish and sea creatures? ____________

3 see a doctor? ____________

4 watch a movie? ____________

5 do sports and exercise? ____________

____

____

Explore It!

Guess the correct answer.

The Dubai Mall is one of the largest shopping malls in the world. There are 1,200 stores, and there's also …

a an aquarium. b a swimming pool. c a skate park.

Find another interesting fact about the Dubai Mall. Then write a question for your partner to answer.

READING

An Online Travel Article

1 **Look at the photo of the town. What do you think happened?**

8.02 **2** **Read the article and check your answer to Exercise 1.**

3 **Find out what the words in bold in the article mean.**

4 EXAM **Read the article again and circle the correct answers.**

1 Until 1985, Pablo lived … in Villa Epecuén.
  A with his family
  B on his own
  C with one of his grandchildren

2 When Villa Epecuén flooded, … of the residents stayed.
  A some   B none   C all

3 Pablo now lives …
  A with his family.
  B with a friend and his dogs.
  C alone with his dogs.

4 Pablo … being the only person in Villa Epecuén.
  A hates   B loves   C doesn't mind

5 Pablo spends time each day …
  A reading the newspaper.
  B shopping for food.
  C sitting in the train station.

6 Pablo has … memories of the town in the past.
  A sad   B happy   C no

Voice It!

5 **Discuss the questions.**

1 Do you know any towns like Villa Epecuén?
2 Look at the questions in the Comments section. Think of two more questions to ask Marisa about Villa Epecuén.

Finished? p125 Ex. 1

Lost Treasures

Last week, our travel writer, Marisa Castillo, visited the town of Villa Epecuén in Argentina and met its only inhabitant, Pablo Novak.

Pablo grew up in Villa Epecuén, and until 1985 he had a normal family life there. On November 10, 1985, after weeks of heavy rain, a lake **flooded** the town and it gradually disappeared under 10 meters of water. All of the town's 1,500 **residents** left. In 2009, the water began to go down and Pablo decided to return.

Now he and his dogs live in an **abandoned** house with no electricity. One of his 21 grandchildren visits him every day and brings him food. He doesn't mind being the only person there. "I am OK here. I am just alone. I read the newspaper. And I always think of the town's golden days," Pablo said.

His **memories** of those golden days brought the town to life for me. As we walked past empty buildings, those places suddenly became family homes, noisy swimming pools, hotels full of **tourists**, and busy parking lots.

Comments

Libby: Did Pablo and the other residents move far away?

Marisa: No, they didn't. They moved to a town called Carhué about seven km away.

Luca: Cool story! Did Pablo's wife want to go back to Villa Epecuén with him?

Marisa: No, she didn't. His wife and family started a new life in Carhué.

Watch video 8.2
What did he do on the weekend?
Did his parents like what he did?

GRAMMAR IN ACTION

Simple Past: Questions

	Yes/No Questions		Short Answers
Did	Pablo and the other residents	[1] *move* far away?	Yes, they **did**. / No, they [3] ______.
	Pablo's wife	[2] ______ to go back?	Yes, she **did**. / No, she [4] ______.

Pronunciation p142

1 **Complete the examples in the chart above. Use the article on page 96 to help you.**

2 **Write simple past questions and answers. Check your answers in the article on page 96.**

1 the lake / flood / Villa Epecuén?

Did the lake flood Villa Epecuén? Yes, it did.

2 the residents / stay / after the flood?

______

______

3 the water / start / to disappear in 2009?

______

______

4 Pablo / return / in 2009?

______

______

8.05 **3** **Complete the conversation with the correct form of the verbs. Listen and check.**

ANNA [1] *Did* you *go* (go) to the ice rink last night?

LALO Yes, I [2] ______.

ANNA [3] ______ you ______ (see) Jack there?

LALO No, I [4] ______. I was with Tom and Kirsten.

ANNA [5] ______ you all ______ (have) a good time?

LALO No, we [6] ______. It was freezing and the music was really bad.

ANNA Oh, no! [7] ______ you ______ (buy) some food later?

LALO Yes, we [8] ______. We bought a pizza at the café.

ANNA [9] ______ you ______ (enjoy) it?

LALO No, we [10] ______. It was disgusting!

ANNA Oh, no! Try the burger place next time.

Get It Right!

Remember to use **Did** and the base verb form in simple past questions.

Did Pablo return? **NOT** ~~*Pablo returned?*~~

8.06 **4** **Look at Simon's list. Write a conversation between Simon and his mom. Listen and check.**

80%

do your homework ✓
cook dinner ✗
buy movie tickets ✓
finish your science project ✗
call Grandpa ✓
clean your bedroom ✗

Use It!

5 **Write simple past questions. Then work with a partner and ask an answer.**

1 you / go / to the swimming pool last Saturday?

Did you go to the swimming pool last Saturday?

2 you and your family / watch / TV last night?

______

______

3 your parents / drive / you to school today?

______

______

4 your best friend / text / you this morning?

______

______

Finished? p125 Ex. 2

VOCABULARY AND LISTENING

Personal Possessions

8.07 **1 Match the words in the box with the photos. Listen, check, and repeat.**

bus pass	☐	laptop	☐
camera	☐	money	☐
concert ticket	1	passport	☐
headphones	☐	phone	☐
ID card	☐	portable charger	☐
keys	☐	tablet	☐

2 Look in your bag. How many of the possessions in Exercise 1 do you have? Compare with your partner.

Use It!

3 Describe a possession you used yesterday. Can your partner guess?

I used this on the bus yesterday.

Your phone?

1
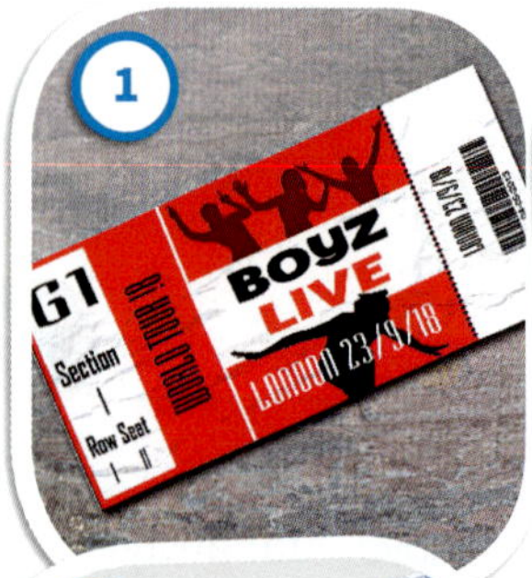

2

3

4

5

6

7

8

9

10

11

12

A Radio Interview

LEARN TO LEARN

Using Photos to Predict Content

Before you listen, look carefully at any pictures. Think about the connection between them.

4 Look at the photos in Exercise 6 and read the sentences. Work with a partner and say what you think the story is about.

8.08 **5 Listen to the radio interview and check your answer to Exercise 4. Were you correct?**

8.08 **6 Listen again. Are the sentences *T* (true) or *F* (false)?**

1 Andres goes out every weekend to look for treasure. F
2 Andres uses special equipment when he does his hobby. ___
3 Detectorists always collect old soda cans. ___
4 When detectorists find treasure, they dance. ___
5 Andres found some very old Roman money. ___

Voice It!

7 Discuss the questions.

1 Do you know anyone with an unusual hobby like Andres?
2 Imagine you find some ancient treasure. How do you feel? What do you do?

GRAMMAR IN ACTION
Simple Past: *Wh*- Questions

Watch video 8.3
What did Nick lose? Where did Nick find them?

Where	did	you	go last weekend?
Who		you	go with?
What		your dad	do?
When		you	take that photo?
How		Andres	find the treasure?

1 Look at the chart above. Put the words in the correct order to write the questions. Then match them with the answers.

1 Andres / find / did / the treasure / when?
When did Andres find the treasure? [b]

2 did / Andres / find / where / the treasure? ______ [ ]

3 Andres / how / feel / did?
______ [ ]

4 he / what / did / do?
______ [ ]

5 send the photos to / did / Andres's dad / who? ______ [ ]

a shocked
b last weekend
c He shouted for his dad and did a dance.
d the people at the local museum
e in a field near his house

8.09 **2 Complete the conversations with the question words and the correct form of the verbs in parentheses. Listen and check.**

A — How much Where

A Hey. Cool headphones!
[1]*Where did* you *get* (get) them?
B I bought them online.
A [2] ______ they ______ (cost)?
B $30.

B — What Which Who

A [3] ______ you ______ (do) on Saturday afternoon?
B I went to the movies.
A [4] ______ you ______ (go) with?
B I went with Lukas.
A [5] ______ movie ______ you ______ (see)?
B We saw the new Avengers movie. It was amazing!

C — When Where

A [6] ______ Sam ______ (lose) his passport?
B He lost it yesterday.
A [7] ______ he ______ (lose) it?
B I don't know, but I know he needs to find it because he's going to Paris tomorrow!

3 Have a conversation like conversation B in Exercise 2. Change the information so it is true for you.

Use It!

4 Think of your favorite possession. Write questions to guess your partner's possession. Then ask and answer. Can you guess?

1 when / get it? *When did you get it?*
2 why / want it? ______
3 where / buy it? ______
4 how much / cost? ______

When did you get it?

I got it for my 13th birthday.

Finished? p125 Ex. 3

SPEAKING
Losing Things

8.10 **1 Listen to the conversation. Where is Billy's bus pass?**

BILLY	I can't find my bus pass, Gemma.
GEMMA	Don't panic.
BILLY	I need it to get home.
GEMMA	Calm down. Let's think. [1] When did you last have it?
BILLY	On the bus this morning.
GEMMA	OK. [2] ______________________
BILLY	I can't remember.
GEMMA	Well, [3] ______________________
BILLY	Yes, I did. I'm certain.
GEMMA	[4] ______________________
BILLY	Maybe.
GEMMA	OK. What's that?
BILLY	Yesterday's lunch.
GEMMA	Gross! What's this?
BILLY	My bus pass. I don't know what to say.
GEMMA	Thanks, maybe?

8.10 **2 Complete the conversation with the phrases from the *Useful Language* box. Then listen and check.**

Useful Language

Did you have it when you (got to school)?
Did you put it (in your bag)?
What did you do with it after that?
When did you last (have/use/see) it?

3 Look at the *Everyday English* box. Find and underline the phrases in the conversation.

WATCH VIDEO 8.4
Everyday English

Calm down. Don't panic.
Gross! Let's think.

4 Work with a partner. Practice the conversation.

PLAN

5 Work with a partner. Plan a conversation about losing something. Decide on these things.

What you lost: ______________________

When you last had/used it: ______________________

Where you were: ______________________

What you did with it: ______________________

Whether you found it: ______________________

SPEAK

6 Practice the conversation with your partner. Remember to use simple past questions and answers, the vocabulary from this unit, and phrases from the *Useful Language* and *Everyday English* boxes.

CHECK

7 Work with another pair. Listen to their conversation and complete the notes.

What did they lose? ______________________

Did they find it? If so, where? ______________________

WRITING
A Blog Post

Tanya's Thoughts on Life, the Universe, and the Rest

A Bad Day!

1 It started this morning. I didn't hear my alarm, so I got up late. I didn't have time for breakfast, and I couldn't find my bus pass, so I ran all the way to school. It got worse!

2 My first class was math – I forgot my book. Guess what? It didn't matter because we had a surprise test. It was really hard. 🙁

3 At lunchtime, I realized I didn't have any money, so I didn't have any lunch. I went to the library instead. Bad news.

4 But the worst thing happened later. After school, I went to the skate park, but I lost my phone, so I can't text, take any selfies, or call anyone. I'm using my brother's laptop to write this. Tragic. 😭

5 Did you all have a good Friday? What did you do? Let me know.

👍 *Friday, June 26 posted at 8:30 p.m.*

1 Read the blog post. Give one reason why Tanya had a bad day. ______________________

____

2 Read the blog post again. Put the events in Tanya's day in the correct order (1–5).

a ☐ She didn't have any lunch.
b [1] She didn't hear her alarm.
c ☐ She lost her phone.
d ☐ She couldn't find her bus pass.
e ☐ She had a math test.

3 Match topics a–e with paragraphs 1–5.

a ☐ in the morning
b [1] when it started
c ☐ the end of the day
d ☐ sign off and ask two questions
e ☐ the middle of the day

Useful Language

I didn't hear my alarm, **so** I got up late.

4 Look at the *Useful Language* box and <u>underline</u> more examples of *so* in the blog post.

5 Join the sentences using *so*.

1 I was late. I ran. I was late, so I ran.
2 I was hungry. I bought a sandwich.
____
3 We didn't have any money. We didn't buy any concert tickets. ______________________
____
4 Emma wanted to apologize. She called me.
____

PLAN

6 Plan your own blog post about a bad day. Think about your answers to these questions and make notes.

When did the bad day start?
What problems did you have?
When did each problem happen?
What did you do?
How did you feel?

Decide what information to include in each paragraph. Use the information in Exercise 3 to help you.

WRITE

7 Write your blog post. Remember to include five paragraphs, the simple past for the questions at the end, and the phrases from the *Useful Language* box.

CHECK

8 Do you …

- use a title for your blog post?
- use *so* to join ideas and explain the results?
- say how you felt on your bad day?

Finished? p125 Ex. 4

HISTORY PROJECT

An Interview

1 **Look at the photos. What's the connection between them?**

8.11 **2** **Listen to Ruby and Jacob's interview. Check your answers to Exercise 1. Were you correct?**

8.11 **3** **Listen again and answer the questions.**

1. How many people were there in Clarissa's family? Ten
2. What was her life like when she was younger? ______
3. What buildings were on Clarissa's street? ______
4. What happened to Cookie? ______
5. In Clarissa's opinion, what are the most important things in life? Do you agree? ______

8.12 **4** **Listen to a teacher talking about questions for a good interview. What are the three types of questions?**

5 **Look at the interview questions 1–6 on page 103. Are they open, closed, or follow-up questions?**

6 **Read the *How To* box. Write the tips (a–h) in the chart.**

Before the Interview	During the Interview	After the Interview
	a	

How to Do a Recorded Interview

- a Keep the interview short.
- b Use open and follow-up questions.
- c Plan your questions.
- d Introduce yourself.
- e Record your interview on your phone.
- f Send a thank you email/letter.
- g Check you have everything you need.
- h Say why you're doing the interview or why you want to interview the person.

7 **Do you think Ruby and Jacob followed all the tips?**

LIVING MEMORIES

Radley Boulevard 1953

Radley Boulevard today

Cookie

Clarissa 1949

Clarissa today

Interview Questions for Clarissa Briggs

Date and time: June 17, 10 a.m.

Place: 937 Houston Street

1 Where did you live as a child? ____________

2 What did you do each day? ____________

3 Why did things change? ____________

4 How did you feel about the change? ____________

5 Who was Cookie? ____________

6 What lessons for life did you learn from that experience? ____________

PLAN

8 **Work in pairs. Choose a person to interview for the Living Memories project. Think about the things you want to know. Then complete the steps below.**

Before the Interview

- Plan and prepare your questions.

During the Interview

- Introduce yourself.
- Record the interview or take notes.
- Listen carefully to the answers.

After the Interview

- Thank the person.
- Type or write up the interview.
- Send the person a copy and a thank you email/letter.

PRESENT

9 **Play your recording for the class or display your written interviews on the wall with the photos. Remember to use polite language, include photos of the person and place in the past and now, and follow the tips in *How to Do a Recorded Interview.***

CHECK

10 **Listen to or read your classmates' interviews and complete the notes. Then discuss in your group.**

Who did they interview?

____

____

Which interview question was the most interesting?

____

____

Write down two interesting or surprising facts that you learned.

____

____

8 REVIEW

VOCABULARY

1 Match 1–6 with a–f to make places in a town.

1 bowling	a park
2 ice	b mall
3 post	c pool
4 shopping	d alley
5 skate	e office
6 swimming	f rink

2 Circle the correct words.

1 Laura always wears her *laptop* / *headphones* when she listens to music.
2 I can't take the bus home. I didn't bring my *passport* / *bus pass*.
3 My *phone* / *concert ticket* isn't working. I can't send any texts.
4 We want to buy some sandwiches. Do you have any *keys* / *money*?
5 They're great photos. Did you use your new *camera* / *charger*?

GRAMMAR IN ACTION

3 Write the simple past questions (1–5) and match them with the answers (a–e).

1 you / have / an egg for breakfast this morning?
______________ ☐

2 you and Mike / go / shopping yesterday?
______________ ☐

3 Teresa / send / you a text this morning?
______________ ☐

4 your new passport / arrive / last week?
______________ ☐

5 your parents / watch / the concert?
______________ ☐

a No, but she called me last night.
b Yes, it did.
c No, I always have toast.
d No, they didn't.
e Yes, we bought some clothes at the mall.

4 Look at the answers and write the questions. Use the question words in the box.

How many	What	When	Where	Who

1 A you / on TV last night?
____
____
B We watched a really exciting movie.

2 A your cousin / her keys?
____
____
B She lost them at the shopping mall.

3 A Ana's grandparents / to Spain?
____
____
B They came here in 1997.

4 A Martin / at the bowling alley?
____
____
B He met Jamie and Emma.

5 A eggs / you?
____
____
B I bought 12.

Self-Assessment

I can name 11 places in a town in English.

I can name 12 personal possessions in English.

I can ask *Yes/No* questions using the simple past.

I can ask *Wh-* questions using the simple past.

LEARN TO LEARN

LEARN TO … IMPROVE YOUR WRITING

When you write something, ask your partner to check it. This improves your writing and your partner's writing.

1 **Read the writing task and Kim's story. Correct Kim's mistakes to help her improve.**

> **WRITING TASK**
>
> **Write a story about a fun day you had in your town.**
>
> - Write between 50 and 70 words.
> - Use the simple past.
> - Use words for places in town and personal possessions.
> - Describe people, places, and things to make it interesting.
> - Give your story a title.
> - Don't forget to use punctuation and check your spelling!

A Nice Day I Had in Town by Kim

Last Saturday it [1]is __was__ my birthday. My [2]parent ______ gave me a skateboard. In the morning, I went to the skate [3]parc ______ to try it. In the afternoon, I met my friend Brad. We love fish, so we visited the aquarium and saw a lot of fish. I didn't [4]took ______ any photos because I [5]leaved ______ my phone at home, but Brad took lots. In the evening, I [6]have ______ dinner with my family in a restaurant.

2 **(Circle) the emojis in the checklist about Kim's writing.**

Checklist for Story Writing Chart

Did he/she …	Kim			My Partner		
1 write about the topic?	(🙂)	😐	😕	🙂	😐	😕
2 write between 50 and 70 words?	🙂	😐	😕	🙂	😐	😕
3 use words for places in town?	🙂	😐	😕	🙂	😐	😕
4 use words for possessions?	🙂	😐	😕	🙂	😐	😕
5 use the simple past?	🙂	😐	😕	🙂	😐	😕
6 make it interesting?	🙂	😐	😕	🙂	😐	😕
7 add a title?	🙂	😐	😕	🙂	😐	😕
8 use punctuation?	🙂	😐	😕	🙂	😐	😕
9 use correct spelling?	🙂	😐	😕	🙂	😐	😕

3 **Work in pairs. Imagine your partner is Kim. Use your answers in the checklist in Exercise 2 to tell her what you like and what she can improve.**

You used words for places in a town. That was good!

Thanks!

You can improve your simple past. You made some mistakes.

OK. Thank you for your help.

SHAPE IT!

4 **Write your own story for the task in Exercise 1.**

5 **Give your partner your story. (Circle) the emojis in the checklist in Exercise 2 about your partner's story.**

6 **Use your answers in the checklist to tell your partner what you like and what they can improve.**

9 What makes a great vacation?

LEARNING OUTCOMES

I can ...

- understand texts about an adventure weekend and vacations
- make suggestions and respond to them
- write an email
- understand how to use the future tenses
- talk about outdoor life and vacations
- make collocations and spidergrams, use place names to find out background information, and make an action plan

Start It!

1 Look at the photo. Do you try new sports or activities when you are on vacation?
2 Before you watch, what do people do on vacation?
3 Where did Juno and Raúl go on vacation? Watch and check.
4 Which vacation do you prefer? Juno or Raúl's? Why?

Watch video 9.1

p109

Grammar in Action 9.2

p111

Grammar in Action 9.3

p112

Everyday English 9.4

p114

Globetrotters 9.5

VOCABULARY
Outdoor Life

a

b

c

d

e

f

g

h

i

j

9.01 **1 Match the activities in the box with the pictures. Then listen, check, and repeat.**

build a shelter	☐	identify plants	☐
catch fish	☐	light a fire	☐
collect wood	☐	pick fruit	a
cook over a campfire	☐	read a map	☐
find food and water	☐	use a compass	☐

9.02 **2 Circle the correct expressions. Listen and check.**

1 A I'm thirsty.
  B OK. *Let's find some water* / *light a fire*.

2 A I'm hungry.
  B Why don't we *build a shelter* / *pick some fruit to eat*?

3 A This plant looks delicious. Let's try it.
  B No. It's important to *collect wood* / *identify plants* before you eat them.

4 A Oh, no! We're lost. Can you *read a map* / *collect wood*?
  B Of course, but we don't know where we are. Let's *cook over a campfire* / *use a compass* first.

LEARN TO LEARN

Collocations

Some verbs and nouns go together in English. Try to learn verbs in a phrase with a noun.

3 Look at the activities in Exercise 1 again. Take turns saying a noun or a verb for your partner to complete the phrase. How many can you remember?

4 Complete the chart with another noun that goes with each verb in Exercise 1.

Verb	Noun	Verb	Noun
build	a house	identify	
catch		light	
collect		pick	
cook		read	
find		use	

Use It!

5 Discuss the questions.

1 Which activities in Exercise 1 can you do?
2 Which ones do you think are the most useful? Why?
3 Which ones do you want to learn?

Explore It!

Guess the correct answer.

Mauro Prosperi ran a marathon in the Sahara Desert in 1994, but he got lost. How long did he survive without water?

a one day **b** ten days **c** three weeks

Find another interesting fact about people's amazing survival skills. Then write a question for your partner to answer.

READING
A Pamphlet

1 **Look at the photos. What do you think the pamphlet is about? What do you want to know about it?**

9.03 **2** **Read the pamphlet. Match the questions (a–d) with the right sections of the pamphlet (1–4).**

a What will you eat?
b Who will take care of you?
c Where will you sleep?
d What will you do during the weekend?

3 **Guess the meaning of the underlined words in the pamphlet.**

4 EXAM **Circle the correct answers.**

Which person …

		You	Adem	Havva
1	will practice their wood skills?	(A)	B	C
2	will learn new things?	A	B	C
3	will organize a cooking competition?	A	B	C
4	will build a shelter?	A	B	C
5	knows about wild food?	A	B	C
6	knows how to track animals?	A	B	C

Voice It!

5 **Discuss the questions.**

1 What do you think is the most interesting part of WILD Weekend?
2 Why it is important to be careful when lighting a fire?
3 Why do we need to identify plants before eating them?

WILD WEEKEND

Do you want a new adventure this summer? Join us at one of our *WILD* centers in Turkey. Every weekend from Friday to Sunday.

1 ☐
In a bed? In a tent? No, you'll sleep in a shelter. You'll build it yourself with leaves and branches.

2 ☐
You won't be near any stores or a supermarket, so you'll find your own food. You'll learn to catch fish, collect fruit, and identify plants to eat.

3 ☐
DAYTIME
Why not try some of our amazing adventure activities?

- Go kayaking or diving in the ocean.
- Go for a bike ride or go horseback riding in the mountains.
- Learn to track animals or practice your wood skills.

EVENING

- Get to know your new friends and compare your *WILD* days.
- Sing, listen to ancient Turkish legends, toast marshmallows over the campfire, drink hot milk with cinnamon, and relax.

4 ☐
MEET YOUR INSTRUCTORS!

Hi! I'm Adem. I'm an expert in extreme survival. I'll teach you survival skills for life. You'll also learn how to track animals and how to work with wood. You'll learn new things about yourself and you'll begin to love outdoor life.

Hi! I'm Havva and I'll help you find, prepare, and cook your own food. You won't want to eat food from a supermarket ever again! Look out for my campfire cooking challenge! Will you be a winner?

Join us for a *WILD WEEKEND!* You'll learn new skills, make new friends for life, and have fun! Will you want to do it again? Of course you will! For more information and booking details, visit our website now!

Finished? p126 Ex. 1

GRAMMAR IN ACTION

Future with *Will/Won't*

Watch video 9.2
Where will he sleep?
What will they do there?

	I/You/He/She/It/We/They
+	I'**ll teach** you survival skills.
+	You [1] 'll sleep in a shelter.
–	You [2] ________ ________ near any stores.
?	[3] ________ you ________ a winner?
?	Yes, you **will**. / No, you **won't**.
?	What [4] ________ you **eat**?

1 Complete the examples in the chart above. Use the pamphlet on page 108 to help you.

2 Complete the summary with *will* or *won't*. Check your answers in the pamphlet on page 108.

WILD Weekend

What [1] will you do?
You [2] ________ sleep in your own bed.
You [3] ________ build a shelter and sleep outdoors.
You [4] ________ buy your food in stores or supermarkets.
You [5] ________ find and cook your own food.
You [6] ________ learn new skills for life.
[7] ________ you have fun? Yes, you [8] ________.

9.04 **3** Complete the TV advertisement with the correct form of *will* and the verbs in the box. Listen and check.

choose get not have
not see ~~spend~~ survive work

TEEN CHALLENGE!

A group of five young teenagers [1] will spend three nights alone on an island.

On tonight's show, the group [2] ________ important information about the challenge, and they [3] ________ five items to take with them.

For three nights, these young teenagers:

- [4] ________ their family or friends.
- [5] ________ phones or laptops.
- [6] ________ together to find shelter, food, and water.

[7] ________ they ________ the toughest three days of their lives? **Watch tonight and find out!**

Use It!

4 You will interview one of the people in *Teen Challenge*. Write questions to ask about how they will survive on the island. Use the ideas below or your own ideas.

1 miss your family and friends?
Will you miss your family and friends?
2 survive without your phone?
____
3 learn new skills?
____
4 sleep in a tent?
____
5 have fun?
____

5 Work with a partner. Ask and answer.

Will you miss your family and friends?

Yes, I will.

Finished? p126 Ex. 2

VOCABULARY AND LISTENING

Vacations

9.05 **1 Match the words with the photos. Listen, check, and repeat.**

apartment	☐	camper	☐
(beach/ski) resort	☐	hotel	☐
B&B (bed and breakfast)	☐	RV (recreational vehicle)	☐
cabin	☐	tent	☐
		youth hostel	1

2 Which two types of accommodation do you think are best for each of these vacations?

1. a cheap beach vacation ______
2. a ski trip ______
3. a comfortable city vacation ______
4. a road trip across the country ______

LEARN TO LEARN

Personalizing Spidergrams

Personalizing a spidergram with colors or pictures can help you remember vocabulary more easily.

3 Make a spidergram with words from Exercises 1 and 2 in your notebook. How many more words can you add?

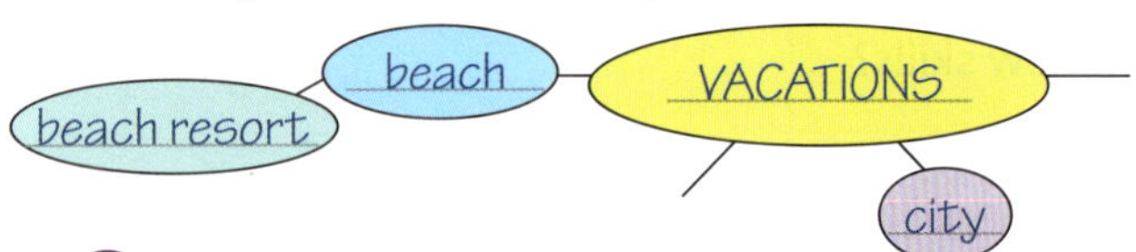

Use It!

4 Write sentences about your ideal type of vacation and place to stay. Compare with a partner.

1. summer or winter vacation
2. adventure vacation or weekend at a hotel

My ideal winter vacation is a ski trip.
I want to stay at a ski resort or in a cabin.

A Conversation

9.06 **5 Listen. What are Matteo and Libby talking about?**

9.06 **6 Listen again. Write *M* (Matteo) or *L* (Libby).**

Who …

1. doesn't want to stay in a small town? ___
2. has a younger brother and sister? ___
3. talks about the tallest building in the world? ___
4. can ski on vacation? ___

9.06 **7 Complete the chart with the correct information. Listen again and check.**

	Matteo and His Family	Libby and Her Parents
1 Accommodation	RV	
2 Start of trip		
3 Length of trip		
4 Destination(s)		

Voice It!

8 Discuss the questions.

1. What is your dream vacation?
2. What kinds of travel accommodation are popular in your country?

GRAMMAR IN ACTION

Present Continuous for Future

Watch video 9.3
Where is the school band going?
How long are they staying there?

	Present Continuous for Fixed Arrangements in the Future
+	I**'m going** to a soccer camp for two weeks in June.
+	They**'re working** in July.
–	She **isn't staying** in a cabin.
?	**Are** they **working** in July? Yes, they [1] *are*. / No, they [2] ______.
?	Where [3] ______ you **staying**? What [4] ______ she **doing** in July?

1 **Complete the examples in the chart above.**

2 **Write questions with the present continuous. Then match them with the correct answers.**

1 where / Matteo / spend / July?
Where is Matteo spending July? [e]

2 what / Matteo's parents / do / on August 1?
______ [ ]

3 Matteo / travel / on his own?
______ [ ]

4 where / Libby / go / on vacation?
______ [ ]

5 when / she / leave?
______ [ ]

a No, he isn't. He's traveling with his family.
b She's going to Dubai.
c She's leaving on July 29.
d They're renting an RV.
e He's spending it in his grandma's town.

Be Going To

	Be Going To for Future Intentions
+	We [1] *'re* ______ **going to visit** a water park.
–	Matteo **isn't** [2] ______ **to travel** in France.
?	**Are** you **going** [3] ______ **go** on vacation this summer?

Pronunciation p142

3 **Complete the examples in the chart above.**

4 **Write questions with *be going to*. Then write the answers.**

1 Matteo and Libby / stay / at home this summer?
Are Matteo and Libby going to stay at home this summer? No, they aren't.

2 who / swim / in six different swimming pools?
______

3 Libby / go up / the tallest building in the world?
______

4 what sport / Matteo / play / in June?
______

Use It!

5 **Write questions and answers with *be going to* to talk about your intentions this summer. Use the ideas below or your own ideas.**

travel   sleep in a tent   go swimming
play tennis   stay with grandparents

Are you going to travel? No, I'm not.

6 **Work with a partner. Ask and answer questions about your arrangements and intentions for this summer.**

What are you doing this summer?

I'm going to Canada in August.

Are you going to sleep in a tent?

Yes, I am.

Finished? p126 Ex. 3

SPEAKING

Making Suggestions and Responding

1 Listen to the conversation. What do they decide to do? 9.09

EVAN: We're having the end-of-school event on Saturday, June 26.
NADIA: Great! [1] What are we going to do?
EVAN: That's why you're both here. Ideas, please!
NADIA: I'm on it. [2] ______________________?
EVAN: [3] ______________________. It's complicated and we'll never agree on a movie.
AVA: OK. Forget that. [4] ______________________?
EVAN: According to my weather app, it's going to rain. [5] ______________________.
AVA: We can have a danceathon indoors or outdoors. Easy!
EVAN: OK. [6] ______________________! So, are you coming on the 26th, Nadia?
NADIA: No, I'm going on vacation. I won't be here.
EVAN: Nadia! You're unbelievable!
AVA: Don't worry. You can count on me!

2 Complete the conversation with the phrases from the *Useful Language* box. Then listen and check. 9.09

Useful Language

How about a (movie night)?
What are we going to do?
Why don't we (have a barbecue)?
I'm not sure about that.
I'd rather not do that.
Let's do that!

Get It Right!

We say: *I'm going on vacation.* **NOT** ~~*I'm going on vacations.*~~

3 Look at the *Everyday English* box. Find and underline the phrases in the conversation.

Watch video 9.4

Everyday English

Easy! Forget that. I'm on it! You're unbelievable!

4 Work with a partner. Practice the conversation.

PLAN

5 Work with a partner. You are organizing an end-of-term event. Plan your suggestions and responses. Use the ideas below or your own ideas.

a picnic a beach sports day a costume party a visit to a theme park

SPEAK

6 Practice the conversation with your partner. Remember to use *will*, *be going to* and the present continuous, the vocabulary from this unit, and phrases from the *Useful Language* and *Everyday English* boxes.

CHECK

7 Work with another pair. Listen to their conversation and complete the notes.

Which end-of-term ideas do they talk about? ______________________

What event do they decide on? ______________________

What event do you want to go to? ______________________

WRITING
An Email

Hi Javi,

1 ☐ It was great to hear from you. I'm really excited about next week, too. I think you'll love England and Wales. They're a bit different from the U.S.A.

2 ☐ Here are the arrangements. We're spending the weekend at home in Chester. We're going to sleep in a tent in the backyard. It won't rain. It never rains in August! Honest! 👍

3 ☐ On Monday, we're going to leave early in the morning to drive to the coast. We're staying in a beach house in Wales for three days. I think it looks amazing. I'm going to go swimming every day, but the water will probably be very cold! ❄️ My dad is going to teach us to catch fish and then we can cook them!

4 ☐ It'll be great to meet you in person. I'm going to meet you at the airport with my parents. Our car is pretty small. Are you going to bring a big bag? It will be a busy week, but it will be fun! See you on August 3! 😀

Martin

1 **Read the email quickly. Why is Martin writing to Javi?**

2 **Match topics a–d with paragraphs 1–4.**

a end the email

b respond to your penpal's last email

c describe the week ahead

d describe the weekend

3 **Complete the *Useful Language* box with *at*, *in*, or *on*. Use Martin's email to help you.**

Useful Language

1 _in_ the morning	4 _____ home
2 _____ August 3	5 _____ Monday
3 _____ August	6 _____ the airport

PLAN

4 **Your penpal is coming to stay for a week. Take notes about these things for an email to your penpal.**

Your arrangements:

____

Things you intend to do:

____

Predictions about what will happen:

____

Plans for meeting your penpal:

____

Decide what information to include in each paragraph. Use the information in Exercise 2 to help you.

WRITE

5 **Write your email. Remember to include four paragraphs, *will*, *be going to* and the present continuous for the future, and phrases from the *Useful Language* box.**

CHECK

6 **Do you ...**

- include arrangements for the weekend and the week ahead?
- make predictions about what will or won't happen?
- say where you are going to meet your penpal?

Finished? p126 Ex. 4

AROUND THE WORLD

READING
A Webpage

Globetrotters

Watch video 9.5
A Summer Camp in ...

- How long is the camp in Costa Rica?
- Which animal will you protect?
- What skills will you learn?

1 **Circle the answer you think is correct.**

1. More than *9* / *11* million American children and teenagers are going to a summer camp this year.
2. The first American summer camp opened more than *50* / *150* years ago.

9.10 **2** **Read the webpage and check your answers to Exercise 1. Write two more things you would like to know about American summer camps.**

____

____

3 **Read the webpage again. Match the sentences with the camps 1–4.**

a. You will work with professional coaches. 3
b. It lasts for three weeks. ___
c. You will spend a month at this camp. ___
d. This camp lasts for two weeks. ___
e. You won't hear any English while you are at this camp. ___
f. You can only do this course if you are not a beginner.

4 **Write the adjectives for nouns 1–6.**

1. beauty beautiful
2. music ___
3. nature ___
4. profession ___
5. success ___
6. wonder ___

Voice It!

5 **Discuss the questions.**

1. Do you think summer camps make you a more independent person?
2. Do you think it is important to be independent? Why?
3. What other skills do you need to be independent?

Your Guide to American Summer Camps

Find a camp

What are you going to do over summer vacation? Here in the U.S.A., more than 11 million children and teenagers are going to summer camp. The first summer camp opened more than 150 years ago, and there are now more than 1,200 summer camps to choose from.

Here are our four favorite camps this week.

1 Tech Camp
Cambridge, Massachusetts

You'll be at one of the best universities in the country, in the heart of technology! In just three weeks, you'll learn to build robots with college students. They'll help you develop useful skills like game and web design. You'll stay in a dormitory on campus and experience a bit of college life.

2 Languages for Life
Atlanta, Georgia

Learn a new language at this summer camp! Choose from Arabic, Chinese, and lots more! You'll live and sleep in the language and culture. You won't speak English for a month! In your free time, why not visit the world's largest aquarium or one of Georgia's wonderful museums?

LEARN TO LEARN

Using Place Names to Find out Background Information

The names of locations in the United States often begin with a town or city, followed by the name of the state. You can look up the location names to learn more about the places.

6 **What country does the webpage focus on?**

7 **Write the city and state where each camp is.**

	City	State
Advanced Soccer Skills	1 ______	5 ______
Languages for Life	2 ______	6 ______
Tech Camp	3 ______	7 ______
Theater School	4 ______	8 ______

8 **Choose one of the locations or another city you know in the United States. Answer the questions.**

1 In what part of the United States is the city?

Northeast   Midwest   Southeast   Northwest   Southwest

2 What is the city famous for?

Explore It!

Is the sentence true or false?

In the state of Georgia, it's illegal to live on a boat for more than 30 days. ___

Find another interesting or unusual law in an American state and write a question for your partner to answer.

Search camps > | **Age** | **State** | **Length**

3 Advanced Soccer Skills
Los Angeles, California

Los Angeles has a long history of sports – the Summer Olympics in 1932 and 1984, and in 2028 the Olympics will be here again! In just one week, our professional coaches will use your natural talent to teach you amazing new soccer skills. Sorry, no beginners!

4 Theater School
Newark, New Jersey

New Jersey is home to one of the most successful performing arts centers in the U.S.A. Develop your musical talents or choose from circus skills, magic, public speaking, or acting! After two weeks here, you'll perform live on the last day.

SHAPE IT!

CULTURE PROJECT

A Webpage

Webpages provide information in a clear and interesting way. Think of an idea for a summer camp. In groups, design a webpage about a camp.

Teacher's Resource Bank

9 REVIEW

VOCABULARY

1 Match the verbs with the nouns.

1	use	a	a map
2	identify	b	a shelter
3	build	c	fish
4	catch	d	plants
5	read	e	a compass

2 Write the words for vacation accommodations.

1 This is part of a larger building. You have your own bedroom, kitchen, and bathroom. ______

2 This is a cheap and simple shelter. You don't sleep in a bed. ______

3 You share a room with other people in this place. ______

4 You travel and sleep in this and you don't need a car. ______

GRAMMAR IN ACTION

3 Complete the sentences with *will/won't* and a verb from the box.

have speak win

1 I know you ______ an amazing vacation in Turkey.

2 She ______ any English in Russia.

3 ______ your country ______ the next World Cup?

4 Complete the conversation with the present continuous form of the verbs in parentheses.

DAN Hi, Gabi. What [1] ______ you ______ (do) on Saturday?

GABI I [2] ______ (meet) Louisa in town. Why?

DAN Matt and Clara [3] ______ (come) to my house to organize a surprise party for Gino.

GABI Really? When [4] ______ you ______ (have) the party?

DAN On September 15. Can you come?

GABI I think so. I [5] ______ (not do) anything that weekend.

DAN Great!

5 Write sentences with the correct form of *be going to*.

1 ______ they ______ to a summer camp this year? (go)

2 I ______ early on Saturday! (not get up)

3 Becca ______ all the food for the party. (cook)

4 We ______ in a cabin this summer. (not stay)

6 Circle the correct verbs.

1 *I'm going to visit / I'll visit* my cousins in Paris in May.

2 Which subjects *are you choosing / will you choose* next year?

3 Jack can't come to the movies tomorrow. *He's working / He'll work.*

4 *Will Kate want / Is Kate wanting* to come to the movies with us tomorrow?

Self-Assessment

I can name ten outdoor life activities in English.

I can talk about places to stay on vacation.

I can use *will* and *won't* to talk about the future.

I can use the present continuous to talk about arrangements and *be going to* to talk about intentions in the future.

LEARN TO ... MAKE AN ACTION PLAN

An action plan can help you improve a little every day.

1 Read the texts and write *S* (Sasha) or *E* (Erin).

Who ...

1 watches movies? S
2 reads blogs? ____
3 watches online videos? ____
4 reads books? ____
5 listens to songs? ____
6 chats with a friend? ____
7 uses an app? ____

SASHA

I have an app on my phone with flashcards. I use it a lot, and sometimes I watch movies in English. I also love American pop music. I find the words of songs online, check their meaning, and sing in my bedroom!

ERIN

I read fashion blogs in English, and a lot of books, too. Also, my best friend Anita and I sometimes chat in English. I don't usually watch movies, because they're difficult, but I watch a lot of videos online.

2 Choose three ways to practice English from Exercise 1. Tell your partner why you want to try them.

I chose "read a blog."

Me, too! Why did you choose that?

Because I love reading online.

3 Write the three things you chose in Exercise 2 and how often you will do them.

read a blog : twice a week
1 ____ : ____
2 ____ : ____
3 ____ : ____

SHAPE IT!

4 Use your answers to Exercise 3 to make an action plan.

Action Plan							
	Sunday	Monday	Tuesday	Wednesday	Thursday	Friday	Saturday
read a blog		✓			✓		
1 ____							
2 ____							
3 ____							

5 Tell your partner about your action plan. Are there any things you can do together?

What are you going to do?

I'm going to watch a movie in English once a week.

We can do that together! You can come to my house.

1 FINISHED?

1 Read the clues and write Esma's family members.

1 This is my mom's dad. grandpa
2 This is my aunt and uncle's son. ________
3 This is my dad's brother. ________
4 This is my mom's mom. ________
5 This is my mom and dad's son. ________
6 This is my dad's sister. ________

2 Find and (circle) the things and family members Jack has. Then complete sentences 1–6.

sbsykmbasketballsiscvkunclauntnotboikanmcousinrtionhfugphonesjdeh

1 He has ________ a basketball.
2 He doesn't have ________ a sister.
3 He ________ an aunt.
4 He ________ a notebook.
5 He ________ a dictionary.
6 He ________ a phone.

3 Put the words in the correct order to make questions. Each question is in a different color. Then look at the fact file and answer the questions.

How	have	she	and
she	green	have	sister
have	Does	eyes	have
she	sisters	a	does
freckles	she	Does	pet
twin	many	Does	brothers
have	she	Does	a

FACT FILE

JENNIFER LAWRENCE
SISTERS 0
BROTHERS 2
EYES green
FRECKLES no
PET Yes

1 Does she have a twin sister?
No, she doesn't have any sisters.
2 ________
3 ________
4 ________
5 ________

4 Read the descriptions and draw the people.

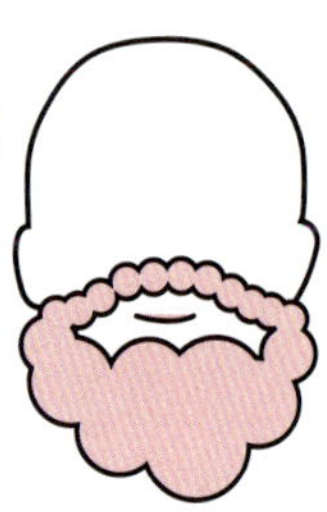

1 He has a beard and a mustache and long, red hair.

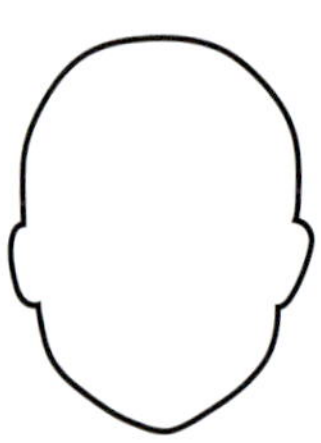

2 She has short, wavy blond hair and freckles.

3 She has brown eyes, glasses, and long, black hair.

2 FINISHED?

1 Look at the pictures and complete the sentences.

I  [1] *get up* ______ at 6:30 a.m. and have my  [2] ______. Then I take a  [3] ______ and I get dressed. After that, I  [4] ______ my teeth.

Before I leave the house, I pack my bag and quickly check my  [5] ______.

2 Put the letters in the correct order to make activities. Write what the people do on the weekend. Remember to use the correct form of the simple present.

1 y a l p | t h i w | d r i f e n s

Isabel *plays with friends.*

2 o d | s i h | w e m o r h o k

Matt ______

3 c t h a w | V T

Mira and Fred ______

4 t o n | o g | o t | c o o l s h

Ada ______

3 Circle words to make questions. Then look at the pictures and answer the questions.

1 whudoeslinsheplayotevideonogegames?

Yes, she does.

2 wdhsdoesbsheklgombforkaybikejhatridet?

______

3 bndoqeuotytheyaslmakefgytonmvideosh?

______

4 lmbdoxdtusrtheyaslikesdfipdtthesclass?

______

5 wdoessgyuashexpyuitplayquenoollinssoccer?

______

4 Read the clues and complete the crossword.

Across

1 I listen to this with my friends.

4 I love to read these.

5 I like to hang out with these people on the weekend.

6 I take these with my phone or camera.

Down

2 I play one of these to make music.

3 I play these games on my computer or cell phone.

3 FINISHED?

1 Circle eight school subjects.

A	M	A	V	O	P	Q	Q	M	J
Y	I	J	F	H	J	E	T	A	I
K	D	R	A	M	A	D	J	T	K
H	I	S	T	O	R	Y	S	H	L
O	I	C	D	R	T	L	M	P	M
U	G	I	H	G	Z	S	U	G	N
J	L	E	N	G	L	I	S	H	T
K	D	N	O	D	A	T	I	A	Y
H	Y	C	L	Y	J	A	C	L	H
F	G	E	O	G	R	A	P	H	Y

2 Read the sentences and write the names.

1 Brian can sing and play the guitar.

2 Oscar can sing and play the piano.

3 Ryan can play the guitar, but he can't sing.

4 Alex can sing very well, but he can't play an instrument.

5 Guillermo can dance very well, but he can't sing or play an instrument.

a  Alex

b  ______

c  ______

d  ______

e  ______

3 Use the code to complete the sentences about Lara. Mark the ones that are true for you.

A	C	D	E	G	H	I	K	L	M	N	O	P	S
✦	□	○	✪	💧	◗	🔔	■	☺	✵	☼	⌘	✈	❖
T	U	V	W										
●	◆	∩	◎										

1 She ☺⌘∩✪❖ ○✦☼□🔔☼💧
She loves dancing. ☐

2 She ◗✦●✪❖ 💧✪●●🔔☼💧 ◆✈
She ______ ☐

3 She ○⌘✪❖☼'● ✵🔔☼○ ◎✦☺■🔔☼💧
She ______ ☐

4 She ○⌘✪❖☼'● ☺🔔■✪ □⌘⌘■🔔☼💧
She ______ ☐

5 She ☺🔔■✪❖ ❖◎🔔✵✵🔔☼💧
She ______ ☐

4 Where are they? Look at the photos and write the correct place.

1 
2 
3 
4 
5 

1 Antoni is in the cafeteria.

2 Alicia is on the ______.

3 Fiona is in the ______.

4 Max and Irina are in the ______.

5 Mr. White and Ms. Green are in the ______.

4 FINISHED?

1 **Complete the chart with the words in the box. Then circle the foods you like to eat.**

apples bananas beans chicken chocolate
fish juice meat rice soda water

Lunch or Dinner	Drink	Snack
		apples

2 **Circle the four countable foods and underline the four uncountable foods.**

heysapplegtuijuicenymeatcarrotxlsiynuricemshiontomatoosbsysbypcbutawatermzxioubbeantyu

3 **Put the letters in the correct order to make a word. Then write a sentence about the photo.**

1 lapsep There aren't any apples.
2 ceiju ______
3 gegs ______
4 trocars ______
5 blatesegev ______

4 **Match photos a–f with descriptions 1–6.**

a  4

d 

b 

e 

c 

f 

1 These are cold, fresh, and healthy, but not sweet.
2 These are cold, fresh, healthy, and sweet.
3 These are hot and healthy.
4 This is cold, sweet, and unhealthy.
5 These are salty and unhealthy, but not hot.
6 This is hot and unhealthy.

5 FINISHED?

1 **Use the code to complete the sentences about Dean's look.**

A	C	D	E	F	G	H	I	J	K	L	M	N	O
✦	☐	○	✪	✓	💧	◗	🔔	∞	■	☺	✵	☼	⌘

P	R	S	T	U	V	W
✈	♥	❖	●	◆	⓿	◎

Dean likes playing sports, so he wears ❖☼✪✦■✪♥❖ [1] sneakers, ❖◗⌘♥●❖, [2] ______, and ●-❖◗🔔♥●❖ [3] ______. At school he wears a ◆☼🔔✓⌘♥✵ [4] ______ and a ☐✦✈ [5] ______.

2 **Match photos a–c with sentences 1–3.**

a

b

c

1 Ingrid is eating an apple and checking her phone. She's wearing a jacket and jeans.
2 Holly is sitting and eating an apple. She's wearing a black jacket.
3 Maria is walking and smiling. She's wearing a jacket and a dress.

3 **Complete the words for 1–5. Then use the letters in circles to find the word for answer 6.**

Ignacio is a fashion photographer. He takes photos of models for magazines. Today he is [1]t a (k) i n g photos of his friend, Naomi. Ignacio often [2]c ___ ( ) ___ ___ here to work with Naomi. She's [3]w ___ ( ) ___ ___ ___ ___ a gray dress and a black hat. She always [4]w ( ) ___ ___ a lot of accessories. Naomi loves clothes and fashion. She [5]s ___ ___ ___ ___ ( ) fashion design at college and she [6] ___ ___ ___ ___ ___ her own clothes.

4 **Read the clues and write the accessories.**

1 You put me on your hands in cold weather. gloves
2 I go on your eyes in the summer. ______
3 You carry me and keep your money inside me. ______
4 You use me in the rain. ______
5 You wear me on your arm. I tell you the time. ______
6 I keep your neck warm. ______

6 FINISHED?

1 **Find five sports words in the box. The letters for each word are in the same color. Put the letters in order and write the words under the correct verb.**

R	E	B	M	B	Y	Y	I	R
C	A	I	G	F	G	K	D	K
L	U	O	D	N	E	C	A	A
C	T	L	H	O	I	G	Y	N

play	go	do
h______	c______	t______
r______		y______

2 **Follow the lines to find the comparisons. Then write the sentences.**

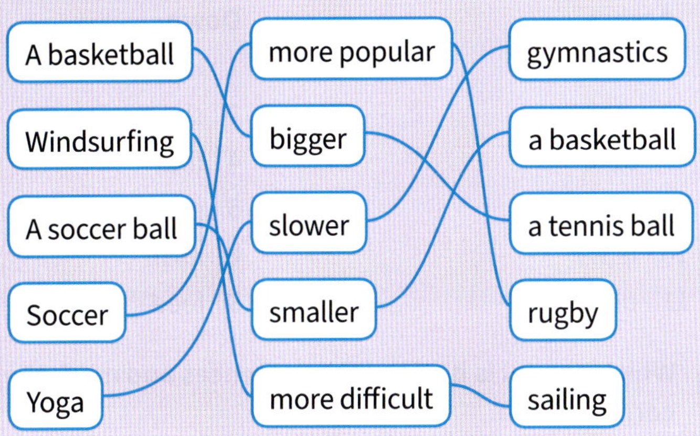

1 *A basketball is bigger than a tennis ball.*
2 ______
3 ______
4 ______
5 ______

3 **Use the chart to write the adjectives. Then complete the questions (a–e) with the superlative form of the adjectives. Answer them for you.**

1	2	3	4	5	6	7	8	9	10	11	12	13
A	B	C	D	E	F	G	H	I	J	K	L	M
N	O	P	Q	R	S	T	U	V	W	X	Y	Z

1

7	1	6	7	12
T	*A*	*S*	*T*	*Y*

2

8	1	3	3	12

3

7	1	12	12

4

9	1	7	5	5	5	6	7	9	1	7

5

5	11	3	5	1	6	9	9	5

a What is ______ food you eat?
b Who is ______ person in your family?
c Who is ______ person in your class?
d What is ______ book you know?
e What is ______ thing you own?

4 **Use the picture to complete the crossword with sports verbs.**

Across
1 Oscar
4 Kyle
5 Melissa

Down
1 Katya and Simon
2 Jimena
3 Dylan

7 FINISHED?

1 **Read the clues and put the letters in the correct order to make words. Write the answers.**

1 This reptile has no arms or legs.
NAKES snake

2 This mammal lives in the ocean.
HELAW ______

3 Some people are scared of this very small animal.
SEMOU ______

4 This bird is the national symbol of the U.S.A.
GALEE ______

5 This animal has a trunk and usually has two tusks.
THAPELEN ______

2 **Sarah went to a safari park. Look closely at her photos and write the animals that were there.**

1 There was a gorilla.
2 There were elephants and a giraffe.
3 ______
4 ______
5 ______

3 **Complete the crossword with the simple past form of the verbs.**

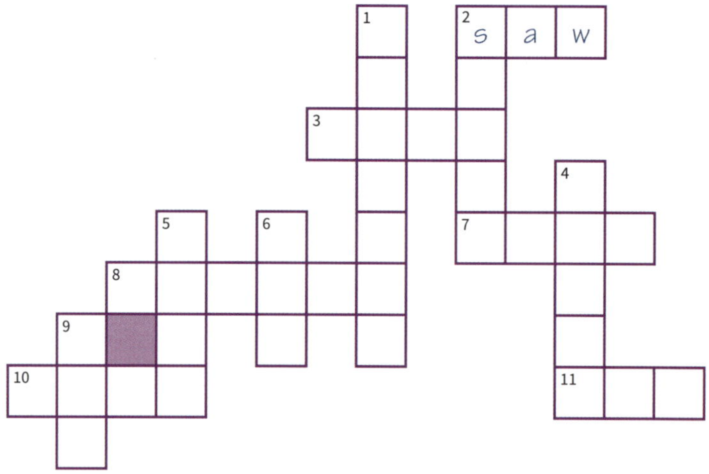

Across		**Down**	
2	see	1	learn
3	make	2	sleep
7	take	4	find
8	become	5	go
10	leave	6	have
11	do	9	feed

4 **Which animal is it? Read the sentences and mark the correct photo.**

This is a wild animal. It is large and heavy. Most people think it isn't cute, and it is very dangerous. It lives on land and in the water.

8 FINISHED?

1 **Write the places 1–5. Then put the letters in the blue boxes in the correct order to make a word. Write the mystery word.**

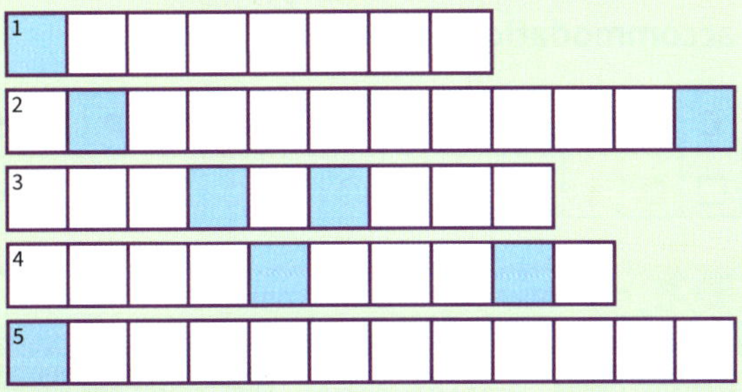

Mystery word: ____________

2 **Circle the words to make questions.**

1 buygulpdodidhuilgeyoursdadjklfoundgefindkolhisqwalletotr?

2 lkifydidaywshechaveklpohadsanydtypizza?

3 miumdidqeidonhyoubvisitklwivbghyourmklawdgrandma?

4 safdidalkshyiheyatgomwenttoasthekfgicexprinkrew?

5 erkldideljoktheytifgofemshoppingoreltogetheriful?

3 **Put the words in the correct order to make questions. Then match the questions with the photos a–e.**

1 did / where / she / that / buy / dress? [b]
Where did she buy that dress?

2 you / see / at / pool? / the / did / who [ ]
____

3 you / do / on / did / what / Monday? [ ]
____

4 when / you / did / your / skateboard? / get [ ]
____

5 locker? / open / how / did / you / the [ ]
____

4 **Look at the pictures and complete the sentences.**

1 Ellie didn't have much  *money*, so she couldn't buy a  ____________.

2 When my  ____________ stopped working, I used my  ____________.

3 You can use your  ____________ or your  ____________ to show who you are.

4 Sam lost his  ____________ and his  ____________ on his way home.

9 FINISHED?

1 Circle ten words. Then write the collocations to make five outdoor activities.

A	D	Y	R	I	L	O	P	K	F
F	M	C	V	N	I	M	K	G	I
C	A	T	C	H	G	D	S	I	S
S	P	R	G	F	H	Y	O	F	H
Z	X	C	V	F	T	H	G	A	Z
C	B	U	I	L	D	H	G	R	F
X	T	A	M	N	F	I	R	E	J
S	H	E	L	T	E	R	W	A	K
G	W	O	O	D	H	G	A	D	W
A	H	T	C	O	L	L	E	C	T

1 catch fish
2 ______
3 ______
4 ______
5 ______

2 What will your life be like in the future? Make predictions with *will* and *won't*. Use the ideas below or your own ideas.

- work hard
- have a dog
- look cool
- become famous
- live in an apartment
- be happy
- have lots of money
- live in a cabin

I won't live in an apartment. I'll live in a big house.

______

______

______

______

______

______

______

3 Put the letters in the correct order to find out these people's plans for the weekend. Write the words.

1 **GAVINAYARTPH:**
Gavin is h a v i n g a p a r t y.

2 **GINOGMWIGMINS:**
Gino is g ______ s ______.

3 **ERINDINGESEFS:**
Erin is s ______ her f ______.

4 **NINAUTSITVIG:**
Nina is v ______ her a ______.

5 **INGEPLANNISTY:**
Inge is p ______ t ______.

4 Use the code to write the types of vacation accommodation.

A	C	E	G	H	I	K	L	M	N	O	P	R	S	T	V
✦	☐	✪	💧	%	◆	◎	☺	✹	☼	⌘	✈	$	❖	●	?

https://www.bookmyhotel.com

HOME | ACCOMMODATION | FLIGHTS | TOURS

1 ✦✈✦$●✹✪☼● apartment
2 ●✪☼● ______
3 ❖◎◆ $✪❖⌘$● ______
4 ☐✦✹✈✪$ ______
5 $? ______
6 %⌘●✪☺ ______

STARTER VOCABULARY BANK

Months

January
February
March
April
May
June
July
August
September
October
November
December

Colors

blue
green
orange
pink
purple
red
yellow
white

1 Ask five students in your class to tell you the date of their birthdays.

When is your birthday?

My birthday is August fifteenth.

Classroom Objects

board

calculator

chair

desk

dictionary

door

notebook

pen

pencil

poster

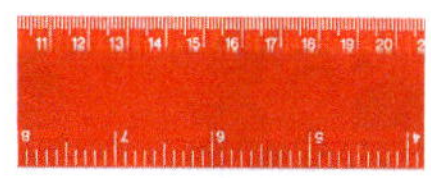
ruler

window

2 Find six classroom objects. Can you see these objects in your classroom? What color are they? Write sentences.

1 *My dictionary is red and blue.*
2 ______
3 ______
4 ______
5 ______
6 ______

D	I	C	T	I	O	N	A	R	Y
F	E	A	N	I	T	O	M	P	E
W	I	L	L	B	E	T	N	O	R
H	J	C	A	S	P	E	N	T	C
A	R	U	B	E	V	B	I	R	U
R	U	L	E	R	T	O	V	E	R
C	H	A	R	T	X	O	R	L	E
I	C	T	O	R	E	K	L	O	P
G	I	O	N	E	R	A	U	H	I
T	R	R	P	P	E	N	C	I	L

LEARN TO LEARN

Using Your Own Language

When you learn a new word in English, write a translation in your own language to help you to remember it.

3 Write a list of the classroom objects in Exercise 2. Write translations in your own language. Then cover the English words. Can you remember them?

1 ______ ______
2 ______ ______
3 ______ ______
4 ______ ______
5 ______ ______
6 ______ ______

1 VOCABULARY BANK

Friends and Family

aunt	granddaughter	husband	sister
brother	grandma	mom	son
cousin	grandpa	nephew	uncle
dad	grandson	niece	wife
daughter			

1 Write true/false sentences about the people in your family. Tell your partner. Can they guess which sentences are false?

1 My grandma is 100 years old.
2
3
4
5

Describing People

beard

blond

brown

freckles

glasses

gray

long

mustache

red

short

tall

wavy

2 Circle the correct words.

1 My baby sister has *a beard / freckles / a mustache.*
2 My grandpa is *tall / wavy / long.*
3 My cousin's eyes are *short / red / brown.*
4 My grandma has *glasses / gray / blond.*

LEARN TO LEARN

Drawing Pictures

Drawing pictures can help you remember new words.

3 Use the words for describing people to describe someone in your family to your partner. Ask your partner to draw the person. Does it look like them?

My brother is tall and has short brown hair and glasses.

2 VOCABULARY BANK

Daily Routines

brush your teeth

check your phone

do your homework

get dressed

get up

go home

go to bed

go to school

have breakfast

pack your bag

take a shower

wake up

1 Match 1–4 with a–d to make sentences.

1 I usually take
2 I pack
3 On weekdays, I wake
4 I go to

a my school bag in the evening.
b a shower in the morning.
c school on the bus.
d up at six o'clock.

Free-Time Activities

chat online	go shopping	make videos	read a book/magazine
download songs	hang out with friends	play an instrument	take photos
go for a bike ride	listen to music	play video games	watch TV

2 Put the letters in order to complete the sentences.

1 My brother *eswtcha VT* ____________ ____________ before he goes to bed.
2 I *og goppshin* ____________ ____________ with my friends.
3 He *tinlses* ____________ to *cimsu* ____________ all the time.
4 He *sketa osotph* ____________ ____________ with his new camera.

LEARN TO LEARN

Word Partners

When you learn new words, learn words that go with them to improve your vocabulary.

3 Make six word partners from the words in the box.

a bike ride   a magazine   do   dressed   get   go for   listen to   music   read   TV   watch   your homework

1 ____________________
2 ____________________
3 ____________________
4 ____________________
5 ____________________
6 ____________________

3 VOCABULARY BANK

School Subjects

art
drama
English
geography
history
information technology (IT)
math
music
nutrition
physical education (PE)
science
Spanish
vocational education

1 **Circle the correct words.**

1 We learn about mountains and rivers in *geography / history*.
2 We draw pictures in *English / art*.
3 We have fun being actors in *drama / science*.
4 In *math / music* we learn about numbers.
5 We run, jump, and play sports in *PE / IT*.

Places in a School

athletic field

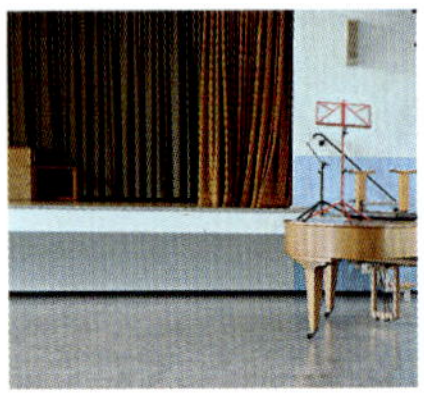
auditorium

cafeteria

classroom

computer lab

gymnasium

library

locker room

office

restrooms

science lab

teacher's lounge

2 **Find and circle six places in a school.**

luartllibraryhotpowofficeaumusicclassroomqoisearestroomsbscienceolockerroomcadramaogymnasiumasi

LEARN TO LEARN

Making a Spidergram

You can use spidergrams to help learn new vocabulary. They show you how words are related.

3 **Which words in the box can you use in a spidergram about each place? Write the words next to the places 1–4.**

board computer desk eat food history lunch math meal mouse online outside PE program running soccer

1 cafeteria: ______
2 athletic field: ______
3 classroom: ______
4 computer lab: ______

4 VOCABULARY BANK

Food and Drink

apples

bananas

beans

carrots

cheese

chicken

chocolate

eggs

fish

juice

meat

rice

soda

water

1 Look at the pictures. How often do you eat or drink these? Compare your answers with your partner.

every day: ______________________ sometimes: ______________________

often: ______________________ never: ______________________

Adjectives

cold	disgusting	healthy	salty	sweet
delicious	fresh	hot	spicy	unhealthy

2 Match the words in the box with the meanings 1–5.

1 This word means something tastes very bad. ______________________
2 This word means something tastes very good. ______________________
3 This word describes something that isn't good for you. ______________________
4 This word describes the taste of sugar. ______________________
5 This word describes something that's good for you. ______________________

LEARN TO LEARN

True or False Sentences

Correcting false statements helps you remember information.

3 Use the adjectives above to write true and false sentences. Say your sentences. Your partner says if they are true or false and corrects the false sentences.

1 ____
2 ____
3 ____
4 ____
5 ____

Chips are sweet.

False. They are salty.

5 VOCABULARY BANK

Clothes

boots

cap

flip-flops

hoodie

jacket

jeans

shirt

shorts

skirt

sneakers

sweatpants

T-shirt

1 Circle the correct words.

1. You *usually wear* / *don't usually wear* a cap indoors.
2. You *wear* / *don't wear* socks with flip-flops.
3. You wear shorts on your *legs* / *feet*.
4. People often wear jeans at *home* / *work*.
5. People usually wear jackets or hoodies in *cool* / *warm* weather.
6. You wear boots on your *hands* / *feet*.

Accessories

belt	earrings	necklace	ring	sunglasses	wallet
bracelet	gloves	purse	scarf	umbrella	watch

2 Put the letters in order to make accessories.

1. It's sunny, so she's wearing a T-shirt and *sesglsunas* ________________.
2. She always wears a gold necklace and *sarering* ________________.
3. It's raining – put on your jacket and take an *umaellbr* ________________.
4. When it's cold, I wear my boots and *ovglse* ________________.
5. Most people keep their money in a purse or a *tellwa* ________________.
6. He always wears a *lebt* ________________ with his jeans.

LEARN TO LEARN

Making a Picture Dictionary

Drawing and labeling pictures helps you remember new vocabulary.

3 Draw a person with six of the accessories above. Label the accessories.

____

____

____

____

____

____

6 VOCABULARY BANK

Sports

basketball

gymnastics

hockey

rock climbing

rugby

running

sailing

swimming

table tennis

track and field

volleyball

windsurfing

yoga

1 Write the verbs in these sentences.

1. They ____________ swimming every Wednesday after school.
2. She ____________ gymnastics on the weekend.
3. Do you ____________ basketball?
4. I ____________ hockey at school.
5. We often ____________ rock climbing in the summer.

Sports Verbs

bounce	climb	hit	kick	pass	score
catch	dive	jump	lift	run	throw

2 Work with a partner. Take turns choosing a sports verb and do the action. Your partner guesses the verb and says a sport that uses it.

LEARN TO LEARN

Remembering Vocabulary Sets

When you learn a new word, write down other forms of the word. This improves your vocabulary.

3 Write words for people who do these sports.

1. climbing ____climber____
2. running ____________
3. gymnastics ____________
4. swimming ____________
5. hockey ____________

7 VOCABULARY BANK

Animals

bear

crocodile

donkey

duck

eagle

giraffe

hippo

horse

lion

monkey

mouse

parrot

snake

whale

1 Complete the categories with the animals. Some animals can go in more than one category.

Land	Air	Water

Adjectives

beautiful	dangerous	large	long	quiet	tiny
cute	heavy	lazy	noisy	smart	wild

2 Put the letters in order to describe the animals.

1 I saw a *eutc* ________ duck in the park.

2 There are *gealr* ________ crocodiles in the water here.

3 There was a *aubfetiul* ________ parrot in the tree.

4 Listen to that *oinys* ________ lion!

LEARN TO LEARN

Remembering New Vocabulary

Using new words in a sentence helps you remember them.

3 Write true sentences about animals. Use the adjectives above.

1 *I love mice because they are tiny and cute.*

2 ________

3 ________

4 ________

5 ________

8 VOCABULARY BANK

Places in Town

aquarium

bowling alley

gym

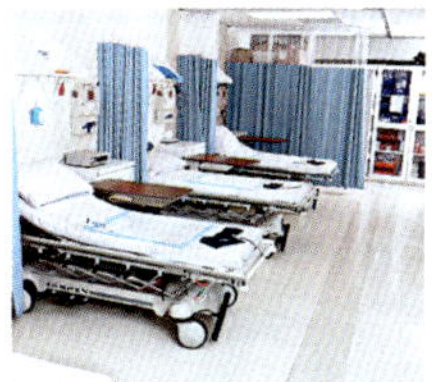

hospital

ice rink

movie theater

parking lot

post office

shopping mall

skate park

swimming pool

1 Match the sentence halves.

1 I went to the post
2 There is a big shopping
3 He loves going to the bowling
4 The water in the swimming
5 We met at the ice

a alley with his friends.
b pool was very cold today.
c rink to go skating.
d office to buy some stamps.
e mall in this city.

Personal possessions

bus pass	headphones	laptop	phone
camera	ID card	money	portable charger
concert ticket	keys	passport	tablet

2 Circle the correct words.

1 I took some *keys* / *money* / *headphones* to the shopping mall to buy some clothes.
2 You need a *concert ticket* / *phone* / *passport* to go to another country.
3 He used his *bus pass* / *tablet* / *portable charger* to get to the gym.
4 You can use *headphones* / *keys* / *cameras* to listen to music.
5 She took a *camera* / *laptop* / *ID card* to take pictures of the fish at the aquarium.

LEARN TO LEARN

Making Real Sentences

When you learn new words, use them to talk about your life. This will help you remember them.

3 Work in pairs. Take turns choosing a personal possession and say when, where, or why you use it.

I use my tablet on the bus to watch videos.

9 VOCABULARY BANK

Outdoor Life

build a shelter	find food and water	pick fruit
catch fish	identify plants	read a map
collect wood	light a fire	use a compass
cook over a campfire		

1 **Look at the outdoor life phrases above and try to remember them. Then cover the list and work in pairs. Take turns saying a verb. Can your partner remember the phrase? Can you remember all ten?**

pick

a shelter?

No! Pick fruit!

Vacations

apartment

(beach/ski) resort

B&B (bed & breakfast)

cabin

camper

hotel

RV

tent

youth hostel

2 **Put the letters in order to make types of accommodation.**

1 We stayed in an *mentparat* ______________ by the ocean.
2 We go to our *cnbia* ______________ every summer and catch fish from the lake.
3 Every winter, we visit a *ksi rorest* ______________ in the mountains.
4 When we stay in our *nett* ______________, we cook over a campfire.
5 We stayed in a *otuhy oeshtl* ______________ to save money.

LEARN TO LEARN

Personalizing Spidergrams

Personalizing a spidergram with colors or pictures can help you remember new vocabulary.

3 **Make a spidergram. Write *Types of Accommodation* in the middle. Add three words for types of accommodation you want to learn and draw pictures next to the words.**

2 MATH

1 **When do you use math in your daily activities?**

2 (2.14) **Read the article. Are any of your ideas from Exercise 1 in the article?**

3 **Match the words in bold in the text with the examples.**

1 ____________________ : 1 kg, two cups
2 ____________________ : $7/8$, $4/5$
3 ____________________ : 45%, 99%

4 **Read the article again and look at the pictures. Answer the questions in blue.**

1 ____________________
2 ____________________
3 ____________________

5 **Are the sentences *T* (true) or *F* (false)?**

1 We don't need fractions in real life. ___
2 We use math every time we tell the time. ___
3 "A quarter" and "half" are examples of percentages. ___

Explore It!

Do the calculation.

Write the number of the month you were born. Multiply by 4. Add 13. Multiply by 25. Subtract 200. Add the day of the month you were born. Multiply by 2. Subtract 40. Multiply by 50. Add the last two numbers of the year you were born. Subtract 10,500.

- The first one or two numbers are the month you were born.
- The next two numbers are the day you were born.
- The last two numbers are the year you were born.

Find another interesting math puzzle and test your partner.

Everyday Math

Your math teacher gives you homework on fractions. "I don't need **fractions** in real life," you think. "What's the point?" In fact, math is everywhere.

Telling Time

"Excuse me, what time is it?" someone asks. You look at your phone. "It's a quarter to four," you reply. This is really a mathematical sentence, and you need to know about fractions! [1]**How many minutes are there in the fractions a quarter, half, and three-quarters of an hour?**

Shopping

You want some new clothes, so you go shopping. You see something nice and a sign says there is 40% off the original price of $20. Then you see another offer … 50% off the original price of $26. [2]**Which item is cheaper?** It helps to know how **percentages** work before you waste money!

Cooking

You want to make your favorite cookies. The recipe asks for two tablespoons of sugar, but you only have a teaspoon. [3]**How many teaspoons make two tablespoons?** You may know the answer, but that's because you understand math and **measurements**!

We use math every day of our lives. So, the next time your math teacher gives you homework, make sure you do it!

4 ART

1 **Look carefully at the photo. What can you see?**

4.12 2 **Read the article. Write what the food represents in the photo.**

1 fruit hot-air balloons
2 broccoli ______ 3 potatoes ______

3 **Are the sentences *T* (true) or *F* (false)?**

1 We need to look at the photo again to understand it. ___
2 The photo shows a dream. ___
3 Warner makes the photos with other people. ___
4 He doesn't eat all the food at the end of the session. ___

4 **Check the meaning of the words in yellow in the article.**

Explore It!

Guess the correct answer.

Carl Warner also makes food photos of famous buildings. What is the main ingredient in his photo of the Taj Mahal?

a chicken b onions c bread

Find another interesting fact about food and art. Write a question for your partner to answer.

Foodscapes

There are many works of art about food. But there are also times when art is food. Literally.

Look at the photo. What can you see? There are some rocks and trees. There are a lot of balloons in the sky. It is a beautiful **landscape**!

Now look again. Those aren't rocks ... they are potatoes! Those aren't trees ... they are pieces of broccoli! And those balloons are all different types of fruit and vegetables!

Don't worry, you aren't dreaming. Photographer Carl Warner loves making landscapes out of food because he loves their connection with the natural world. He calls them "foodscapes," and the results are amazing.

Warner takes three days to prepare a photograph. First, he decides which ingredients to use. Then he builds the **scene** with his team. Next, he takes photos in **layers**. There is a lot of fresh food, so he works quickly under the hot lights. What happens to the food at the end of a session? He shares it with his team, of course!

Warner wants to make people smile. However, he also wants to **promote** a good diet. With these **surreal** images, he makes us think about food in a different way.

6 PE

1 Discuss the questions.

1 What sports do you play?

2 Which of these skills do you need to play your favorite sport?

bouncing catching jumping kicking teamwork

3 Read the article again and match the sentence halves.

1	Olga and Maya are	a	more Type II muscle tissue than Olga.
2	Type I muscle tissue is	b	both runners.
3	Type II muscle tissue gets	c	better for stamina.
4	Maya has	d	tired fast.

6.12 **2 Read the article. Check the meaning of the words in bold. Then match them with the definitions.**

1 ________________: the ability to do something difficult for a long time

2 ________________: very strong

3 ________________: takes part in a competition

Explore It!

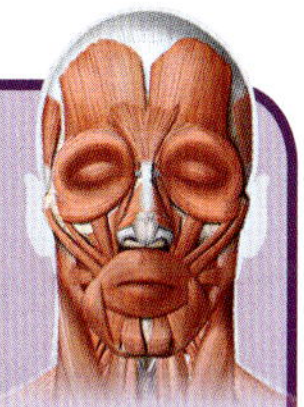

Guess the correct answer.

What's the fastest muscle in the body?

a eye b tongue c finger

Find another interesting fact about muscles. Then write a question for your partner to answer.

FAST OR SLOW?

Meet Olympic athletes Olga and Maya. They have a lot in common, but they are also very different.

Olga **competes** in an event with three different parts: the triathlon. She swims 1.5 km, then cycles 40 km, and finishes with a 10-km run!

Maya runs the 100-meter race. She is much faster than Olga. But she can't do a triathlon.

Olga has more **stamina** and Maya has more speed. But why? What's different inside their bodies?

The difference is in the types of muscles they use.

Type I Muscle Tissue (Slow-Twitch)

This muscle doesn't have a lot of power, but it can keep going. Marathon runners use Type I muscle tissue.

Type II Muscle Tissue (Fast-Twitch)

This is much more **powerful**, but it gets tired fast – in less than a minute. Sprinters use Type II muscle tissue.

Now, the difference is obvious. Olga trains her slow-twitch muscles more and Maya has a lot more fast-twitch muscle.

So, which is better?
Which muscles do you have more of?

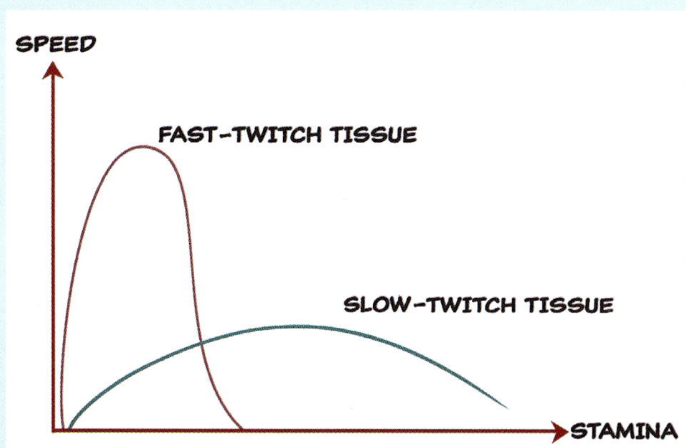

8 HISTORY

1 **Look at the picture. How old are the paintings?**

8.13 **2** **Read the article and check your answer to in Exercise 1.**

3 **Find the synonyms in bold in the text.**

1 amazing ______
2 hole ______
3 profound ______
4 something you find ______

4 **Match questions a–f with paragraphs 1–6.**

a What did they find?
b Did the boys keep their promise?
c Where did the boys make the discovery?
d How did the boys feel?
e When did the discovery take place?
f How did they make the discovery?

5 **Read the article again and put the events in order.**

a ☐ The boys saw a hole in the ground.
b ☐ Archaeologists came to see the paintings.
c ☐ The boys saw pictures of animals in a cave.
d ☐ The boys threw stones down a hole.

Explore It!

Guess the correct answer.

Cave artists used … as paint.

a plants b charcoal c food

Find another interesting fact about the Lascaux cave paintings. Then write a question for your partner to answer.

The Lascaux Cave Paintings

1 ☐

On September 12, 1940, four teenage boys made an amazing discovery. What do you think they discovered? Read on to find out …

2 ☐

The boys were in the woods near the village of Montignac, France. One of them, Marcel Ravidat, saw a hole in the ground a few days earlier. They believed it was the entrance to a secret tunnel that people in the village talked about.

3 ☐

First, they looked inside the hole. Then they threw stones through the **opening** to see how **deep** it was. They decided to go in and carefully climbed down 15 meters. At the bottom, there was a cave. They were amazed by what they saw.

4 ☐

There were **incredible** paintings all over the walls, including hundreds of pictures of red, black, brown, and yellow animals. The animals looked like they were moving in the dark.

5 ☐

The boys were excited, but also worried about getting out. They left the cave and promised to keep their **discovery** a secret.

6 ☐

No, the whole village soon found out, and archaeologists came to visit. The cave paintings were about 17,000 years old. Can you imagine that? They are still some of the best examples of prehistoric art ever discovered.

PRONUNCIATION

UNIT 1

/h/

1.07 **1 Listen and repeat.**

/h/ have Hey! home husband

1.08 **2 Listen and (circle) the option you hear.**

1 (hat) / at
2 hair / air
3 has / as
4 hand / and

1.09 **3 Listen and repeat the sentences.**

1 Hunter has brown hair and he is happy.
2 Hey! How are things?

4 Practice saying the sentences in Exercise 3.

UNIT 2

/s/, /z/, and /ɪz/

2.05 **1 Listen and repeat.**

/s/ speak**s** /z/ doe**s** /ɪz/ chang**es**

2.06 **2 Listen and write A (/s/ or /z/) or B (/ɪz/).**

1 goes A
2 brushes ___
3 eats ___
4 teaches ___

3 Add *-s* or *-es* to the verbs and put them in the correct column.

breaks catch___ choose___ go___ read___ think___ watch___

/s/ **or** /z/	/ɪz/
breaks	

2.07 **4 Listen, check, and repeat.**

5 Cover the chart in Exercise 3 and take turns saying a verb from the box. Your partner says the verb with the *-s* ending.

UNIT 3

Can

3.03 **1 Listen and repeat.**

1 /kən/ She can play the piano.
2 /kən/ Can he read music?
3 /kæn/ Yes, he can.
4 /kænt/ She can't go.

3.04 **2 Listen and (circle) the option you hear.**

1 I (*can*) / *can't* hear you.
2 Pablo *can* / *can't* help you with your homework.
3 They *can* / *can't* count to 20 in Russian.
4 *Can* / *Can't* you use your phone at school?

3 Read the conversation. Write the numbers (1–7) in the correct column.

/kən/	/kæn/	/kænt/
1		

BETH Hi, Tim. [1]Can I ask you some questions?
TIM Yes, you [2]can. Of course.
BETH Great. [3]Can you swim?
TIM No, I [4]can't.
BETH [5]Can you draw or paint?
TIM Yes, I [6]can.
BETH And [7]can you speak Spanish?
TIM *Sí!* I mean, yes.

3.05 **4 Listen and check. Then practice the conversation.**

UNIT 4

Word Stress

1 How many syllables do these words have?

apples 2
disgusting ☐
salty ☐
unhealthy ☐
vegetable ☐
water ☐

4.06 **2 Listen and check.**

3 Match the words in Exercise 1 with the stress patterns (1–3).

1 Oo apples
2 oOo ___
3 Ooo ___

4.07 **4 Listen, check, and repeat.**

UNIT 5

-ing

1 Listen and repeat. (5.03)

play**ing** stand**ing** sing**ing**

2 Match the sentence halves. Then listen, check, and repeat. (5.04)

1 Martin is writing — a around the world.
2 Amir is catching — b salsa.
3 Ysabella is traveling — c a letter.
4 Oscar is dancing — d fish in the sea.

3 Practice saying the sentences in Exercise 2.

UNIT 6

-er

1 Listen and repeat. (6.04)

better	1	faster		older	
bigger		happier		smaller	
easier		healthier		smarter	

2 Match the words in Exercise 1 with the stress patterns. Write 1 or 2 in the box.

1 Oo 2 Ooo

3 Listen and write the words with *-er* endings. Then practice saying the sentences. (6.05)

1 Jane is *smaller* than her ______________.
2 Bossaball is ______________ than ______________.
3 My ______________ is ______________ now that he plays rugby.

UNIT 7

/t/, /d/, and /ɪd/

1 Listen and repeat. (7.06)

/t/ lik**ed** /d/ play**ed** /ɪd/ want**ed**

2 Listen and write A (/t/ or /d/) or B (/ɪd/). (7.07)

1 looked A
2 wanted
3 danced
4 needed

3 Write the simple past form of the verbs in the box and put them in the correct place in the chart.

call climb hunt start want watch

/t/ **or** /d/	/ɪd/
called	

4 Listen, check, and repeat. (7.08)

5 Cover the chart in Exercise 3 and take turns saying a verb from the box. Your partner says the past form of the verb. Check your partner's pronunciation.

UNIT 8

Intonation in *Yes/No* Questions

1 Listen and repeat. (8.03)

1 Did Pablo move?
2 Did they go to the swimming pool?

2 Mark where your voice goes up in the questions.

1 Did Alex play basketball at the gym?
2 Did you take the letter to the post office?
3 Did Fred and George buy anything?
4 Did your brother go to the library?

3 Listen, check, and repeat. (8.04)

UNIT 9

Going To

1 Listen and repeat. (9.07)

1 Are you **going to** the airport?
2 I'm **gonna** watch a movie.

2 Listen and choose the option you hear. Then practice saying the sentences. (9.08)

1 He's *going to* / *gonna* order pizza.
2 Are they *going to* / *gonna* Turkey?
3 I'm not *going to* / *gonna* tell you the secret.
4 Are you *going to* / *gonna* help me?
5 She's *going to* / *gonna* the supermarket.
6 Is he *going to* / *gonna* talk to the teacher?

IRREGULAR VERBS

Infinitive	Simple Past	Past Participle
be	was / were	been
beat	beat	beaten
become	became	become
begin	began	begun
break	broke	broken
bring	brought	brought
build	built	built
buy	bought	bought
catch	caught	caught
choose	chose	chosen
come	came	come
cost	cost	cost
cut	cut	cut
do	did	done
draw	drew	drawn
drink	drank	drunk
drive	drove	driven
eat	ate	eaten
fall	fell	fallen
feel	felt	felt
fight	fought	fought
find	found	found
fly	flew	flown
forget	forgot	forgotten
get	got	gotten
give	gave	given
go	went	gone
grow	grew	grown
have	had	had
hear	heard	heard
hide	hid	hidden
hit	hit	hit
hold	held	held
keep	kept	kept

Infinitive	Simple Past	Past Participle
know	knew	known
leave	left	left
lose	lost	lost
make	made	made
meet	met	met
pay	paid	paid
put	put	put
read	read	read
ride	rode	ridden
ring	rang	rung
run	ran	run
say	said	said
see	saw	seen
sell	sold	sold
send	sent	sent
show	showed	shown
shut	shut	shut
sing	sang	sung
sit	sat	sat
sleep	slept	slept
speak	spoke	spoken
spend	spent	spent
stand	stood	stood
swim	swam	swum
take	took	taken
teach	taught	taught
tell	told	told
think	thought	thought
throw	threw	thrown
understand	understood	understood
wake	woke	woken
wear	wore	worn
win	won	won
write	wrote	written

ACKNOWLEDGEMENTS

The authors and publishers acknowledge the following sources of copyright material and are grateful for the permissions granted. While every effort has been made, it has not always been possible to identify the sources of all the material used, or to trace all copyright holders. If any omissions are brought to our notice, we will be happy to include the appropriate acknowledgements on reprinting and in the next update to the digital edition, as applicable.

Key: **CLIL** = Content and Language Integrated Learning, **F** = Finished, **SU** = Starter Unit, **U** = Unit, **VB** = Vocabulary Bank

Text

U1: Text about the brother Bibi and Bichu. Reproduced with kind permission; Text about Cortes Circus family. Copyright © The Wallenda Cortes Circus family. Reproduced with kind permission; **U3:** Text about Cuban Ballet school. Reproduced with kind permission.

Photography

The following photographs are sourced from Getty Images:

SU: lukbar/Stock/Getty Images Plus; bowdenimages/iStock/Getty Images Plus; Panya/iStock/Getty Images Plus; Jose Luis Pelaez Inc/Blend Images; lattesmile/iStock/Getty Images Plus; LysenkoAlexander/iStock/Getty Images Plus; Peter Dazeley/Photographer's Choice/Getty Images Plus; Adrian Weinbrecht/Cultura; **U1:** Peter Beavis/Stone; Morsa Images/DigitalVision; FG Trade/E+; Stephanie Hager - HagerPhoto/Photodisc; Voisine/iStock/Getty Images Plus; Jon Anderson/Moment Open; bobbieo/iStock/Getty Images Plus; Echo/Juice Images; Image Source; Jutta Klee/Canopy; Compassionate Eye Foundation/Photodisc; Kemter/E+; STOCK4B-RF; Panya/iStock/Getty Images Plus; EMMANUEL DUNAND/AFP; lolaira/E+; Vladimir Sagadeev/iStock/Getty Images Plus; Bernd Vogel/Corbis; jopstock/Moment; Gem Hall; Eamonn McCormack/WireImage; Frederick M. Brown/FilmMagic; Kevin Mazur/WireImage; Ben Pruchnie/WireImage; Sean Justice/The Image Bank; Bruce Laurance/The Image Bank; View Pictures/UIG via Getty Images; Westend61; Carboxylase/Shutterstock; Jinxy Productions/Blend Images; Fuse/Corbis; Kiko Jimenez/EyeEm; Bruno Vigneron/Getty Images Entertainment; SEBASTIAN KAULITZKI/Science Photo Library; FRED TANNEAU/AFP; Manakin/iStock/Getty Images Plus; Sean Locke/EyeEm; mocoo/iStock/Getty Images Plus; **U2:** Prasit photo/Moment; Vstock LLC/Vstock; Timothy Allen/Photolibrary; Picavet/Photodisc; wrangel/iStock/Getty Images Plus; Dragos Cosmin photos/Moment Open; Fabian Krause/EyeEm; Gordon Esler/Photographer's Choice/Getty Images Plus; monkeybusinessimages/iStock/Getty Images Plus; Tetra Images; kali9/E+; 7romawka7/iStock/Getty Images Plus; Hill Street Studios/DigitalVision; mocoo/iStock/Getty Images Plus; **U3:** Frédéric Soltan/Corbis News; Cristian Lungu/Moment; Michael Marquand/Lonely Planet Images; AWelshLad/E+; Westend61; Photography taken by Mario Gutiérrez/Moment; Education Images/UIG via Getty Images; Eric Lafforgue/Art In All Of Us/Corbis via Getty Images; Digital Vision/Photodisc; Paolo Negri/Photographer's Choice/Getty Images Plus; Homiel/iStock/Getty Images Plus; Peerapat Tandavanitj/Moment; Absodels; Keren Su/The Image Bank; mocoo/iStock/Getty Images Plus; Natalia Kuprova/iStock/Getty Images Plus; Nikiteev_Konstantin/iStock/Getty Images Plus; **U4:** Photo Josse/Leemage/Corbis Historical; paulprescott72/iStock Editorial/Getty Images Plus; CreativeBrainStorming/iStock/Getty Images Plus; EasyBuy4u/E+; Richard Coombs/EyeEm; ahavelaar/iStock/Getty Images Plus; rosabernardes/RooM; cookelma/iStock/Getty Images Plus; nathan4847/iStock/Getty Images Plus; Juanmonino/E+; Ekaterina_Marory/iStock/Getty Images Plus; Jill Clardy/Moment Open; Lisovskaya/iStock/Getty Images Plus; efired/iStock/Getty Images Plus; Adrienn Medvegy/EyeEm; fcafotodigital/E+; Holden Worrell/EyeEm; Tom Cockrem/Lonely Planet Images/Getty Images Plus; Jamie Stamey/iStock/Getty Images Plus; Blaine Harrington III/Corbis Documentary; Edwin Remsburg/VW Pics via Getty Images; Russell Monk/The Image Bank; Jon Lovette/Photographer's Choice RF; fcafotodigital/E+; KatarzynaBialasiewicz/iStock/Getty Images Plus; mevans/iStock/Getty Images Plus; Marco Livolsi/EyeEm; Ragnar Schmuck; structuresxx/iStock/Getty Images Plus; 4nadia/iStock/Getty Images Plus; margouillatphotos/iStock/Getty Images Plus; Karlevana/iStock/Getty Images Plus; Andreas Berheide/EyeEm; phloxii/iStock/Getty Images Plus; ivo_13/iStock/Getty Images Plus; ValentynVolkov/iStock/Getty Images Plus; Rengim Mutevellioglu/Moment; jantroyka/iStock/Getty Images Plus; pedphoto36pm/iStock/Getty Images Plus; PauloVilela/iStock/Getty Images Plus; Penny Tweedie/The Image Bank/Getty Images Plus; mocoo/iStock/Getty Images Plus; **U5:** Mehmet Hilmi Barcin/E+; primeimages/E+; mocoo/iStock/Getty Images Plus; Andy Roberts/Caiaimage; Jorge Fernández/LightRocket via Getty Images; Image Source/DigitalVision; davidcreacion/iStock/Getty Images Plus; Mochipet/iStock/Getty Images Plus; Sol de Zuasnabar Brebbia/Moment; lightasafeather/iStock/Getty Images Plus; Richard Boll/Photographer's Choice RF; Ryan McVay/Photodisc; AndreyGorulko/iStock/Getty Images Plus; kenneth-cheung/E+; pepifoto/E+; Saowakon Sukrak/EyeEm; malerapaso/iStock/Getty Images Plus; s-cphoto/E+; AnthonyRosenberg/iStock/Getty Images Plus; Fernando Trabanco Fotografía/Moment; ProArtWork/E+; Maria Taglienti-Molinari/Hulton Archive; Willowpix/E+; Willowpix/E+; Juanmonino/E+; PeskyMonkey/iStock/Getty Images Plus; Thomas Barwick/DigitalVision; Echo/Juice Images; Cultura RM Exclusive/Stefano Gilera; Miya Bhai/EyeEm; ImagesBazaar; Aaron Joel Santos/Aurora; tolgart/iStock/Getty Images Plus; transiastock/iStock/Getty Images Plus; VCG Wilson/Corbis via Getty Images; mai111/iStock/Getty Images Plus; Education Images/UIG via Getty Images; cheekudigital/iStock/Getty Images Plus; photosindia; Jihan Abdalla/Blend Images; anitha devi/iStock/Getty Images Plus; Fgorgun/iStock/Getty Images Plus; Oleg Golovnev/EyeEm; **U6:** RyanJLane/E+; groveb/E+; Marcia Straub/Moment; Ben Welsh/Design Pics; miki-tiger/iStock/Getty Images Plus; ian600f/iStock/Getty Images Plus; Luka/Cultura; AAGAMIA/The Image Bank; Jon Feingersh/The Image Bank; Polhansen/iStock/Getty Images Plus; Westend61; kosmos111/kosmos111; PeopleImages/DigitalVision; Pete Saloutos/Image Source; Mehmet Hilmi Barcin/E+; vinhdav/iStock/Getty Images Plus; Vladimir Godnik; Lou Jones/The Image Bank/Getty Images Plus; NurPhoto; Stuart Franklin/Getty Images Sport; Markus Gann/EyeEm; Ty Allison/Photographer's Choice; lzf/iStock/Getty Images Plus; Hero Images; somnuk krobkum/Moment; kevinruss/iStock/Getty Images Plus; MARC MUELLER/AFP/Getty Images; BRENDAN SMIALOWSKI/AFP/Getty Images; Keshav Singh/Hindustan Times via Getty Images; Klaus Vedfelt/DigitalVision; Lars Niki/Getty Images for The North Face; nenadpitarevic/iStock/Getty Images Plus; RunPhoto/Photodisc; 2e812ac3_768/iStock/Getty Images Plus; Nongluk Charoenpronwattanakun/EyeEm; RUSSELLTATEdotCOM/DigitalVision Vectors; Don Mason; **U7:** Inaki Relanzon/Nature Picture Library; Mostafa Gabr/EyeEm; Gerald & Buff Corsi/Visuals Unlimited; Dave Fleetham/Design Pics/Perspectives; Anup Shah/Stockbyte; Tim Platt/Stone; CreativeNature_nl/iStock/Getty Images Plus; Jeffrey Coolidge/DigitalVision; Barrie Thomas/EyeEm; Paul A. Souders/Corbis Documentary; ERNESTO BENAVIDES/AFP/Getty Images; Eric VANDEVILLE/Gamma-Rapho via Getty Images; A-Digit/DigitalVision Vectors; Jurgen & Christine Sohns; Jennifer Borton/DigitalVision Vectors; Fiona Davis/EyeEm; esancai/iStock/Getty Images Plus; John Crux Photography/Moment Open; baona/E+; Alan Tunnicliffe Photography/Moment; Tim Flach/Iconica; PomInOz/iStock/Getty Images Plus; Arun Roisri/Thailand; Jane Burton/Dorling Kindersley; GlobalP/iStock/Getty Images Plus; Barry Bland/Barcroft Media/Getty Images; Paul Souders/Corbis Documentary; guenterguni/E+; Adriano La Naia/EyeEm; Yuri_Arcurs/E+; TIMOTHY A. CLARY/AFP; Jeff R. Bottari/Getty Images Entertainment; Barcroft Media; Ysanne Slide/Moviestore collection Ltd/Alamy Stock Photo; Serjio74/iStock/Getty Images Plus; Kauriana/iStock/Getty Images Plus; ChrisGorgio/iStock/Getty Images Plus; krugli/iStock/Getty Images Plus; perysty/iStock/Getty Images Plus; Ace_Create/DigitalVision Vectors; Fabian Berg/EyeEm; JuliarStudio/iStock/Getty Images Plus; luplupme/iStock/Getty Images Plus; Science Picture Co/Collection Mix: Subjects; James Gritz/Photographer's Choice RF; Sexto Sol/Stockbyte; stockcam/E+; Dirk Wüstenhagen Imagery/Moment Open; José Luis Ruiz/Moment; Edgardo Contreras/Photodisc; **U8:** Eg Project/Photonica; Walter Zerla/Blend Images; asiseeit/E+; Andres Benitez/EyeEm; Streeter Lecka/Getty Images; alxpin/iStock/Getty Images Plus; kevinjeon00/E+; Chris Ryan/OJO Images; ihoe/iStock/Getty Images Plus; Vostok/Moment & Vostok/Moment; Jon Hicks/Corbis Documentary; Spaces Images/Blend Images; Yongyuan Dai/The Image Bank; Dmitry Berkut/iStock/Getty Images Plus; ENRIQUE MARCARIAN/REUTERS/Newscom; Hemant Mehta; David De Lossy/Valueline/Getty Images Plus; Tetra Images; Richard Boll/Photographer's Choice; FlamingPumpkin/E+; rasikabendre/iStock/Getty Images Plus; s-cphoto/E+; daizuoxin/iStock/Getty Images Plus; Chuck Cross/EyeEm; Ryan McVay/Photodisc; pbombaert/Moment; Nick Dolding/The Image Bank; j_markow/iStock/Getty Images Plus; Bloom Productions/Taxi; pixelfusion3d/iStock/Getty Images Plus; jashlock/iStock/Getty Images Plus; seb_ra/iStock/Getty Images Plus; ti-ja/iStock/Getty Images Plus; Haywood Magee/Picture Post; Folb/Topical Press Agency/Getty Images; Igor Golovniov/EyeEm; oxygen/Moment; Pinghung Chen/EyeEm; Tomsmith585/iStock Unreleased; George Marks/Retrofile RF; PeopleImages/E+; damircudic/E+; mocoo/iStock/Getty Images Plus; **U9:** Hybrid Images/Cultura; Shing Chak Wong/EyeEm; Eye Ubiquitous/UIG via Getty Images; David De Lossy/Photodisc; ©Studio One-One/Moment Open; Burak Karademir/Moment; Ismailciydem/iStock/Getty Images Plus; Siphotography/iStock/Getty Images Plus; Diana Mayfield/Lonely Planet Images; ©fitopardo.com/Moment; Westend61; DarthArt/iStock Editorial/Getty Images Plus; Michael Blann/DigitalVision; Photawa/iStock Editorial/Getty Images Plus; Billy Currie Photography/Moment; HAGENMULLER Jean-Francois/Hemis.fr; coryz/E+; SeventyFour/iStock/Getty Images Plus; Stephen

Spraggon/Photolibrary; Hero Images; KatarzynaBialasiewicz/iStock/Getty Images Plus; Hero Images; Kontrec/E+; tupungato/iStock/Getty Images Plus; Compassionate Eye Foundation/Robert Kent/DigitalVision; Zsolt Hlinka/Moment; John Giustina/Iconica; Hill Street Studios/Blend Images; Letizia Le Fur/ONOKY; BrankoPhoto/iStock/Getty Images Plus; mocoo/iStock/Getty Images Plus; Inti St. Clair, Inc.; ozgurdonmaz/iStock/Getty Images Plus; **F1:** Vladimir Godnik; Vera Anderson/WireImage; **F2:** bubaone/DigitalVision Vectors; Gareth Morgans/StockFood Creative; kenex/DigitalVision Vectors; Dorling Kindersley/Dorling Kindersley; lushik/DigitalVision Vectors; Hero Images; Gang Zhou/E+; Compassionate Eye Foundation/Chris Ryan/Tax; Barry Austin/DigitalVision; **F3:** Michael Moeller/EyeEm; intraprese/iStock/Getty Images Plus; April30/E+; Davizro/iStock/Getty Images Plus; Wavebreakmedia/iStock/Getty Images Plus; Lisay/iStock/Getty Images Plus; Viktorcvetkovic/E+; Bill Reitzel/Stockbyte; Mike Kemp; AlekZotoff/iStock/Getty Images Plus; **F4:** kelly bowden/Moment; Carol Yepes/Moment; Tim Grist Photography/Moment; Burcu Atalay Tankut/Moment; Creative Crop/DigitalVision; Creativ Studio Heinemann; Photographer Nick Measures/Moment; **F5:** Westend61; Ronnie Kaufman/DigitalVision; Roy JAMES Shakespeare/Photodisc; Gpointstudio/Cultura; **F7:** acceptfoto/iStock/Getty Images Plus; Rob Lind/EyeEm; Tier Und Naturfotografie J und C Sohns/Photographer's Choice; mmozzies/iStock/Getty Images Plus; claudialothering/RooM; Moiz_Cukurel/iStock/Getty Images Plus; PILLAIBALANMADHAVAN/iStock/Getty Images Plus; Vicki Jauron, Babylon and Beyond Photography/Moment; imaginima/E+; **F8:** Denny Soetiono/EyeEm; Vostok/Moment; Михаил Руденко/iStock/Getty Images Plus; Sorapong Chaipanya/EyeEm; Rondeau Laetitia/EyeEm; Raphael Brian Espineli/EyeEm; baona/iStock/Getty Images Plus; Jasmin Merdan/Moment; Image Source; yulkapopkova/iStock/Getty Images Plus; **F9:** Peter John Dickson/Moment Mobile; **VB0:** Symphonie/The Image Bank; Chumphon Wanich/EyeEm; Erik Rank/The Image Bank; View Pictures/Universal Images Group; Nora Carol Photography/Moment; Dorling Kindersley; Peter Dazeley/Photographer's Choice; Tim Hall/Taxi; Steve Gorton and Alex Wilson/Dorling Kindersley; imaginima/E+; **VB1:** Jamie Garbutt/Taxi; PeopleImages/E+; Morsa Images/DigitalVision; Westend61; Moritz Otto/EyeEm; Andreas Kuehn/DigitalVision; Sam Diephuis; Patricia Hamila/EyeEm; XiXinXing/iStock/Getty Images Plus; Emma Early/EyeEm; Supawat Punnanon/EyeEm; **VB2:** Rasulovs/iStock/Getty Images Plus; Maskot; Sean Justice/Corbis/VCG/Getty Images Plus; bymuratdeniz/E+; Nomad/E+; Jose Luis Pelaez Inc/DigitalVision; kali9/E+; sophie adams, cardiff, uk/Moment; Compassionate Eye Foundation/Rob Daly/OJO Images Ltd/DigitalVision; Tetra Images; Flashpop/DigitalVision; **VB3:** Tom Merton/DigitalVision; xavierarnau/E+; Caiaimage/Chris Ryan/OJO+; Westend61; Justin Yoast/EyeEm; SilviaJansen/E+; fanjianhua/Moment; Hero Images; Caiaimage/Sam Edwards; Stella; Erik Isakson; Ariel Skelley/Photodisc; **VB4:** Arisara Tongdonnoi/EyeEm; RedHelga/E+; Arisara Tongdonnoi/EyeEm; Dorling Kindersley:Charlotte Tolhurst/Dorling Kindersley/Getty Images Plus; IvonneW/iStock/Getty Images Plus; Paul Poplis/Photolibrary; Kuzmik_A/iStock/Getty Images Plus; Barry Wong/The Image Bank; John Borthwick/Lonely Planet Images; koya79/iStock/Getty Images Plus; Science Photo Library; annick vanderschelden photography/Moment; Skarie20/iStock/Getty Images Plus; LAL/The Image Bank; **VB5:** Nophamon Yanyapong/EyeEm; Radionphoto/iStock/Getty Images Plus; clu/E+; NAKphotos/iStock/Getty Images Plus; mattiestudio/iStock/Getty Images Plus; Issaurinko/iStock/Getty Images Plus; malerapaso/iStock/Getty Images Plus; OxfordSquare/iStock/Getty Images Plus; akova/iStock/Getty Images Plus; mawielobob/iStock/Getty Images Plus; ersinkisacik/iStock/Getty Images Plus; Ng Sok Lian/EyeEm; **VB6:** baona/iStock/Getty Images Plus; Vedrana Sucic/EyeEm; Steve Smith; Patrik Giardino/Corbis; Hero Images; Alistair Berg/DigitalVision; PeopleImages/E+; Marc Princivalle for imagesconcept.com/Moment; Peter Noyce/LOOP IMAGES/Corbis Documentary; Aksonov/E+; Mike Kemp; Johner Images; Andrii Afanasiev/EyeEm; **VB7:** Andrea Croati/EyeEm; Kryssia Campos/Moment; sjharmon/E+; Chris Beavon/Moment; Jim Adams/500px; Jens Huelsmeier/EyeEm; Joe McDonald/Corbis Documentary; Travelographer 1/500px; Vicki Jauron, Babylon and Beyond Photography/Moment; Images from BarbAnna/Moment; silversaltphoto.j.senosiain/Moment Open; Ryan Petersen/EyeEm; Tim Melling/Moment; **VB8:** damircudic/E+; cscredon/E+; tma1/E+; Aliraza Khatri's Photography/Moment; Steve Debenport/iStock/Getty Images Plus; SimplyCreativePhotography/E+; Billy Hustace/The Image Bank; Oleksiy Maksymenko/All Canada Photos; Westend61; Hero Images; Nongnuch Leelaphasuk/EyeEm; **VB9:** Toby Howard/Moment; photo by Chris Axe/Moment; pchoui/E+; Vadim Sushchenko/iStock/Getty Images Plus; juhy13/E+; Noel Hendrickson/DigitalVision; buzbuzzer/iStock; Yuriy_Kulik/iStock/Getty Images Plus; DaveLongMedia/E+; **CLIL2:** rolleiflextlr/iStock/Getty Images Plus; kitthanes/iStock/Getty Images Plus; Jupiterimages/PHOTOS.com>>/Getty Images Plus; porcorex/E+; stock_colors/iStock/Getty Images Plus; **CLIL4:** Cosmin Rechitan/EyeEm; **CLIL6:** TREVOR JOHNSTON/Eye Meets World Photography; QAI Publishing/UIG via Getty Images; Hero Images/DigitalVision; **CLIL8:** Ralph Morse/The LIFE Premium Collection/Getty Images; Universal History Archive/UIG via Getty Images.

The following photographs are sourced from other libraries/sources:

U1: Copyright © The Wallenda Cortes Circus family; Copyright © Gem Hall; **U1–U9:** Carboxylase/Shutterstock; **U3:** Copyright ©Cuban Ballet school; **U8:** ENRIQUE MARCARIAN/REUTERS/Newscom; **VB0:** Copyright © Cambridge University Press; **CLIL4:** Carl warner/Fairbank Literary; **ICONS:** Prithvi/Noun Project; Agni/Noun Project; mikicon/Noun Project; Baboon designs, US/Noun Project; Tanguy Keryhuel, FR/Noun Project; Icons Bazaar/Noun Project; Adrien Coquet, FR/Noun Project; Vectors Market/Noun Project; TukTuk Design/Noun Project; iconsphere, ID/Noun Project; i cons, US/Noun Project; Kim Eriksson/Noun Project; Lloyd Humphreys, DK/Noun Project; Delwar Hossain, BD/Noun Project; Kirby Wu, TW/Noun Project; Magicon, HU/Noun Project; Baboon designs, US/Noun Project.

Illustration

SU: Alex Herrerías; **U1:** Alex Herrerías; Chelen Écija; Antonio Cuesta Cornejo; **U2:** Alex Herrerías; Chelen Écija; Antonio Cuesta Cornejo; **U3:** Alex Herrerías; Chelen Écija; Antonio Cuesta Cornejo; **U4:** Alex Herrerías; Chelen Écija; Antonio Cuesta Cornejo; **U5:** Alex Herrerías; Chelen Écija; Antonio Cuesta Cornejo; Mark Duffin; **U6:** Chelen Écija; **U7:** Mark Duffin; **U8:** Alex Herrerías; Chelen Écija; Mark Duffin; **U9:** Alex Herrerías; Chelen Écija; **F6:** Alex Herrerías; **CLIL2:** Antonio Cuesta Cornejo; **CLIL6:** Alex Herrerías.

Video Stills

The following stills are sourced from Getty Images:

U1: andresr/Vetta; monkeybusinessimages/Creatas Video- New Getty+/Getty Images Plus; **U2:** ImagesBazaar/Photo- New Gettylibrary Video- New Getty; **U3:** Klaus Vedfelt/Image Bank Film; Ariel Skelley/Image Bank Film: Signature; **U4:** chizheffsky/Creatas Video- New Getty+/Getty Images Plus; monkeybusinessimages/Creatas Video- New Getty+/Getty Images Plus; Yellow Dog Productions Inc./Image Bank Film; **U5:** Yellow Dog Productions Inc./Image Bank Film; **U6:** 3sbworld/Creatas Video- New Getty+/Getty Images Plus; **U7:** Mark Kostich/Creatas Video- New Getty; DDCoral/Creatas Video- New Getty+/Getty Images Plus; **U8:** HeroImagesFootage/Creatas Video- New Getty; **U9:** Faithfulshot/DigitalVision.

The following stills are sourced from other libraries:

SU–U9: Lucentum Digital

Typesetting: Aphik, S.A. de C.V.

Cover Design and Illustrations: Collaborate Agency

Audio Recordings: Eastern Sky Media Services, Inc. and City Vox New York

Video Production: Lucentum Digital

The authors and editors would like to thank all the teachers and consultants who have contributed to the development of the course, in particular:

Mexico: Ana Belém Durán Gutiérrez; Nelly Marina Elizalde; Julio Andrés Franco Del Campo; Nimbe García Haro; Raoul Josset Paquette; Adriana Maldonado Torres; Ana Edith Ramos Ramírez

Brazil: Beatriz Affonso; Alessandra Bautista; Ana Carolina De Luca; Esdras Fattobene; Maria Claudia Ferreira; Itana Lins; Maria Helena Meyer; ; Valéria Moraes Novoa; Odinéia Morandi; Regina Pedroso De Araujo; Andrea Perina; Simone Rodrigues; Jacqueline Saback; Clice Sales; Silvia Teles

Turkey: Belgün Akçelik; Peggy Alptekin; Hayri Arslan; Ayşe Aylin Kündüroğlu; Nihan Çalışkan; Selin Dinçkal Erkenci; Bengü Özbek; Saliha Şimşek

Contributing Authors: Liz Walter and Kate Woodford

Versioner: Suzanne Harris

American English Consultant: Multimodal Media

Freelance Editors: Mandie Drucker, Jacqueline French, Meredith Levy, and Cara Norris-Ramirez

SHAPE IT! 1

COMBO

WORKBOOK

Vicki Anderson and Lynn Durrant

CAMBRIDGE
UNIVERSITY PRESS

CONTENTS

STARTER

Welcome!

VOCABULARY AND READING

Months, Cardinal and Ordinal Numbers, and Colors

1 Complete the sentences with the months in the box and ordinal numbers.

April	August	February	~~January~~
June	March	November	October

1 January is the first month.
2 ______ is the ______ month.
3 ______ is the third month.
4 ______ is the ______ month.
5 May is the ______ month.
6 ______ is the sixth month.
7 July is the ______ month.
8 ______ is the ______ month.
9 September is the ______ month.
10 ______ is the tenth month.
11 ______ is the ______ month.
12 December is the ______ month.

2 Complete the crossword with seven more colors.

ACROSS →
2 three letters
3 four letters
4 six letters
7 five letters
8 five letters

DOWN ↓
1 five letters
5 six letters
6 four letters

An Online Profile

3 Read about Dasha and Carlos. Where are their friends from?

Home **Profile** Photos Events

INTERNATIONAL STUDENT PROFILE DAY!

Hello! My name's Dasha. I'm from Warsaw in Poland. I'm 12. How old are you? In this photo, I'm with my two best friends. Polina is Polish, but Marta isn't Polish. She's Brazilian. My favorite color is green. What's your favorite color?
My birthday is April 10. When's your birthday?
My dream is to be a doctor! What's your dream?
Write soon!

Hi, Dasha! I'm Carlos. I'm Mexican, from Mexico City. I'm 11. In this photo, I'm with my best friends. They're not Mexican. Yusuf is from Turkey, and David is from England. My favorite color is blue. It's June 5 tomorrow, and it's my birthday! My dream is to be a singer! Who's your favorite singer?
Let me know! :)

4 Read the profiles again and complete the chart.

Name	Birthday	Favorite Color	Dream
Dasha	April 10	green	1 doctor
2 ______	3 ______	4 ______	singer

5 Circle the correct answers.

1 Dasha is from *China* / *Poland*.
2 Her birthday is in the *fourth* / *seventh* month of the year.
3 Carlos is from *Turkey* / *Mexico*.
4 His birthday is in the *sixth* / *twelfth* month of the year.
5 *David* / *Carlos* is 12 tomorrow.

GRAMMAR IN ACTION AND VOCABULARY

Subject Pronouns and Possessive Adjectives

1 ☆ **Complete the chart with the subject pronouns in the box.**

it they we ~~you~~

Singular	Plural
I	3 ______
1 *you*	you
he / she / 2 ______	4 ______

2 ☆ **Write the subject pronoun.**

1 Dasha *she*
2 photos ______
3 school ______
4 Carlos ______
5 Polina and Marta ______
6 Yusuf and I ______

3 ☆ **Which plural pronoun can we use for objects and people?**

______

4 ☆ **Complete the sentences with the possessive adjectives in the box.**

her his its my our ~~their~~ your

1 Yusuf and Carlos are at school. They're in *their* classroom.
2 He's from Poland. ______ name's Max.
3 I'm 12 years old, and ______ best friend, Alba, is 11.
4 We're from China. ______ nationality is Chinese.
5 You're 13. ______ birthday is in April.
6 My teacher is Maria. ______ birthday is in August.
7 This school is nice. ______ classrooms are big!

Verb *To Be*

5 ☆☆ **Complete the profile with the correct form of *to be*.**

My name 1 *is* Sofía. I 2 ______ from Chile. My best friend 3 ______ Ana. She 4 ______ (not) from Chile. She 5 ______ from Brazil. My favorite singer 6 ______ Lorde. My favorite songs 7 ______ *Green Light* and *Royals*. They 8 ______ incredible!

Question Words

6 ☆ **Match questions 1–5 with answers a–e.**

1 Where are you from? [*c*]
2 How old are you? [ ]
3 When's your birthday? [ ]
4 Who's your best friend? [ ]
5 What's your favorite number? [ ]

a May 10.
b It's 15.
c ~~I'm from Miami.~~
d Alba.
e I'm 11.

Classroom Objects

7 ☆ **Look at the pictures. Circle the correct words.**

1 It's a *board* / *(calculator)*.
2 They're *chairs* / *desks*.
3 It's a *window* / *door*.
4 They're *pens* / *pencils*.
5 It's a *pen* / *pencil*.
6 They're *rulers* / *notebooks*.

LISTENING AND GRAMMAR IN ACTION

An Introduction

1 S.01 ☆ **Listen and circle the correct answer.**

Elena's from *Spain / Brazil*.

2 S.01 ☆ **Listen again. Number the instructions in the order you hear them (1–4).**

a
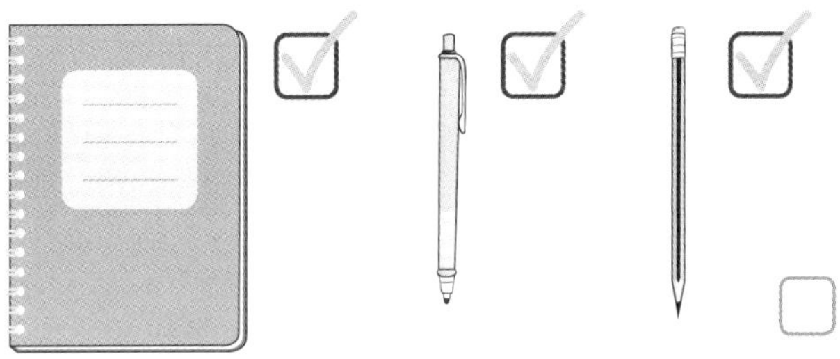

b
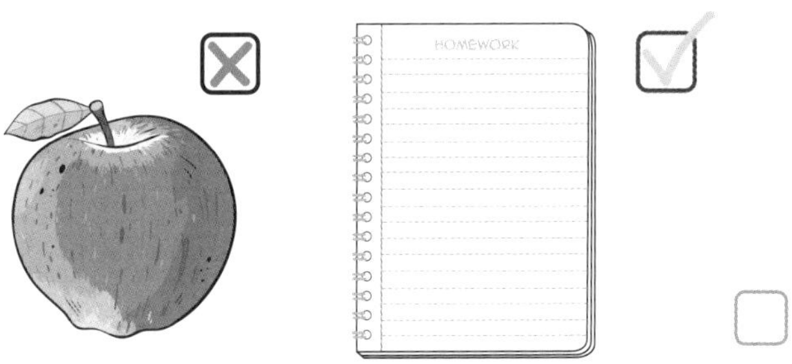

c

1

d
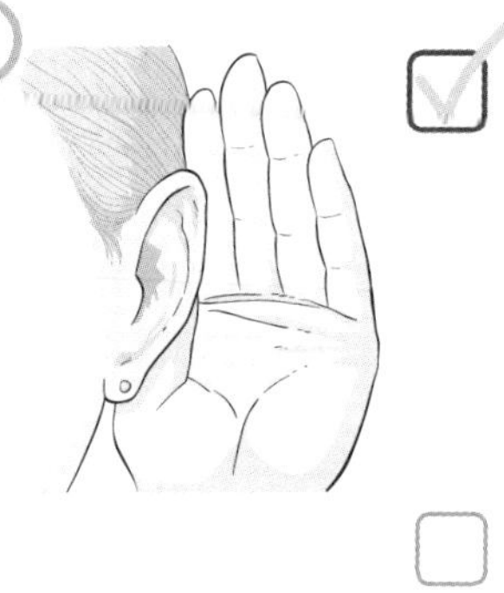

3 S.01 ☆☆ **Listen again. Are the sentences *T* (true) or *F* (false)?**

1 This is Elena's first day at school. T
2 She's from the capital of Brazil. ____
3 She's the only student from Brazil in her class. ____
4 Her notebook is on her desk. ____
5 Her pens and pencils are in her bag. ____
6 The ruler on the desk is hers. ____

Whose + Possessive Pronouns

4 ☆☆ **Complete the sentences with the correct possessive pronouns.**

1 Whose dictionaries are these?
They're their dictionaries. They're theirs.
2 Whose ruler is this?
It's my ruler. It's ____.
3 Whose books are these?
They're our books. They're ____.
4 Whose poster is that?
It's her poster. It's ____.
5 Whose chairs are those?
They're your chairs. They're ____.
6 Whose calculator is this?
It's his calculator. It's ____.

Imperatives

5 ☆☆ **Put the words in the correct order to make sentences.**

1 write / Don't / notebook / my / in
Don't write in my notebook.
2 board / the / Write / the / words / on
____
3 late / Don't / for / be / class
____
4 teacher / to / Listen / the
____
5 eat / in / class / Don't
____
6 book / your / Close
____

6 ☆☆☆ **Write two more instructions for your class.**

____

WRITING

An Informal Letter

1 ☆ **Read Jenny's letter. Who is from Australia?**

____

20 Marsh Street
Newark, NJ 07114

October 20

Dear Lucy,

1 My name is Jenny Watts, and I'm 12. I'm from Newark, New Jersey in the United States.

2 My school is great. The classroom is green, orange, and white. It's very nice, with a lot of posters on the walls. Our teacher is friendly, and I'm happy in my new class.

3 My best friend isn't in my class. She goes to a different school. She isn't American like me. She's Australian. Her name is Sarah.

4 My favorite object is my new red and blue notebook. My favorite number is five – my birthday is May 5! My dream is to be a famous singer like you!

Sincerely,

Jenny

2 ☆ **Read the letter again. Match topics a–d with paragraphs 1–4.**

a favorite object, number, birthday, and dream ☐
b name, age, and where she's from [1]
c best friend and nationality ☐
d school and class ☐

3 ☆ **Match phrases 1–3 with functions a–c.**

1 Sincerely, ☐
2 Our teacher is friendly, <u>and</u> I'm happy in my new class. ☐
3 Dear Lucy, ☐

a to start a letter
b to end a letter
c to join two ideas in one sentence

PLAN

4 ☆☆ **Write an informal letter. Decide what information to include in each paragraph. Use the information in Exercise 2 to help you.**

WRITE

5 ☆☆☆ **Write your letter. Remember to include four paragraphs, the address and date, and expressions from the *Useful Language* box (see Student's Book, p9).**

CHECK

6 **Do you …**

- introduce yourself and give your name, age, and nationality?
- use *and* to join ideas?
- say what your dream is?

1 What is your family like?

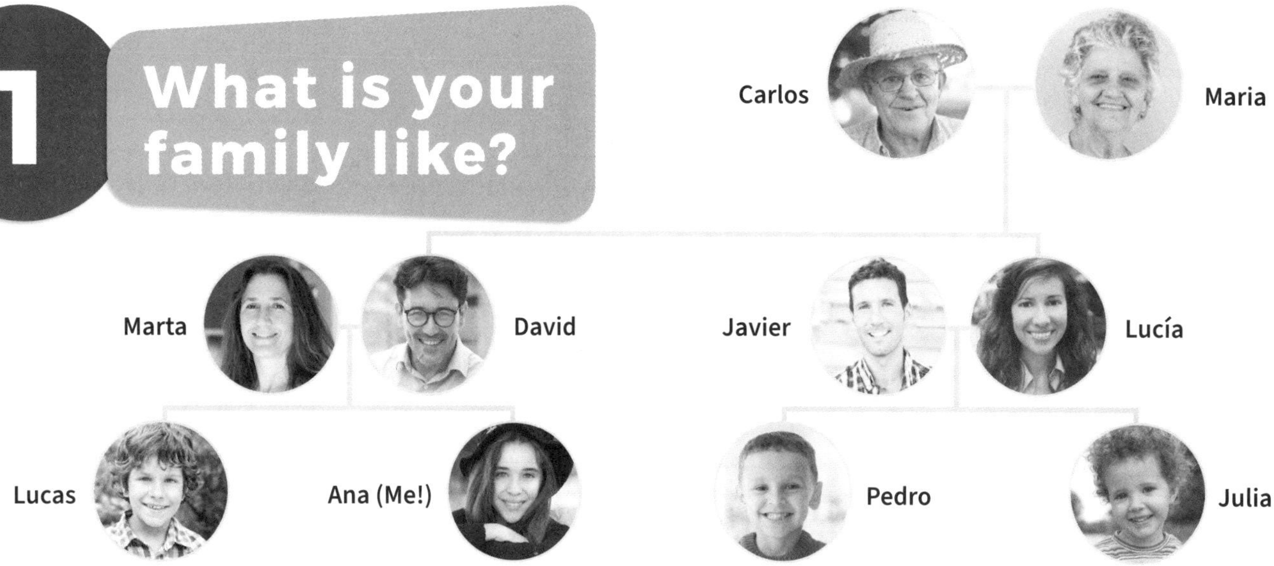

VOCABULARY

Family Members

1 ☆ **Find 14 more words for family in the word search. Look at the words in Exercise 2 to help you.**

W	G	N	E	P	H	E	W	G	S	O	N
B	R	O	T	H	E	R	D	F	T	S	E
R	A	D	G	U	J	I	N	K	M	W	K
A	N	U	T	S	S	K	J	I	E	A	Y
V	D	W	H	B	C	U	N	C	L	E	D
G	M	O	M	A	K	E	H	K	M	Y	A
D	A	T	S	N	H	D	A	D	W	D	U
G	R	A	N	D	P	A	C	Q	I	F	G
R	G	U	W	J	O	P	R	T	F	Q	H
B	D	N	I	E	C	E	I	M	E	P	T
F	G	T	K	H	O	S	N	G	X	V	E
C	O	U	S	I	N	S	I	S	T	E	R

2 ☆ **Match 1–8 with a–h to make family word pairs.**

1 brother [f]
2 nephew [ ]
3 husband [ ]
4 grandpa [ ]
5 uncle [ ]
6 dad [ ]
7 son [ ]
8 grandson [ ]

a mom
b wife
c daughter
d aunt
e grandma
f ~~sister~~
g granddaughter
h niece

3 ☆ **Which family word in Exercise 1 can be male or female?** ____________

4 ☆☆ **Look at Ana's family tree. Complete her sentences with the correct family words.**

1 Carlos is my *grandpa* and María is my ____________.
2 Marta is my ____________ and David is my ____________.
3 Javier is my ____________ and Lucía is my ____________.
4 Lucas is my ____________.
5 Pedro and Julia are my ____________.

5 ☆☆ **Circle the correct answer to complete the riddle.**

GUS Hi! I'm Gus, and my sisters are April, May, and June. This is my mom.

MOM Hi! I'm a mom with four children. My daughters are April, May, and June, and this is my son. His name is ________.

a July   b September   c Gus

Explore It!

Guess the correct answer.

____________ is the most popular boy's name in the United States in the last 100 years.

a Robert   b John   c James

Find another interesting fact about names. Write a question and send it to a classmate in an email, or ask them in the next class.

READING

A Webpage

1 Read the webpage. What is it about? Circle the correct title.

a A Big Family
b A Small Family
c A Family from Canada

2 Read the webpage again and underline the words. Then check their meaning and complete the sentences.

dentist	everyone	fun	~~neighbors~~	whole

1 Your house is next to mine. We're neighbors.
2 My aunt is a ______. Her job is to look at teeth!
3 A ______ day is 24 hours long.
4 My favorite day is Sunday with friends and family. It's ______!
5 This lesson is for all students. It's for ______.

3 Read the webpage again. Are the sentences *T* (true) or *F* (false)?

1 Tom is American. T
2 His mom is a teacher. ___
3 His family is typical because it's big. ___
4 His cousins live on a different street. ___
5 The family is together in the morning and evening. ___
6 Tom is happy at home. ___

4 Circle the options that are true for you.

1 My family is *big* / *small*.
2 My favorite time of day is the *morning* / *evening*.
3 My neighbors *are* / *aren't* at my birthday parties.

Tom is from Durham, North Carolina, in the United States. He's seven years old today! His parents' names are Helen and Richard. His mom is a dentist, and his dad is a middle school teacher.

Tom's family isn't very typical. He has two brothers and three sisters, and his grandma and grandpa live with them, too. Tom's aunt, uncle, and four cousins have a house in front of his. The whole family lives on the same street!

Tom's favorite times are the morning and the evening. That's when his family is all together for breakfast and dinner – there are ten people around the table!

Birthdays in Tom's family are fun, too. They have a birthday party every month! Today, everyone is at Tom's party: his family, his friends, and his neighbors.

Is Tom happy in his big family? Yes, he has good friends at school, and a lot of brothers, sisters, and cousins at home!

GRAMMAR IN ACTION

To Have: Affirmative and Negative

1 ☆ **Circle the correct options.**

1 Richard and Helen (have) / *has* six children.
2 My grandma *have* / *has* a red car.
3 I *don't* / *doesn't* have a big family.
4 My dad *don't* / *doesn't* have any cousins.
5 My friend's parents *have* / *has* a big house.
6 Uncle Bill *don't* / *doesn't* have any children.

2 ☆☆ **Complete the text with the correct form of *to have*.**

My name is Claudia. I'm from Mexico, but I live in Australia with my family. I [1] ___have___ a big family. I [2] ________ five brothers and two sisters. My parents [3] ________ a big house – it's perfect for a big family! My dad's name is Javier. He [4] ________ a lot of brothers and sisters, too. My mom is named Sandra. She [5] ________ a brother in Mexico – that's my Uncle Sergio. I [6] ________ any aunts or uncles in Australia. They're all in different countries. My best friend, Helen, is Australian. She [7] ________ any brothers or sisters. It's only her! She [8] ________ a small family, but they're really fun! ☺

3 ☆☆ **Write the words in the correct order to make sentences. Then match them with pictures a–e.**

1 bike / I / have / a / don't
I don't have a bike. [b]
2 My / have / grandpa / doesn't / a / cell phone
________ [ ]
3 home / We / pets / at / four / have
________ [ ]
4 best friends / at / school / two / I / have
________ [ ]
5 My / two / has / boards / classroom
________ [ ]

Possessive *'s*

4 ☆☆ **Complete the sentences with the possessive *'s* and a family word.**

1 My mom ___'s mom___ is my grandma.
2 My cousin ________ is my uncle.
3 My dad ________ is my uncle.
4 My mom ________ is my aunt.
5 My brother ________ is my mom.
6 My dad ________ is my grandpa.

5 ☆☆☆ **Find four facts about a famous family. Write four sentences about them. Use the correct form of *to have* and the possessive *'s*.**

Angelina Jolie has six children.
____
____
____
____

VOCABULARY AND LISTENING

Describing People

1 ☆ **Complete the list with the words in the box.**

blond	freckles	~~gray~~	tall	wavy

Describing People

Eyes: [1] *gray* , brown
Hairstyle: long, short, [2] ____________
Hair color: [3] ____________ , brown, gray, red
Height: [4] ____________ , short
Other features: beard, [5] ____________ , glasses, mustache

2 ☆ **Match the descriptions (1–4) with the photos (a–d).**

1 glasses and long wavy hair
2 long hair and a beard
3 long blond hair
4 short brown hair and glasses

a

b

c

d

A Conversation

1.01 **3** ☆☆ **Listen to the students talking about their families. Write *Paul's family*, *Emma's family*, *Jon's family*, or *Sue's family* under the correct pictures.**

1

____

2

____

3

____

4

____

1.01 **4** ☆☆ **Listen again. Circle the correct answers.**

1 Paul has (*four*) / *five* brothers and sisters.
2 Paul *has* / *doesn't have* blond hair.
3 Emma's sister *has* / *doesn't have* freckles.
4 Emma has a friend with *long* / *short* hair.
5 Jon has *one brother* / *two brothers*.
6 Jon's mom *is* / *isn't* short.
7 Sue has *one tall brother* / *two tall brothers*.
8 *Sue's* / *Tony's* hair is red.

5 ☆☆☆ **Describe a friend. Include information from each category in Exercise 1.**

My friend's name is Cindy. She has brown eyes and long red hair.

GRAMMAR IN ACTION

To Have: Questions

1 ☆ **Complete the chart with *have*, *has*, *do*, *does*, *don't*, or *doesn't*.**

[1] Do you _have_ any cousins?	Yes, I [2] ______.	No, I [3] ______.
[4] ______ they have red hair?	Yes, they [5] ______.	No, they [6] ______.
Does she [7] ______ green eyes?	Yes, she [8] ______.	No, she [9] ______.
How many sisters [10] ______ he have?	He [11] ______ two sisters.	

2 ☆ **Complete the questions with the correct form of *to have*. Then match them with answers a–f.**

1 _Do_ you _have_ any brothers and sisters? [b]
2 ______ your niece ______ brown hair? [ ]
3 ______ you and your family ______ a big house? [ ]
4 ______ your dad ______ a beard? [ ]
5 ______ your parents ______ a car? [ ]
6 ______ your house ______ a lot of rooms? [ ]

a No, he doesn't.
b ~~No, I don't~~.
c Yes, they do.
d Yes, she does.
e Yes, it does.
f No, we don't.

3 ☆☆ **Complete the conversation with the correct form of *to have* and the words in parentheses.**

BETH Hi, Jan. [1] _Do you have_ (you) a lot of homework?
JAN No, I [2] ______.
BETH Good. I have some questions about a school project. [3] ______ (you) any brothers and sisters?
JAN Yes, I [4] ______. I have two brothers. They're twins.
BETH [5] ______ (they) green eyes like you?
JAN Yes, they [6] ______!
BETH Cool! And [7] ______ ______ (your mom) brown hair like you?
JAN No, she [8] ______. She has blond hair.

4 ☆☆☆ **Read the answers from an interview with a famous actor. Write questions with *to have*. Use *How many* when necessary.**

1 _Do you have a big house?_
Yes, I do. My house is very big.

2 ______?
Yes, we have five children, including twins!

3 ______?
We have three boys and two girls.

4 ______?
My wife has a horse, and the children have two rabbits.

5 ______?
Yes, I do. I have two Oscars!

WRITING

An Informal Email

1 ☆ **Look at the photos and read the email. Which photo is of Kylie and Kate? Mark (✓) the correct photo.**

a

b

TO: Ed

FROM: Kate

Hi Ed,

1 How are things? I'm in a new school, and I have a new friend. This email is about her.

2 I have a lot of friends in my class, but one girl [1]'s / 've my best friend. Her name [2]'re / 's Kylie. We say we [3]'re / 've twins – we look the same! We have brown hair and green eyes, and we have the same birthday! It [4]'s / 're funny! And we both have a little brother. My brother [5]'re / 's ten and Kylie's brother [6]'s / 're nine.

3 The photo is of Kylie and me playing basketball. Kylie's a lot of fun and a great friend.

4 Do you have good friends at your new school? Do you have a best friend? Email me soon!

That's all for now,

Kate

2 ☆☆ **Circle the correct contractions in the email.**

3 ☆☆ **Read the email again. Are the sentences *T* (true) or *F* (false)?**

1 Kate and Kylie are best friends. T
2 They are in different classes. ____
3 Their birthdays are on the same day. ____
4 Kate doesn't have brown hair. ____
5 Kylie doesn't have green eyes. ____
6 They both have a little brother. ____
7 Kate's brother is ten. ____

4 ☆☆ **Match topics a–d with paragraphs 1–4 in the email.**

a extra information about a photo [3]
b description of a new friend at school [ ]
c introduction and reason for writing [ ]
d Kate's questions for Ed [ ]

PLAN

5 ☆☆ **Write an informal email to a friend about a new school friend. Make notes about these things:**

your friend's name and age

____

your friend's physical description and family

____

6 **Decide what information to include in each paragraph. Use the information in Exercise 4 to help you.**

WRITE

7 ☆☆☆ **Remember to include four paragraphs, the verbs *to be* and *to have*, and expressions from the *Useful Language* box (see Student's Book, p17).**

CHECK

8 **Do you …**

- use expressions to start and end your email?
- give information about your friend in the second paragraph?
- use information from a photo in the third paragraph?
- ask questions in the last paragraph?

1 REVIEW

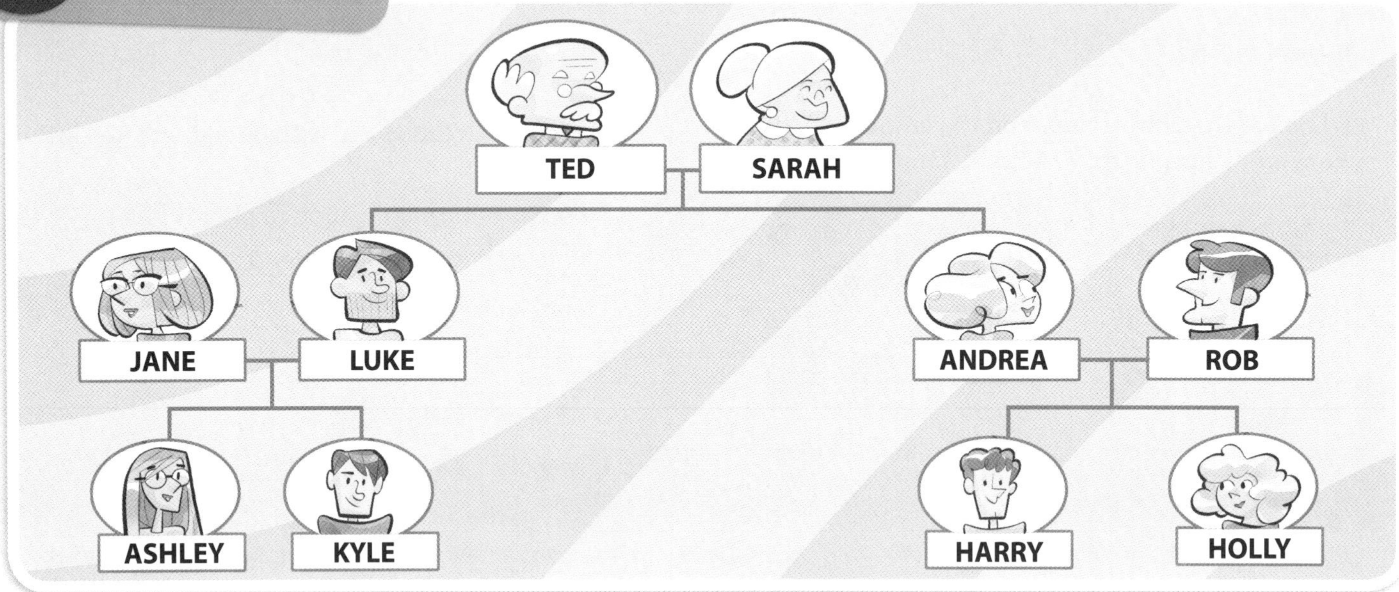

VOCABULARY

1 Look at the family tree. Are the sentences *T* (true) or *F* (false)? Correct the false sentences.

1 Ashley is Kyle's brother. ____

____

2 Jane is Luke's sister. ____

____

3 Ted is Ashley's grandpa. ____

____

4 Luke is Andrea's cousin. ____

____

5 Jane is Kyle's mom. ____

____

6 Luke is Jane's brother. ____

____

7 Kyle and Harry are Ted's grandsons. ____

____

8 Sarah is Luke's and Andrea's grandmother. ____

____

9 Rob is Ashley and Kyle's dad. ____

____

10 Holly is Jane's and Luke's niece. ____

____

2 Circle the word that doesn't fit.

1 mustache / beard / (tall)
2 wavy / glasses / short
3 blond / freckles / brown
4 blue / green / short
5 long / blond / red
6 brown / tall / wavy

GRAMMAR IN ACTION

3 Circle the correct options.

Victor and Anna [1]*has / have* a big house. It [2]*has / have* a big yard and seven rooms. They [3]*has / have* one daughter named Siena. They [4]*don't have / have* any sons. Anna and Siena [5]*has / have* blond hair. Anna [6]*has / have* blue eyes, and Siena [7]*has / have* brown eyes. Victor [8]*has / have* three sports cars. They're his favorite! Anna [9]*don't have / doesn't have* a sports car, but she [10]*has / have* a mobile home!

4 **Write questions with the correct form of *to have*. Use *How many* when necessary. Then look at Exercise 3 on page 14 and answer the questions.**

1 Victor and Anna / a big yard?

2 rooms / their house?

3 they / sons?

4 Siena / blond hair?

5 sports cars / Victor?

6 Anna / mobile home?

CUMULATIVE GRAMMAR

5 **Match questions 1–8 with answers a–h.**

1 Do your grandparents have a big yard? ☐
2 What do we have for homework? ☐
3 How many cousins do you have? ☐
4 Do you have an English dictionary? ☐
5 Does your dad have a beard? ☐
6 When do we have our exam? ☐
7 Is that Amalia's baby brother? ☐
8 Wow! How many books do your parents have? ☐

a I have four.
b Yes, they do. It's my favorite place!
c I don't know. I think they have hundreds!
d No, he doesn't! But he has a mustache.
e Yes, I do.
f We have the exercises on page 14.
g No! It's her nephew. He's her sister's baby.
h I'm not sure. I think it's in November.

2 What's your day like?

VOCABULARY
Daily Routines

1 ☆ **Complete the crossword. Use the clues.**

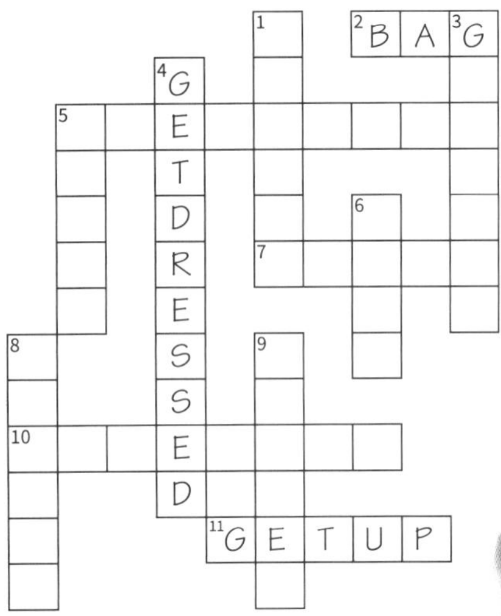

ACROSS →

2 You pack your *bag* with your books for school.

5 I have ______ with my family. We have cereal.

7 After school, you check your ______ for messages.

10 In middle school, you do your ______ every evening.

11 First you wake up. Then you *get up* .

DOWN ↓

1 I ______ at seven o'clock, but I get up at 7:15.

3 At night, you ______ and sleep.

4 In the morning, I *get dressed* . I put on my school clothes.

5 I ______ my teeth after breakfast and before I go to bed.

6 After school, I go ______ on the bus.

8 I go to ______ from Monday to Friday, but not on the weekend!

9 I take a ______ when I get up and after sports.

2 ☆ **Complete the daily routines with the verbs in the box.**

brush check do get (x2) go (x3) have pack take wake

1 *get* up		7 ______ to school	
2 ______ dressed		8 ______ my phone	
3 ______ my teeth		9 ______ to bed	
4 ______ breakfast		10 ______ up	
5 ______ home		11 ______ a shower	
6 ______ my bag		12 ______ my homework	

3 ☆☆ **Complete the text with the correct form of the phrases from Exercise 2.**

This is my ideal school day. I [1] *wake up* at nine o'clock, and I [2] ______ for messages. I [3] ______ at 9:15, I take a shower, and I [4] ______. These are my favorite clothes. Then I [5] ______ (cereal). At ten o'clock, I brush my teeth, I [6] ______ with my books, and I [7] ______ on the bus. I have three classes, and I go home to have lunch. I don't have any homework! After dinner, I check my phone again and I [8] ______.

4 ☆☆☆ **Write about your ideal school day. Use Exercise 3 to help you.**

This is my ideal school day. I ...

______

______

______

Explore It!

Guess the correct answer.

People in the United States *get dressed / take a shower* in eight minutes.

Find another interesting fact about daily routines in your country. Write a question and send it to a classmate in an email, or ask them in the next class.

READING

A Profile

1 ☆ **Read the profile. Is this sentence *T* (true) or *F* (false)?**

Dylan has 25 hours of classes a week. ______

A Day in the Life of a Child Actor

Dylan Roberts is 14, and he's a child actor. He makes movies and doesn't go to school. He always has classes with special teachers called on-set teachers. Child actors usually have 15 hours of classes a week (schools have 25), but it isn't easy! Dylan often has a lot of work to do.

Dylan talks about his typical day:

"I get up at six in the morning and get dressed. At 6:15, a car takes me to the movie set. I have breakfast at work, and then I practice the day's scenes for an hour. At 8:00, they do my hair and makeup. Filming starts at 9:00. Then, at 11:00, I have a break for half an hour. After that, I go to the teacher's room for classes. I don't have any homework. At 6:00 in the evening, I go home or to a hotel. I take a shower, have dinner, read my part of the movie for tomorrow, and go to bed. It's a busy day!"

2 ☆☆ **Read the profile again and <u>underline</u> these words. Then check their meaning in a dictionary and complete the sentences.**

break   busy   filming   ~~makeup~~   on-set teacher

1 Here's the green *makeup* for your eyes.
2 After three classes, we have a ______ to have lunch.
3 All the actors are ready for ______ today.
4 I have an ______ for extra English classes.
5 Our weekends are very ______ with a lot of things to do!

3 ☆☆ **Read the profile again. (Circle) the correct answer.**

1 Dylan is a child actor. He *goes* / *(doesn't go)* to school.
2 Dylan's special teacher is an *on-set teacher*/ *actor*.
3 A child actor *has* / *doesn't have* a lot of work to do.
4 Dylan has breakfast at *home* / *work*.
5 Dylan's first classes are *before* / *after* filming.
6 He doesn't have any *homework* / *breaks*.

4 ☆☆ **What's your opinion? Read the statements and write *Yes* or *No*.**

1 It's easy to be a child actor. ______
2 Fifteen hours of classes a week is a good idea. ______
3 Dylan's day is fun. ______
4 Not having homework is great. ______

GRAMMAR IN ACTION

Simple Present: Affirmative and Negative

1 ☆ Circle the correct options.

1 Dylan is a child actor and he *make* / *makes* movies.
2 Child actors *don't* / *doesn't* live at home when they are in a movie.
3 They *have* / *has* dinner in a hotel.
4 We *study* / *studies* English.
5 Maya *have* / *has* breakfast at school.
6 On-set teachers *teach* / *teaches* small classes.

2 ☆ Write the third person singular of the simple present.

have	watch	meet	go
1 has	2 ______	3 ______	4 ______

play	brush	do	hurry
5 ______	6 ______	7 ______	8 ______

3 ☆☆ Complete the text with the simple present form of the verbs in parentheses.

Veera is 12. She [1] goes (go) to school in Finland, and her class [2] ______ (have) 18 students. School [3] ______ (start) at 9:45 a.m., and it [4] ______ (end) at 2:45 p.m. There are three or four classes a day. In Finland, students [5] ______ (not have) homework or exams. Veera [6] ______ (have) a lot of free time. After school, she [7] ______ (meet) her friends and they [8] ______ (go) to a sports club for lunch. Veera [9] ______ (love) sports, and she [10] ______ (play) on the school soccer team. Her dream is to be a soccer player!

Adverbs of Frequency

4 ☆ Match the adverbs of frequency with the correct meanings.

1 always [c]
2 usually [ ]
3 often [ ]
4 sometimes [ ]
5 never [ ]

a ✓✓
b ✗
c ✓✓✓✓
d ✓
e ✓✓✓

5 ☆ Are these statements true for you? Write *T* (true) or *F* (false).

1 I often do my homework with my friends. ____
2 I always check my phone when I wake up. ____
3 My best friend sometimes has lunch at my house. ____
4 I never go to bed late on the weekend. ____
5 I usually have lunch with my grandparents on Sundays. ____

6 ☆☆ Write the words in the correct order to make sentences.

1 makes / dad / often / dinner / My
My dad often makes dinner.
2 I / brush / after / teeth / always / my / breakfast
______
3 go / at / They / lunchtime / usually / home
______
4 sometimes / We / class / are / for / late
______
5 I / check / in / never / my / class / phone
______
6 does / in / the / Dan / park / homework / his / usually
______

VOCABULARY AND LISTENING

Free-Time Activities

1 ☆ **Complete the free-time activity phrases.**

1 play an ins t r u m ent
2 go for a b ___ e r ___ e
3 read a book or a ma ________ e
4 chat on ____ e
5 play v ____ o g ____ s
6 make v ______ s
7 take ph ____ s
8 download s ____ s
9 listen to m ____ c
10 go sh ________ g
11 hang out with fr _____ s
12 watch __ V

2 ☆☆ **Complete the sentences with the correct form of phrases from Exercise 1.**

1 Laura often ___ *downloads songs* ___ from the Internet – she doesn't buy CDs.
2 When I ______________ with my friends, we talk for hours on our computers or phones.
3 I usually meet and ______________ in the park after school.
4 Luke's sister plays the guitar, but he doesn't ______________ .
5 I use my phone to ______________ – my friends are the actors. I sometimes put them on YouTube!
6 They never ______________ now. They always find movies and series online.

Street Interviews

3 2.01 ☆ **Listen to the interviews. Circle the correct answer.**

The interviews are about different …

a school activities.
b free-time activities.
c instruments.

4 2.01 ☆☆ **Listen again and number the activities in the photos in the order you hear them (1–3).**

a

b

c

5 2.01 ☆☆ **Listen again and write *A* (Alyssa), *C* (Caleb), or *D* (Destiny).**

1 __A__ does his/her activity every day.
2 ____ and ____ do their activities on the weekend.
3 ____ does his/her activity early in the morning.
4 ____ does his/her activity with animals.
5 ____ uses the Internet for his/her activity.
6 ____ wants to do his/her activity as a job.

6 ☆☆☆ **Write about one of your free-time activities. Use the questions below to help you.**

Where? How often? When? Who with?

GRAMMAR IN ACTION

Simple Present: Questions

1 ☆ **Complete the questions with *Do* or *Does*. Then match them with answers a–f.**

1 ___Do___ you see your friends on the weekend? [b]
2 ______ your parents like the same music? [ ]
3 ______ your sister watch TV a lot? [ ]
4 ______ your cousin hang out with you? [ ]
5 ______ all your family members play an instrument? [ ]
6 ______ this schedule have ten subjects? [ ]

a No, they don't.
b ~~Yes, I do~~.
c Yes, he does.
d Yes, we do.
e No, she doesn't.
f Yes, it does.

2 ☆☆ **Write the words in the correct order to make questions. Use the photos to help you.**

1 friends / you / online / Do / your / chat / with / ?
Do you chat online with your friends?
2 download / your / Does / best friend / songs / ?
______
3 go / for / Do / you / Sundays / a / bike / ride / on / ?
______
4 shopping / Do / you / go / a lot / ?
______
5 play / games / your / dad / video / Does / ?
______
6 your / books / Does / read / aunt / ?
______

3 ☆☆ **Answer the questions in Exercise 2 for you. Use short answers.**

1 ______ 4 ______
2 ______ 5 ______
3 ______ 6 ______

Wh- Questions

4 ☆ **(Circle) the correct question words.**

1 (*What*) / *When* do you do on the weekend?
2 *Where* / *Who* do you go after school?
3 *What* / *Who* does Eric have lunch with?
4 *Where* / *What* do you usually meet Ava?
5 *How often* / *Who* do they go shopping?
6 *Where* / *What time* do you wake up on Mondays?

5 ☆☆ **Read the interview with a tennis player. Complete the questions using the words in parentheses.**

JADE What time [1] *do you get up* (you / get up), Alina?
ALINA Very early! At six o'clock.
JADE [2] ______ (you / get up) early on weekends, too?
ALINA No, not always.
JADE And how often [3] ______ (you / hang out) with friends?
ALINA I see my friends twice a week.
JADE [4] ______ (your friends / come) to your matches?
ALINA Yes, sometimes they do.
JADE Great! And [5] ______ (your parents / watch) you, too?
ALINA Yes. My dad comes to all my matches.
JADE Nice! And [6] ______ (other people / ask) you to do interviews?
ALINA No, they don't! I'm not famous!

WRITING

An Article

1 ☆ **Read the article. (Circle) the correct title.**

a What does Zev do on the weekend?

b What is Zev's daily routine?

Zev is an American student. He's 12 years old. In his free time, he's a photographer. Zev's photos are of animals and objects. He often makes photo stories. He uses digital technology and his imagination.

1 This is a typical day in Zev's life. He always gets up at 7:00 and takes a shower. At 7:30, he has breakfast. At 7:45, he brushes his teeth and packs his bag. He then goes to school at 8:00.

2 In the afternoon, Zev goes home. At 3:00, he usually has lunch and does his homework. He goes for a walk with his sister at 5:00 and looks for ideas for his photo stories.

3 From 6:30 to 8:00 in the evening, Zev makes his photo stories and puts them on his website. He sometimes chats online with his friends, but he never stays up late. At 9:30, Zev goes to bed.

One day, I want to take photos like Zev!

2 Match topics a–c with paragraphs 1–3.

a description of Zev's evening routine ☐

b description of his morning routine ☐

c description of his afternoon routine ☐

3 ☆ **Read the article again. What time does Zev do these things?**

1 gets up *7:00*

2 has breakfast ______

3 packs his bag ______

4 goes to school ______

5 has lunch ______

6 goes for a walk ______

7 makes his photo stories ______

8 goes to bed ______

4 ☆ **Find and underline five adverbs of frequency in the article.**

5 ☆☆ **Rewrite the sentences with the correct punctuation.**

1 how does Zev make his photo stories

How does Zev make his photo stories?

2 zevs sister doesnt take photos

______

3 zevs friends look at his photo stories

______

4 wow I think the photos are great

______

PLAN

6 ☆☆ **Write an article about someone's day. Choose a person with a different daily routine than yours. It can be a friend or someone from your family. Decide what information to include in each paragraph. Use the information in Exercise 2 to help you.**

WRITE

7 ☆☆☆ **Write your article. Remember to include the information in the correct order, the simple present, adverbs of frequency, and correct punctuation from the *Useful Language* box (see Student's Book, p29).**

CHECK

8 Do you …

- include an interesting title with a question?
- introduce the person, their nationality, and what they do?
- describe the person's morning, afternoon, and evening routines?
- end the article with a sentence about you and your ambition?

2 REVIEW

VOCABULARY

1 Complete the text with the words in the box.

brush do dressed get go (x2) have pack shower up

I wake [1] __________ at 6:30, and I [2] __________ up at 7:00. Then I take a [3] __________ and [4] __________ my teeth. I get [5] __________ and [6] __________ my bag for school. At 7:30, I [7] __________ breakfast with my mom and dad. I [8] __________ to school at 8:30 and finish at 3:30. In the afternoon, I [9] __________ my homework, and then I have some free time. In the evening, I have dinner with my parents, and then I [10] __________ to bed at about 10:00.

2 Match the verbs with the activities.

1 chat	☐	a songs
2 download	☐	b a bike ride
3 go for	☐	c online
4 listen to	☐	d a book or a magazine
5 hang out with	☐	e music
6 read	☐	f friends
7 go	☐	g TV
8 watch	☐	h shopping

GRAMMAR IN ACTION

3 Complete the sentences with the simple present form of the verbs in parentheses.

1 I __________ (not wake up) early on the weekend.
2 Martin __________ (go) to school at 9:00 every day.
3 We __________ (not do) our homework at school.
4 Tom's dad __________ (make) videos of his birthday every year.
5 Isabela __________ (not have) a big breakfast, only fruit.
6 Theo __________ (not play) the guitar very often.

4 Complete the sentences with the missing words. Circle the correct options.

1 Daniel __________ shopping with his mom.
a sometimes goes b goes sometimes
2 I __________ video games with my brother.
a play often b often play
3 My dad __________ to rock music!
a listens never b never listens
4 We __________ with friends on the weekend.
a always hang out b hang out always
5 They finish their homework, and they __________ TV.
a watch often b often watch

5 Complete the questions and answers with the simple present form of the verbs in parentheses. Add *Wh-* question words where necessary.

1 **A:** _____ you _____ (brush) your teeth every day? **B:** Yes, I _____.
2 **A:** _____ your mom _____ (pack) your bag for you? **B:** No, she _____.
3 **A:** _____ your cousins _____ (play) an instrument? **B:** No, they _____.
4 **A:** _____ time _____ Chris _____ (go) home? **B:** At 7:00.
5 **A:** _____ often _____ you _____ (read) a book? **B:** Every month.
6 **A:** _____ _____ you _____ (go) on Sundays? **B:** I often go to the park with my family.

CUMULATIVE GRAMMAR

6 Complete the conversation with the missing words. Circle the correct options.

ROSA [1] _____ do you do in your free time?
MIRA I [2] _____ my best friend or go with my brother for a bike ride.
ROSA [3] _____ you see your best friend every day?
MIRA Yes, most days. [4] _____'s your best friend?
ROSA That's Susan, but I [5] _____ her all the time.
MIRA [6] _____ often do you see her?
ROSA It depends, but usually every weekend. We sometimes [7] _____ basketball on Saturdays.
MIRA Hey! I play, too. What [8] _____ do you meet on Saturdays?
ROSA Usually in the afternoon.
MIRA [9] _____ to hang out one Saturday?
ROSA Sure! [10] _____ your phone? Here's my number.
MIRA Yes, I [11] _____. OK, great!

1 a What b Where
2 a meet usually b usually meet
3 a Does b Do
4 a Who b When
5 a don't see b doesn't see
6 a When b How
7 a play b plays
8 a often b time
9 a You want b Do you want
10 a Have do you b Do you have
11 a do b do have

3 How do we learn?

VOCABULARY

School Subjects

1 ☆ **Complete the subjects with the correct letters.**

1 Eng l ish
2 Spani _ h
3 vocatio _ al educati _ n
4 m _ th
5 musi _
6 ar _
7 d _ ama
8 geo _ raphy
9 histor _
10 nut _ ition
11 P _
12 sci _ nce
13 I _

2 ☆ **Write the correct school subjects from Exercise 1.**

1 music

2 ______

3 ______

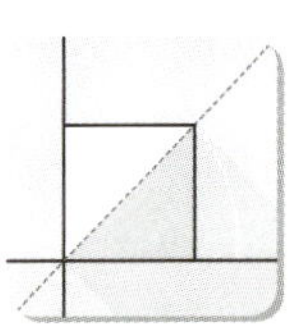

4 ______

5 ______

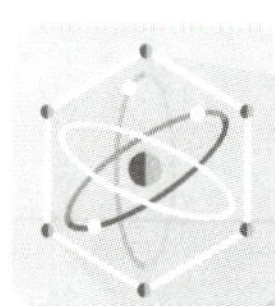

6 ______

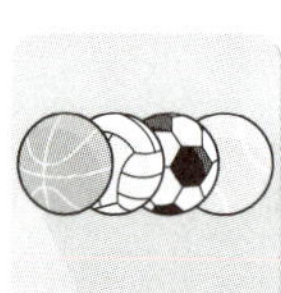

7 ______

8 ______

3 ☆☆ **Write the subjects for the definitions.**

1 You learn to play an instrument. music
2 You learn a language that people speak in a lot of countries in South America. ______
3 You learn about people, countries, and places. ______
4 You learn about things in the past. ______
5 You learn about numbers, shapes, and space. ______
6 You learn a language that people speak in the UK and the United States. ______
7 You learn about food and what is good or bad to eat. ______
8 You do experiments. ______

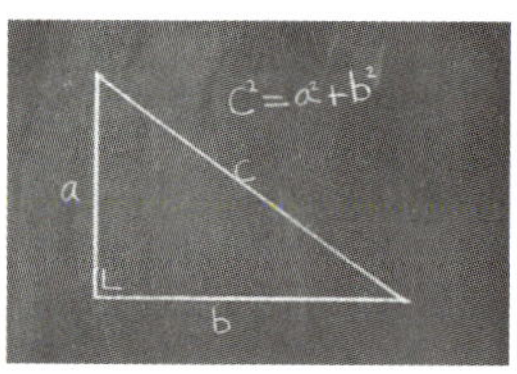

4 ☆☆ **Write the names of these subjects in your language. Write *S* if they are similar to the words in English, or *D* if they are different.**

1 science ______ ___
2 geography ______ ___
3 drama ______ ___
4 art ______ ___

Explore It!

Guess the correct answer.

One school in Lucknow, India, has a lot of students. How many students does it have?

a about 15,000 b about 27,000 c about 52,000

Find another interesting fact about school subjects in another country. Write a question and send it to a classmate in an email, or ask them in the next class.

READING

A Webpage

1 ☆ **Read the webpage about schools in Singapore. Why don't teachers like posters in math classrooms?**

____

HOME | STORIES | PHOTOS

SCHOOLS IN SINGAPORE

STUDENTS FROM SINGAPORE OFTEN GET VERY GOOD SCORES IN MATH AND SCIENCE ON INTERNATIONAL TESTS.

In math classes, students can use technology to answer the different math problems. Their answers go on the whiteboard at the front of the class. All students can see and talk about their classmates' answers.

A lot of math classrooms don't have posters on the walls. Teachers don't think posters help students learn.

Students can't talk to each other a lot. They work alone, but they can ask the teacher questions when they don't understand something.

In science classes, students can work on their projects once a week. In one class, they can build a robotic arm, and in another class, students can make a small radio.

In many high schools in Singapore, students don't do a lot of drama, language, music, or art. Some teachers say, "Art subjects aren't very important. Students need to be good at science and math. They need these subjects for their adult life."

Is this a good or a bad idea? What do you think?

2 ☆☆ **Read the webpage again and underline these words. Then check their meaning in a dictionary and complete the sentences.**

~~adult~~ alone build scores whiteboard

1 In many countries, you're an adult when you're 18.

2 My teacher always writes the answers on the ______.

3 I never get good ______ on geography tests. Maps are difficult!

4 We want to ______ a robot for our project.

5 **A:** Do you need help?

B: No, thanks. I always do my homework ______.

3 ☆☆ **Answer the questions.**

1 What subjects are students from Singapore often good at?
math and science

2 What do teachers show on the whiteboard?
______

3 How do students work in math classes?
______

4 How often do students work on science projects?
______

5 Which subjects are not very important in many schools?
______

4 ☆☆☆ **Answer the questions with your own ideas.**

1 "Art subjects aren't very important." What do you think?
______

2 Which subjects do you think are important? Why?
______

GRAMMAR IN ACTION

Can for Ability and Permission

1 ☆ **Circle the options that are true for you.**

1 In our classes, we *can* / *can't* put posters on the walls.

2 At break time, we *can* / *can't* play and talk to friends.

3 We *can* / *can't* talk in science classes.

4 We *can* / *can't* build interesting things for our projects.

5 Sometimes we *can* / *can't* work in groups in our English classes.

2 ☆☆ **Complete the sentences. Use *can/can't* and the verbs in parentheses.**

1 My dad _can't sing_ because he doesn't have a good voice, but he __________ amazing pictures. (sing / draw)

2 My cousin __________ good photos, but she __________ videos. She's really bad at it! (take / make)

3 My mom __________ salsa very well, and she __________ the guitar, too. She's really good at it! (dance / play)

4 My little brother's four. He __________ English very well, but he __________ it. (speak / read)

3 ☆☆ **Complete the texts with *can/can't* and the verbs in parentheses.**

My favorite subject is history. I like it because we 1 _can work_ (work) in groups – it's great when we 2 __________ (do) projects together. But we work alone when we have an exam – we 3 __________ (talk). After the exam, we usually take a break, and we 4 __________ (hang out) with friends.

RAJ

My favorite teacher is Mr. Bell, our geography teacher. I like his classes because we 5 __________ (ask) questions when we need to. We have options, too: sometimes we 6 __________ (choose) our homework, and we 7 __________ (bring) interesting things to class. But we 8 __________ (be) late – Mr. Bell doesn't like that!

PAULA

4 ☆☆ **Write questions and short answers with *can*.**

1 students / check their phone / in class? (✗)
Can students check their phone in class?
No, they can't.

2 students / ask questions / in class? (✓)

3 Kate / play the piano? (✓)

4 María / speak two languages? (✗)

5 students / work in groups / in math classes? (✓)

6 he / do ballet? (✗)

5 ☆☆ **Are these statements true for you? Write *T* (true) or *F* (false).**

1 I can speak two languages. ____

2 I can dance salsa. ____

3 I can ride a bike. ____

4 I can play the guitar. ____

5 I can sing. ____

VOCABULARY AND LISTENING

Places in a School

1 ☆ **Read the definitions. Then circle the correct places in the spidergram.**

1 You can do outdoor sports here.
2 You can buy and eat food here.
3 You can do PE here.
4 Teachers can plan their lessons here.
5 You can leave your bag here.
6 You can read books and study here.
7 You can wash your hands here.

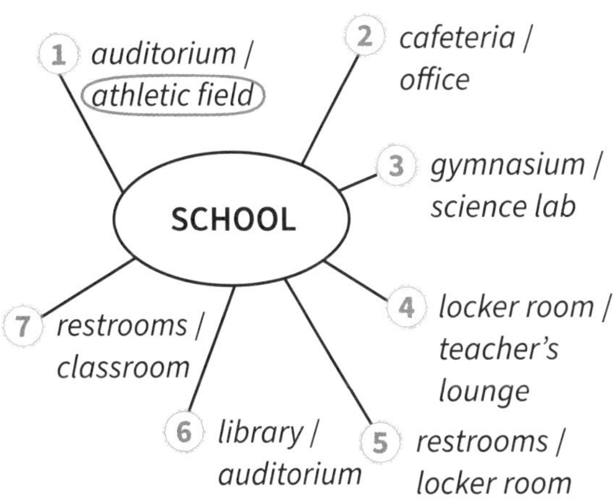

2 ☆☆ **Complete the text with places from Exercise 1.**

Mondays!

I don't like my schedule on Mondays! At 8:45, I go to the [1] *office* and say hello to my aunt – she works at the school. Then I go to the [2] ______________ and put my sports shoes in my locker. After that, my class goes to the [3] ______________ and we do experiments. I don't like science! At break time, I usually go to the [4] ______________ for some food. Then we have PE in the [5] ______________ and then lunch. In the afternoon, it's music and drama. At 4:15, we go to the [6] ______________ and get a book to read – that's OK because I like books, but I'm always happy on Mondays at 4:30 because I can go home!

A Radio Program

3 3.01 ☆☆ **Listen and number the places in the order you hear them (1–6).**

a 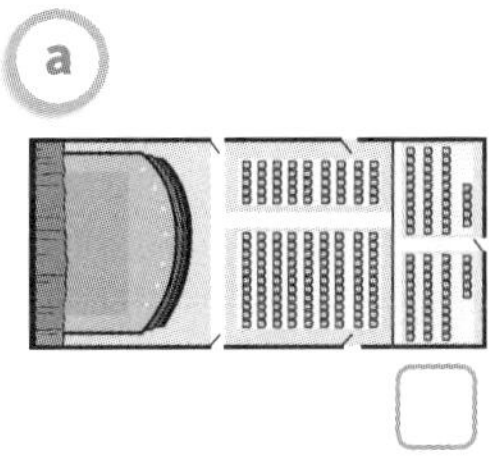
auditorium

b 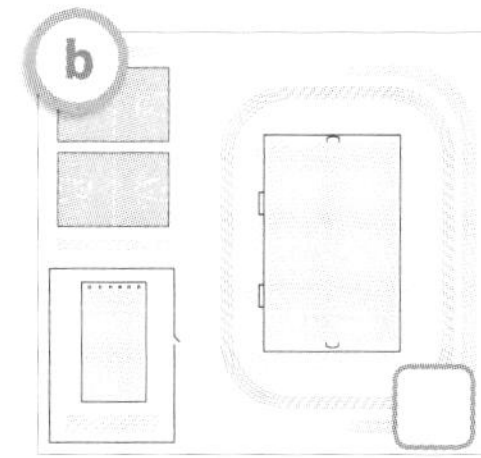
athletic field

c 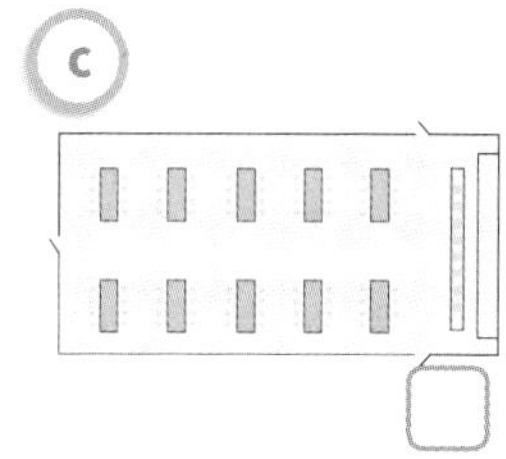
cafeteria

d 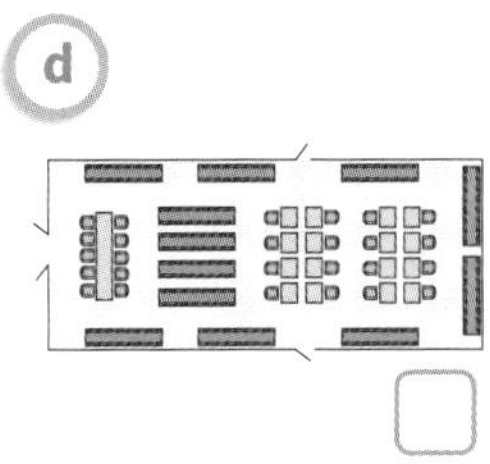
library

e 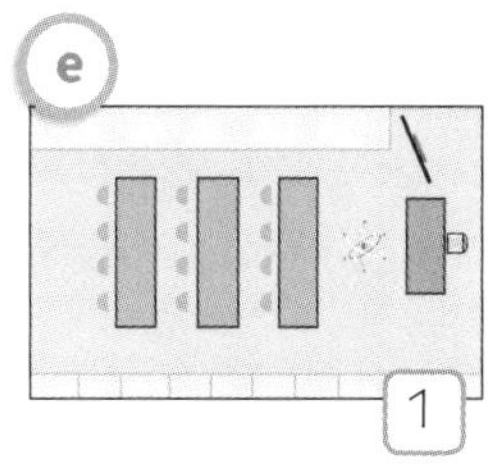

science lab

f 
music classroom

4 3.01 ☆☆ **Listen again. Are the sentences *T* (true) or *F* (false)?**

1 Alex likes the science lab. T
2 He likes the magazines from the library. ____
3 Alex's favorite subject is PE. ____
4 The music classroom is Alex's favorite place. ____
5 Marina has lunch in the cafeteria. ____
6 She likes all the places in the school. ____

GRAMMAR IN ACTION

Verb Forms: *(Don't) Like, Don't Mind, Love, Hate + -ing*

1 ☆ **Match the verbs with the emojis.**

1 love [b] 2 like [ ] 3 don't mind [ ]
4 don't like [ ] 5 hate [ ]

a b c d e

2 ☆☆ **Write sentences with the correct form of the verbs.**

1 I / like / go / to the music club
I like going to the music club.
2 We / hate / have / a lot of homework
____
3 Tariq / not mind / play / sports in the gymnasium
____
4 Gina / love / play / soccer / on the athletic field
____
5 They / not like / learn / history
____

3 ☆☆ **Complete the text with the correct form of the verbs in parentheses.**

I have a twin brother, but we're very different! He [1] *hates getting up* (hate / get up) early, but I [2] _______ (not mind / do) it for school. He [3] _______ (love / play) sports, and I [4] _______ (like / play) video games. I [5] _______ (not like / go) to parties. I [6] _______ (like / stay) at home. My brother [7] _______ (love / hang out) with his friends and [8] _______ (have) a good time. He [9] _______ (not mind / study) sometimes, but he doesn't love it. I [10] _______ (love / learn) new things, especially about science.

Object Pronouns

4 ☆ **Complete the chart with the object pronouns.**

Subject	I	you	he	she	it	we	they
Object	1 *me*	2 ___	3 ___	4 ___	5 ___	6 ___	7 ___

5 ☆ **Circle the correct option.**

1 **A:** Do you like drama? **B:** Yes, I like (*it*) / *them*.
2 Mr. Patel isn't in the office. Can you call *her* / *him*?
3 I have a problem. Can you help *me* / *it*, please?
4 Is Amaya here? I can't see *you* / *her*.
5 **A:** Do you like video games? **B:** I hate *it* / *them*.
6 What classes do we have today? Can you give *us* / *you* the schedule, please?

6 ☆☆ **Look at the pictures and then complete the text with the correct subject or object pronouns.**

Me (Josh) **Lucas**

¡HOLA!

Lucas' mom **Spanish**

I'm Josh, and Lucas is my best friend. [1] *We* (Josh + Lucas) 're in the same class and [2] _______ (Lucas) lives near [3] _______ (Josh). Lucas' mom is Spanish. [4] _______ (Lucas' mom) speaks Spanish with [5] _______ (Lucas) at home, but [6] _______ (Josh) speak English with [7] _______ (Lucas + Lucas' mom). We learn Spanish at school, and Lucas helps [8] _______ (Josh) with my homework. Spanish is difficult, but I like [9] _______ (¡HOLA!).

WRITING

A Description

1 Read Sanjiv's description. Does he like his school?

My School

1 *Tracks and Subjects*

I study at a very big school. Students can take different tracks, <u>such as</u> science or arts. I'm on the science track. I study English, math, and science, and technology subjects, <u>like</u> computer science. That's my favorite subject.

2

I really like the teachers. They teach regular classes, but they also teach some after-school clubs, <u>like</u> astronomy and dance. I like being with my teachers after class.

3

We have six classes a day and homework. I don't mind doing some homework, but I don't like a lot of it! I really like working with my classmates on group projects. I don't like working alone!

4

Our school has great places for classes and activities. <u>For example</u>, we have a big gymnasium, a cafeteria, a computer lab, and three science labs. I love studying here.

2 **Write the correct heading for each paragraph in the description.**

Great Teachers ~~Tracks and Subjects~~
School Places School Routine

3 **Read the description again. Then complete the text below with the phrases in the box.**

computer science doing a lot of homework
~~the teachers at his school~~ working alone

Sanjiv likes 1 *the teachers at his school* and
2 ______ . He doesn't like
3 ______ or
4 ______ .

4 **Look at the <u>underlined</u> words and phrases in Sanjiv's description. What does he use them for? Circle the correct answer.**

a to join ideas
b to show different times
c to give examples

PLAN

5 **Write a description of your school. Make a spidergram of your school in your notebook and use the plan below.**

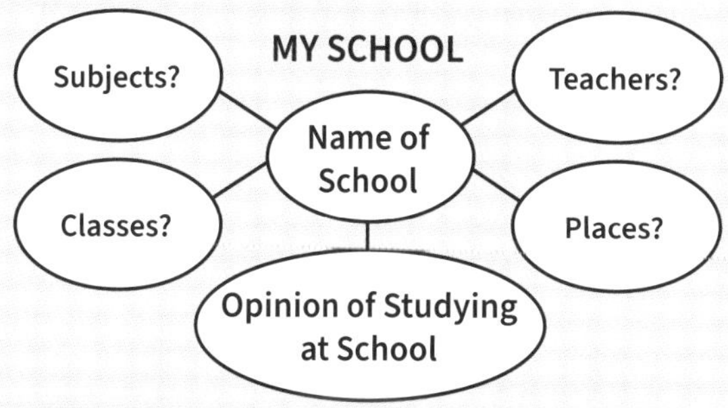

6 **Decide what information to include in each paragraph. Use your spidergram and the information in Exercise 2 to help you.**

WRITE

7 **Write your description. Remember to include four paragraphs, *can/can't*, and expressions from the *Useful Language* box (see Student's Book, p41).**

CHECK

8 **Do you ...**

- give the name of the school in the opening sentence?
- include all of the information from your spidergram?
- give your opinion about studying at the school in your closing sentence?

3 REVIEW

VOCABULARY

1 Complete the school subjects.

1 Languages: E________, S______
2 Numbers: m___
3 The past: h_______
4 Countries: g_________
5 In a lab: s_______
6 Art subjects: d_____, m_____, a__
7 Sports: p________ e__________
8 IT: i____________ t___________
9 Food: n________

2 Find 12 places in a school in the word search.

O	L	H	W	L	I	B	R	A	R	Y	P	S	O
T	E	A	C	H	E	R	S	L	O	U	N	G	E
C	Y	C	A	F	E	T	E	R	I	A	I	U	T
L	O	C	K	E	R	R	O	O	M	E	G	M	W
A	Z	G	Y	M	N	A	S	I	U	M	F	R	P
S	A	T	H	L	E	T	I	C	F	I	E	L	D
S	P	A	U	D	I	T	O	R	I	U	M	T	W
R	S	C	I	E	N	C	E	L	A	B	A	B	T
O	O	H	O	P	R	E	S	T	R	O	O	M	S
O	C	T	B	G	N	G	T	O	F	F	I	C	E
M	W	B	U	F	T	A	P	F	Y	E	I	D	B
C	O	M	P	U	T	E	R	L	A	B	N	F	T

GRAMMAR IN ACTION

3 Look at the chart. Complete the sentences with *can*/*can't* and the correct verbs.

			¡HOLA!
 **Jon**	✓	✗	✓
 **Lisa**	✗	✓	✓

1 Jon ______________ the guitar.
2 Lisa ______________ the guitar.
3 ______________ Jon ______________ songs in English? ______________, he ______________.
4 ______________ Lisa ______________ songs in English? ______________, she ______________.
5 Jon and Lisa ______________ Spanish.

4 Look at the symbols. Write sentences using (*don't*) *like*, *don't mind*, *love*, *hate* + *-ing*.

1 We /  / talk to / our teachers ______________________________
2 I /  / do / homework ______________________________
3 She /  / listen / to music ______________________________
4 They /  / have / lunch at school ______________________________
5 He /  / be / late for class ______________________________

5 Match questions 1–6 with answers a–f.

1 Does Tom like soccer? ☐
2 Does Beth play video games? ☐
3 Can you help Suzi? ☐
4 Is Harry in your class? ☐
5 Is this party for you and your friends? ☐
6 Do you like reading? ☐

a No, it isn't for us!
b No, he hates it!
c I don't mind it.
d Yes, she loves them.
e Yes, I can help her.
f Yes, he is.

CUMULATIVE GRAMMAR

6 Complete the conversation with the missing words. Circle the correct options.

DENIZ Hi, Kate! [1] ________ soccer today?
KATE No, I [2] ________ . It's Wednesday today.
DENIZ When [3] ________ practice?
KATE On Tuesdays and Thursdays, and on the weekend [4] ________ have games.
DENIZ Oh! And [5] ________ your parents watch your games?
KATE It depends. [6] ________ come and see me.
DENIZ Hey, [7] ________ do we finish school today?
KATE At three o'clock! It's Wednesday, remember?
DENIZ Oh, great! Harry and I [8] ________ for a bike ride after school on Wednesdays.
KATE [9] ________ Harry now?
DENIZ He's in the library. He [10] ________ a math project to finish.
KATE Well, I love [11] ________ my bike. [12] ________ I go with you?
DENIZ Sure!

	a	b	c
1	Do you have	Have you	You have
2	doesn't	don't have	don't
3	do you have	have you	you have
4	always we	we always	it always
5	does	do	are
6	They sometimes	Them sometimes	Sometimes them
7	when	who	what
8	go usually	usually goes	usually go
9	What's	Where's	Who's
10	has	have	don't have
11	riding	ride	rides
12	Do	Can	Have

4 What do you like to eat?

VOCABULARY

Food and Drink

1 ☆ Complete the chart with the words in the box.

~~apples~~	bananas	cheese	chicken
eggs	fish	juice	rice
soda			

Food from Plants	Food from Animals	Drinks
apples	______	______
______	______	______
______	______	______
	______	

2 ☆☆ Circle the correct answers in the quiz.

ALL ABOUT FOOD AND DRINK

1 Which food is NOT usually a cake?
  a chicken **b** chocolate
2 Which of these is NOT protein?
  a meat **b** carrots
3 Which of these is NOT from fruit?
  a juice **b** chocolate
4 Which of these is NOT from a plant?
  a meat **b** rice

3 ☆☆ Complete the food words in the text.

I'm Zara from Malaysia. I usually have kaya toast with [1]e *g g s* for breakfast. I have lunch at school. Lunch is usually rice and [2]me____ or [3]ch________ curry with vegetables. I drink [4]ju______ made from oranges and purple [5]ca________ and red [6]ap________. It's yummy! My mom cooks dinner. I love her [7]fi____ curry with [8]be______. We always drink [9]w________.

4 ☆☆☆ What is your favorite food for breakfast, lunch, and dinner? Write about what you eat. Use Exercise 3 to help you.

I usually have . . . ____________________

____

____

____

Explore It!

Guess the correct answer.

Which country grows millions of bananas?

a the United States
b Ecuador
c China

Find another interesting fact about food in your country. Write a question and send it to a classmate in an email, or ask them in the next class.

READING
An Article

1 ☆ **Read the article and match the foods in the box with the photos (1–3).**

blinis	herring with potatoes	mooncakes

Welcome to My Festival!

1 ____________

2 ____________

3 ____________

Hugo:
Midsummer Eve, Sweden

I love this festival in June. It's at the beginning of summer vacation. We go to the country, and in the morning, we get some flowers for our hair. Then we dance to traditional music. Lunch is outside, and it's big! We always eat herring (a type of fish) with potatoes. Later, people play instruments and dance all night!

Mei Lin:
Moon Festival, China

My favorite festival is in September, when we can see the first full moon of the month. We make paper lights and go to the park. And of course, we eat a mooncake or two! These are small round cakes (like the moon!) that have different fillings. I like the chocolate one. We give them to our friends and eat them together.

Daria:
Maslenitsa Pancake Festival, Russia

This great festival is in February. We have fun activities for seven days! We do some sports, play music, dance, and eat a lot of food. I love having blinis. They are Russian pancakes made with butter, eggs, and milk. We eat them with different toppings. My favorite topping is salmon and cream cheese. Yummy!

2 ☆☆ **Read the article again and <u>underline</u> these words. Then check their meaning in a dictionary and complete the sentences.**

country	fillings	full moon	pancakes	~~toppings~~

1 What are your favorite *toppings* on a pizza? I love extra cheese!
2 Every four weeks, we can see the ____________ in the sky. It's completely round.
3 *Empanadas* are popular in South America. They have different ____________ inside, such as meat or vegetables.
4 I love going to the ____________ and looking at the trees and flowers.
5 We need milk and butter to make ____________.

3 ☆☆ **Read the article again and complete the chart.**

Festival	Country	Month	Special Food
Midsummer Eve	Sweden	1 *June*	2 ________
Moon Festival	3 ________	4 ________	mooncakes
Maslenitsa	5 ________	February	6 ________

4 ☆☆☆ **Answer the questions with your own ideas.**

1 Which of the festivals is your favorite? Why?
____
2 Think of a festival in your country. When is it? What food do you have?
____

GRAMMAR IN ACTION

Countable and Uncountable Nouns

1 ☆ **Write the correct headings in the chart: *Countable* or *Uncountable*.**

1 ______	2 ______
cheese water bread rice ______ ______	apple egg tomato ______ ______ ______

2 ☆ **Complete the chart in Exercise 1 with the words in the box.**

bean carrot chocolate fish ~~rice~~ taco

A/An, Some/Any

3 ☆ **Circle the correct options.**

1 We use *a* or *an* with *countable* / *uncountable* nouns.
2 We use *some* and *any* with *singular* / *plural* countable nouns and uncountable nouns.
3 We use *some* in *affirmative* / *negative* sentences.
4 We use *any* in *affirmative* / *negative* sentences and questions.

4 ☆☆ **Complete the sentences with the words in the box.**

~~apple~~ chocolate eggs juice sandwich

1 Do you have ___apple___ for your snack?
2 We don't have any ______ for an omelet.
3 I'm hungry. Do you have a ______ for me?
4 Drink some ______ with your breakfast.
5 Can we have some ______ after dinner?

5 ☆☆ **Complete the conversation with *a*, *an*, *some*, or *any*.**

KIM What can we have for dinner? Do we have [1] ___any___ rice?
DAN No, we don't have [2] ______ rice, but we have [3] ______ pasta.
KIM Pasta with cheese! Do we have [4] ______ cheese?
DAN No. I can see [5] ______ tomato and [6] ______ egg, but that's all! Let's go to the store.
KIM OK. Can you write a list? We need [7] ______ cheese, [8] ______ milk, and [9] ______ tomatoes. Is that all?
DAN No. We don't have [10] ______ drinks. We need [11] ______ juice.
KIM Right! And [12] ______ chocolate!

6 ☆☆☆ **What is your favorite dinner? What do you have at home to make it and what do you need? Write sentences with *a*, *an*, *some*, and *any*.**

I want ______ for dinner.
I have ______
I don't have ______
I need ______

VOCABULARY AND LISTENING

Adjectives

1 ☆ **Complete the adjectives with the missing vowels. Then match adjectives 1, 5, 7, and 10 with the photos (a–d).**

1 hot [d]
2 d_l_c___s
3 _nh___lthy
4 d_sg_st_ng
5 sw___t [ ]
6 sp_cy
7 c_ld [ ]
8 h___lthy
9 fr_sh
10 s_lty [ ]

a

b

c

d

2 ☆☆ **Circle the correct options.**

1 Careful! The milk is *cold* / *hot*!
2 I don't like beans. They're *delicious* / *disgusting*!
3 Ice cream is perfect for a hot day. It's *hot* / *cold* and *sweet* / *spicy*.
4 Water is a *healthy* / *unhealthy* drink, but soda is *healthy* / *unhealthy*.
5 I like having *disgusting* / *fresh* fruit for breakfast.

A Quiz

4.01 **3** ☆ **Listen to the family. Do they answer all the questions in the quiz?**

____

4.01 **4** ☆ **Listen again. Match the foods (1–3) with the restaurants (a–c).**

1

kebab

2
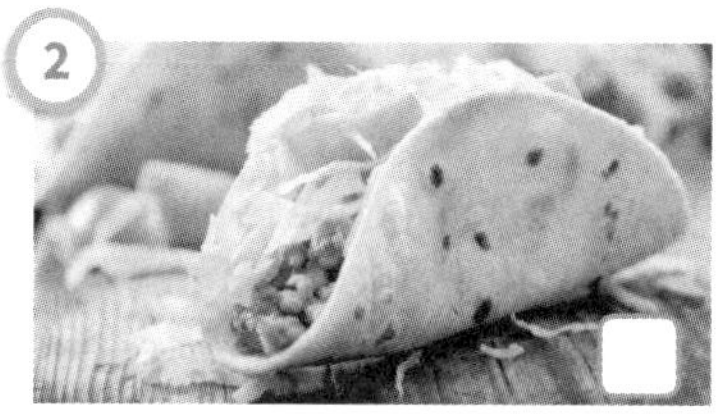

taco

3

curry

a La Cantina b Kumkapi c Bangkok Garden

4.01 **5** ☆☆ **Listen again. Are the sentences *T* (true) or *F* (false)?**

1 The restaurants in the quiz are new. T
2 The names of the restaurants are in the first question. ___
3 The girl thinks Turkish food is sweet. ___
4 "Fresh" and "healthy" describe two of the three types of food. ___
5 The boy thinks kebabs are delicious. ___
6 The children both want to go to the Mexican restaurant. ___

6 ☆☆☆ **Do you prefer Mexican, Turkish, or Thai food? Look on the Internet for more information about these types of food. Write your ideas.**

I prefer ________ food because it's ________

____

____

____

GRAMMAR IN ACTION

There Is/Isn't, There Are/Aren't

1 ☆ Look at the picture of the restaurant. Circle the correct options.

1 There is / *isn't* a picture on the wall.
2 There *is some* / *isn't any* water in the glasses.
3 There *is some* / *isn't any* food on the tables.
4 There *are some* / *aren't any* children.
5 There *are* / *aren't* eight people.
6 There *is* / *isn't* a window in the picture.

2 ☆☆ Look at the picture and complete the questions and answers with the correct form of *there is/there are*.

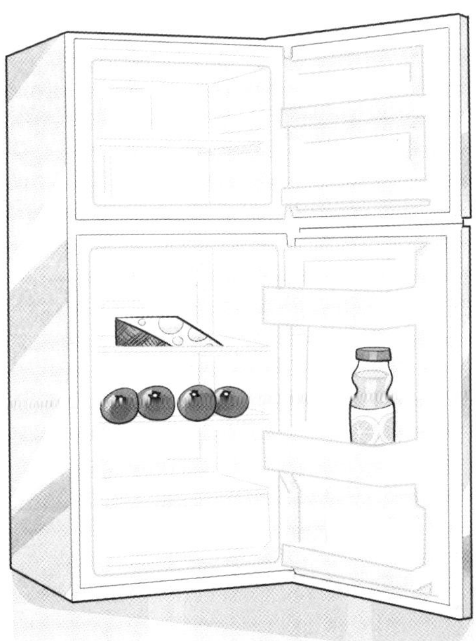

1 Is there ________ any juice?
Yes ________, there is ________.
2 ________ any bananas?
________, there ________.
3 ________ any tomatoes?
________, there ________.
4 ________ any cheese?
________, there ________.
5 ________ any milk?
________, there ________.

Much/Many, A Lot Of

3 ☆☆ Circle the correct options.

My sister loves cooking, and she has [1]*a lot of* / *much* ideas for delicious meals. I like cooking, too, but I don't have [2]*many* / *much* time to help her. She often uses [3]*a lot of* / *much* fruit and vegetables. She loves healthy food. Tonight, she wants to make pasta for dinner, but there isn't [4]*many* / *much* pasta, and there aren't [5]*many* / *much* tomatoes in the fridge. The good thing is that there are [6]*a lot of* / *much* restaurants near home!

4 ☆☆ Complete the questions in the quiz with *much* or *many*. Then circle the correct answers.

HOW MUCH DO YOU KNOW?

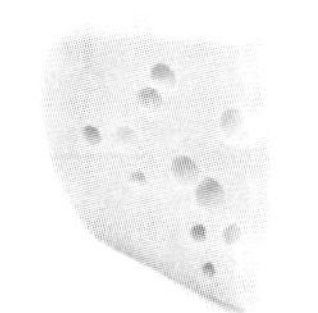

1 How ________ milk is there in 1kg of cheese?
a two liters b five liters

2 How ________ water is there in a banana?
a 74% b 90%

3 How ________ sugar is there in an average glass of orange juice?
a about 21 g b about 50 g

4 How ________ coffee beans are there in a 1-kg bag of coffee?
a about 1,500 b about 8,800

5 ☆☆☆ Look in your fridge and answer the questions.

1 How much fruit is there?
____
2 How many vegetables are there?
____

WRITING

A Description

1 ☆ **Look at the menus and read the description. Which menu is from Eva's favorite place, a or b?**

a

b
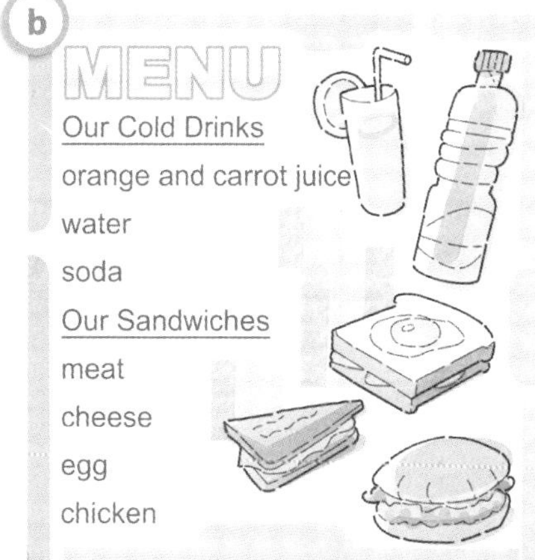

My Favorite Place to Eat

by Eva García

1 My name's Eva [1]*and* / *but* I'm from Chile. My favorite place to eat is a small café called Buenas Migas. I go there every Friday with my best friend and our parents.

2 Buenas Migas is near my house. There isn't a lot of space inside the café [2]*and* / *or* it doesn't have many tables, [3]*or* / *but* there are some more tables outside. We sit outside when the weather's nice.

3 You can eat different sandwiches, and they're all delicious! They have egg, cheese, chicken, [4]*but* / *or* meat sandwiches and they're all healthy. My favorite is the egg sandwich.

4 To drink, you can have water, soda, [5]*but* / *or* juice. Their orange and carrot juice is always fresh. It's definitely my favorite drink!

2 ☆☆ **Circle the correct options in the description.**

3 ☆☆ **Circle the correct options.**

We use [1]*but* / *or* when there is a choice (usually between two things).

We use [2]*but* / *and* to contrast different information.

We use [3]*or* / *and* to add similar information.

4 ☆☆ **Read the description again. Match topics a–d with paragraphs 1–4.**

a food (including your favorite) 3

b introduction: who you are, what the description is about ☐

c drinks (including your favorite) ☐

d the place: where it is and what it is like ☐

PLAN

5 ☆☆ **Write a description of your favorite place to eat. Make notes about the place. Say where it is, when you go there, and what it is like. Decide what information to include in each paragraph. Use the information in Exercise 4 to help you.**

WRITE

6 ☆☆☆ **Write your description. Remember to include four paragraphs, *there is* / *there are*, countable and uncountable nouns, and expressions from the *Useful Language* box (see Student's Book, p53).**

CHECK

7 **Do you ...**

- introduce yourself and say where you are from and the name of your favorite place?
- say what your favorite type of food and drink is?
- use adjectives to describe food?

4 REVIEW

VOCABULARY

1 Write the food or drink words. Use the picture to help you.

1 They are a vegetable. They are long and orange. _ _ _ _ _ _ _

2 You can make cheese from this drink. _ _ _ _

3 It's usually brown and it's sweet. It's made from cacao. _ _ _ _ _ _ _ _ _

4 It's usually on top of pizza. _ _ _ _ _ _

5 They come from chickens. _ _ _ _

6 It's a yellow fruit. There are a lot in Ecuador. _ _ _ _ _ _ _

7 You make this drink with fruit or vegetables. _ _ _ _ _

8 It's a drink, but we also use it to take a shower. _ _ _ _ _

2 Match the opposites.

1 healthy	☐	a	disgusting
2 delicious	☐	b	sweet
3 cold	☐	c	unhealthy
4 salty	☐	d	hot

GRAMMAR IN ACTION

3 Circle the correct option: *C* (countable) or *U* (uncountable).

1	apple	*C / U*
2	cheese	*C / U*
3	water	*C / U*
4	sandwich	*C / U*
5	bread	*C / U*
6	milk	*C / U*
7	potato	*C / U*
8	chocolate	*C / U*
9	banana	*C / U*
10	bean	*C / U*

4 Complete the text with *a*, *some*, or *any*.

It's my mom's birthday today, and my dad and I want to make her a nice meal. We don't have [1] ________ chicken, but we have [2] ________ meat to cook with [3] ________ rice. There's [4] ________ bottle of water in the fridge and we have [5] ________ fruit juice, too. There are [6] ________ carrots and [7] ________ tomatoes as well. We have [8] ________ book for my mom. She loves reading.

5 Complete the conversation with the words and phrases in the box.

Are there any	How many	Is there	
much	some	there are	There aren't

NATHAN Let's make dinner.
ANDREA OK. We can cook some chicken with vegetables. [1] __________ vegetables?
NATHAN Yes, [2] __________. We have three carrots and some tomatoes.
ANDREA [3] __________ tomatoes are there? I need three.
NATHAN [4] __________ three – only two.
ANDREA OK. [5] __________ any cheese? We can have the tomatoes with some cheese.
NATHAN Yes, there's [6] __________ cheese!
ANDREA Great. And how [7] __________ chicken is there?
NATHAN A lot! We can eat chicken for dinner, breakfast, and lunch!

CUMULATIVE GRAMMAR

6 Complete the conversation with the missing words. Circle the correct options.

VICTOR Mom, what [1] __________ for dinner?
MOM There's [2] __________ soup and fish. Do you want that?
VICTOR Yes, I'm hungry! And [3] __________ can I have to drink?
MOM [4] __________ some soda.
VICTOR Do we have any juice? I don't like [5] __________ soda.
MOM Take a look in the fridge. I think there [6] __________ two bottles of juice there.
VICTOR Yes! And it's orange juice – delicious! Do you want some juice, too?
MOM No, thanks. I [7] __________ like it very much. I prefer water. [8] __________ any apples for after your dinner?
VICTOR No, there [9] __________ any, but there are some bananas. I [10] __________ eat those.
MOM You're hungry! There's [11] __________ food, and you can eat all of it!
VICTOR OK, Mom. Yes, I'm really hungry!

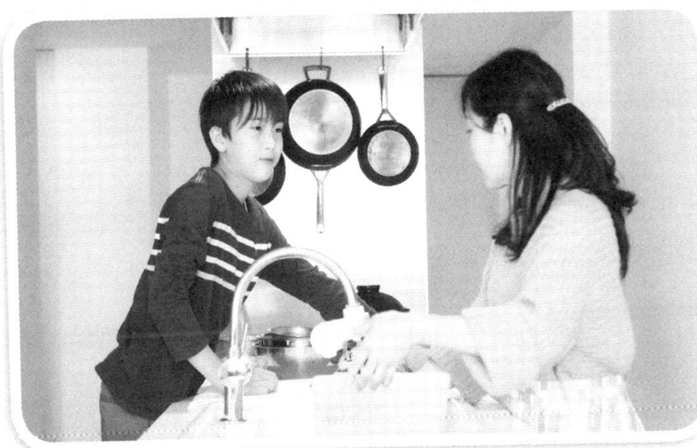

1 a there is b is there c are there
2 a some b a c an
3 a where b what c when
4 a There are b There is c There has
5 a drink b drinking c drinks
6 a are b have c is
7 a do b don't c 'm not
8 a Are there b Is there c Are they
9 a aren't b isn't c haven't
10 a am b do c can
11 a much b a lot of c many

5 What's your style?

VOCABULARY

Clothes

1 ☆ **Look at the photos and (circle) the correct words.**

1 *boots* / *(sneakers)*

2 *hoodie* / *T-shirt*

3 *jeans* / *sweatpants*

4 *boots* / *flip-flops*

5 *shorts* / *skirt*

6 *T-shirt* / *jacket*

2 ☆ **Look at the picture. Complete the text with the words in the box.**

boots	cap	jacket	shirt
shorts	sneakers	sweatpants	~~T-shirt~~

Laura's favorite outfit is a [1] T-shirt ______, [2] ______, [3] ______, and a [4] ______. Alex's favorite outfit is a [5] ______ and a [6] ______, [7] ______, and [8] ______.

3 ☆☆☆ **What can you wear? Write at least three clothes items for each situation.**

1 Your friends ask you to go to the mountains with them in December.

I can wear ______

2 It's July and you have a picnic with your parents.

______

3 It's Saturday afternoon and you want to visit your grandma.

______

Explore It!

Guess the correct answer.

A *kurta* is a long shirt without a collar. Men and women from *South America* / *South Asia* / *Europe* wear kurtas.

Find another interesting fact about clothes in your country. Write a question and send it to a classmate in an email, or ask them in the next class.

READING

An Online Diary

1 Read Marina's online diary. Who doesn't like purple?

____

Marina'sFashionFriends.com

Sunday, 10:30 a.m.

It's Sunday morning and I'm writing this post from the park. I'm here with my family. I can see a group of girls. They're talking and having some snacks. One girl looks great! I want her clothes! She's wearing purple jeans, an orange T-shirt, a black cap, and some fabulous purple sneakers.  I think those sneakers are in a store around the corner! Hmm … do I have got the money to buy them?

2:00 p.m. (and back online!)

I'm at home and guess what? I have those beautiful sneakers!

6:00 p.m.

Comments

Ethan: Hi, Marina! I always read your diary, and I usually like your ideas. But sorry … I don't like purple. I think it's a horrible color! It's a nice day today and I'm at a park, too. I'm wearing my new sweatpants, and a T-shirt, but it's hot now, and I'm not wearing my cap. What are you wearing?

Ada: Where can I buy those sneakers? I want some, too. Ethan, purple is THE color! I have six purple T-shirts and a pair of purple shorts! I'm wearing my favorite purple T-shirt today!

8:00 p.m.

Ada, they're selling them in World of Sneakers. I'm wearing them now!
Now I need some jeans. 
Sorry, Ethan, purple is THE color!

New post tomorrow!

2 Read the diary again and underline these words. Check their meaning in a dictionary and then complete the sentences.

beautiful corner ~~fabulous~~ guess what pair

1 I love my green boots. They're fabulous !
2 ______________ ? We're in the same class!
3 The store isn't far away. It's around the ______________ .
4 Sara's new skirt is ______________ . I want one!
5 You need to get a new ______________ of shoes.

3 Read the diary again. Circle the correct answers.

1 It's Sunday and Marina *is* / *isn't* at home.
2 She likes *one girl's* / *some girls'* sneakers.
3 Ethan *usually likes* / *doesn't usually like* Marina's posts.
4 Marina and *Ethan* / *Ada* want to buy the sneakers.
5 Ada *has some* / *doesn't have any* purple clothes.
6 Marina tells *Ethan* / *Ada* the name of a sneakers store.

4 Answer the questions with your own ideas.

1 Do you think fashion is important? Why / Why not?

____

____

2 Where do you get your ideas about what to wear? For example, from online diaries, friends, magazines, TV, movies, stores?

____

____

GRAMMAR IN ACTION

Present Continuous

1 ★☆☆ **Write the words in the correct order to make sentences.**

1 on TV / I'm / fashion show / a / watching
I'm watching a fashion show on TV.

2 her / She / isn't / doing / homework
____

3 the park / sitting / Marina / is / in
____

4 a / Ethan / isn't / cap / wearing
____

5 playing / We're / basketball
____

6 same / skirt / the / buying / They're
____

2 ★☆☆ **Complete the message with the correct form of the verb *to be*.**

60%

< Back

Hi Dad! I [1] *'m* sitting on the school bus and it [2] ______ (not) moving! The bus driver [3] ______ talking on the phone, and he [4] ______ (not) looking very happy. Oh, and it [5] ______ raining! Can you come? Juan [6] ______ playing hockey, and Mom [7] ______ (not) answering the phone.
Thanks, Dad!

3 ★☆☆ **What are they doing? Look at pictures 1–4 and write sentences using the words in boxes a and b.**

a dance ~~read~~ ride write

b a bike ~~a magazine~~ on the board to music

1 *He's reading a magazine.*
2 ____________________
3 ____________________
4 ____________________

4 ★★☆ **Match questions 1–6 with answers a–f.**

1 Are you listening to me? *b*
2 Is Anton wearing his new sneakers? ☐
3 Is Claudia studying? ☐
4 What are they eating? ☐
5 Which movie is Pedro watching? ☐
6 Where are you having your lunch? ☐

a *Wonder Woman*.
b ~~Yes, I am~~!
c In the cafeteria.
d No, she isn't.
e Cold pizza. Yuck!
f Yes, he is.

5 ★★★ **Answer the questions.**

1 What are you wearing today?
____

2 What is your best friend doing now?
____

6 ★★★ **Find out what two people in your family are doing now. Write sentences in the present continuous.**

My sister's watching TV.
____
____
____

VOCABULARY AND LISTENING

Accessories

1 ☆ **Complete the accessory words in the spidergram.**

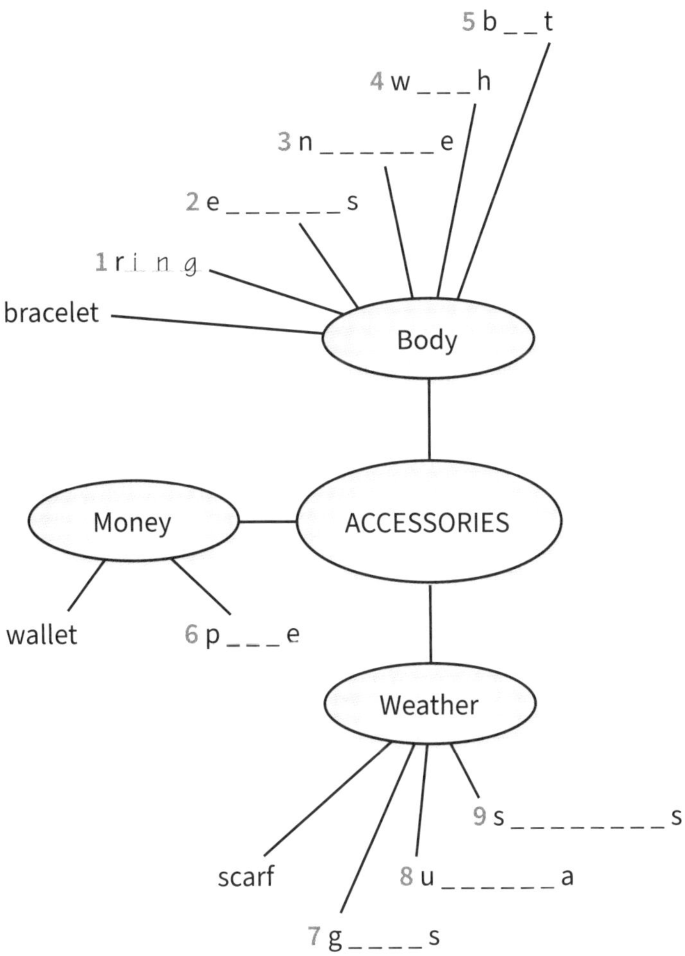

2 ☆☆ **Complete the sentences with words from Exercise 1.**

1 Those new jeans look big. You need a belt.

2 José always wears ______ when it's sunny.

3 Madison carries her wallet and phone in her ______.

4 I don't wear a ______ because there's a clock in the classroom.

5 It's raining, and I don't have my ______!

6 In cold weather, my grandma always wears ______ and a ______.

7 My dad has a big ______, but he never has any money in it!

An Interview

5.01 **3** ☆ **Listen to the interview. Mark (✓) the two things that Alba paints.**

5.01 **4** ☆☆☆ **Listen again. Answer the questions.**

1 Who is Alba painting this week?

Her baby brother.

2 Where does she get her ideas from?

______

3 What does she put in the mini boxes?

______

4 What is inside the box for her friend?

______

5 What does the interviewer want?

______

5 ☆ **Alba is making you a box (big or small). Write two things you want to put in it. Use the ideas below or your own ideas.**

a bracelet	a ring	a wallet	a watch	gloves

I'd like ______ and ______.

GRAMMAR IN ACTION

Simple Present and Present Continuous

1 ☆ **(Circle) the correct options.**

2 We use the *simple present* / *present continuous* to talk about things happening now.

3 We use the *simple present* / *present continuous* to talk about facts, habits, and routines.

2 ☆ **Complete the chart with the words and phrases in the box.**

at the moment	every Monday	never	~~on Fridays~~	right now	sometimes	this week	this morning	today	usually

Facts, Habits, and Routines	Things Happening Now
on Fridays	

3 ☆☆ **Write sentences with the simple present or present continuous.**

1 Some people / wear / sports clothes / on the weekend

Some people wear sports clothes on the weekend.

2 I / look for / some jeans / right now

______

3 They / make / the costumes for the show / now

______

4 Naomi / usually / buy / red clothes

______

5 We / never / go shopping / on Saturdays

______

6 A lot of people / wear / hats / at the moment

______

4 ☆☆ **Complete the conversation with the simple present or present continuous form of the verbs in parentheses.**

DANA What [1] *are you doing* (do), Paula?

PAULA I [2] ______ (look) at my clothes. Some of them are very small now. I [3] ______ (often / need) new clothes in the summer.

DANA Oh! Can I have this skirt?

PAULA Well, I [4] ______ (always / give) my small clothes to my little sister, but she [5] ______ (not wear) skirts, so it's yours!

DANA Thanks! Where [6] ______ (you / usually / buy) your clothes?

PAULA At a store near home. My mom [7] ______ (shop) there right now.

DANA [8] ______ (they / sell) accessories, too? I [9] ______ (look for) a bracelet at the moment.

PAULA Yes, they do! They [10] ______ (sell) lovely bracelets. We can go shopping there together next time!

5 ☆☆☆ **Answer the questions.**

1 What do you do with your old clothes and accessories?

______

2 What clothes are you wearing a lot at the moment?

______

3 What do you usually wear in the evening during the week?

______

WRITING

A Description of a Photo

1 ☆ **Read the description and look at the photo. Write the names of the people (a–e).**

a Damir
b ______
c ______
d ______
e ______

A Photo of a Day Out

By Alyssa

1 This is a photo of my friends and me. We're on a school trip to a national park. It's cold but sunny.

2 The boy on the left is Damir. He [1]*looks* / *'s looking* down. He often [2]*looks* / *is looking* down because he hates photos! He [3]*wears* / *'s wearing* a black and gray hoodie. Next to Damir is Peter. He's in a pink shirt and a gray sweater. The boys [4]*don't wear* / *aren't wearing* jackets in the photo. Then that's me in the middle, with a jacket and a checked shirt. Carmen's next to me. She [5]*wears* / *'s wearing* her favorite denim jacket and a big scarf. Gina's on the right. She has a gray T-shirt, a green jacket, and a scarf. Gina's the only one in a hat.

3 This is one of my favorite photos. We [6]*laugh* / *'re laughing* because it's a fun day. I like this photo because there are trees in the back and we all look happy. We always [7]*have* / *are having* a great time!

2 ☆☆ **Circle the correct form of the verbs (1–7) in the description.**

3 ☆☆ **Read the description again. Complete the sentences with the words in the box.**

Alyssa	boys	girls	Peter	~~trees~~

1 The trees are in the back.
2 ______ is in the middle. Carmen and ______ are next to her.
3 The ______ are on the left.
4 The ______ are on the right.

4 ☆☆ **Match topics a–c with paragraphs 1–3.**

a why it is a favorite photo ☐
b people in the photo, where they are, and what they're wearing ☐
c who is in the photo and where the photo is ☐

PLAN

5 ☆☆ **Write your own description of a photo of a day out. Choose your photo and make notes. Decide what information to include in each paragraph. Use the information in Exercise 4 to help you.**

WRITE

6 ☆☆☆ **Write your description. Remember to include the information in the correct order, the simple present and present continuous, and expressions from the *Useful Language* box (see Student's Book, p65).**

CHECK

7 **Do you …**

- describe the people in the photo, including the clothes and accessories they are wearing?
- describe the people's positions in the photo?
- say why you like the photo?

5 REVIEW

VOCABULARY

1 **Circle the word that doesn't fit.**

1 sweatpants / T-shirt / jeans
2 sneakers / shorts / boots
3 shorts / boots / skirt
4 jacket / hoodie / cap
5 shirt / skirt / shorts
6 flip-flops / boots / sneakers

2 **Complete the crossword. Use the pictures.**

ACROSS →

3

6

8

9

10
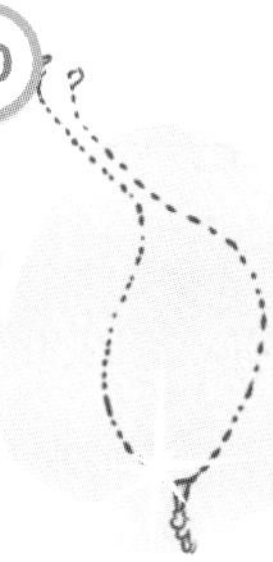

11

DOWN ↓

1

2

4
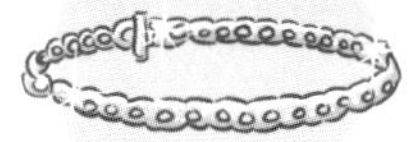

5

7

8

GRAMMAR IN ACTION

3 **Complete the sentences with the present continuous form of the verbs in the box.**

do	look	make	not rain	not wear	watch

1 **A:** What ______ you ______ now?
B: I'm doing my homework.
2 At the moment, I ______ for a new jacket with my dad.
3 They ______ a TV show about the history of fashion.
4 We ______ our school clothes today – it's Sunday.
5 My grandma ______ me a new dress for my birthday.
6 You don't need an umbrella. It ______ .

4 Circle the correct options.

MAYA What [1]*do you usually do / are you usually doing* on the weekend?

ISAAC We [2]*sometimes visit / are sometimes visiting* my grandparents, but they [3]*travel / 're traveling* around Europe at the moment.

LILY [4]*Is Jimi having / Does Jimi have* lunch at home this month?

TOM Yes. He usually [5]*has / is having* lunch at school, but this month he [6]*goes / 's going* home early.

HUGO [7]*Does Dad do / Is Dad doing* the shopping now?

CALEB No, it's Sunday. The stores [8]*close / are closing* early on Sundays.

CUMULATIVE GRAMMAR

5 Complete the conversation with the missing words. Circle the correct options.

ADAM Hi, Mom. [1] ________ are you?

MOM Hi, Adam! I'm [2] ________ the shopping with Dad.

ADAM Oh, OK! Listen, [3] ________ for a bike ride this afternoon with Tom and his brother?

MOM Sure! We don't have [4] ________ plans.

ADAM Great! But [5] ________ a problem. I can't [6] ________ my sneakers, or my hoodie. Where are they?

MOM I [7] ________ know. They're your things.

ADAM Oh! The sneakers are under my bed, but I can't see my hoodie. Can you buy [8] ________ a new one, please?

MOM A new one? I don't have [9] ________ time now, and you have a hoodie! You need to look for [10] ________.

ADAM Ugh! I hate [11] ________ things.

MOM I know, but how often [12] ________ things when you look for them?

ADAM Hmm, I guess so. OK, talk to you later.

	a	b	c
1	When	Where	What
2	does	do	doing
3	can I go	I can go	do I go
4	any	some	a
5	there are	there's	it's
6	find	to find	finding
7	not	'm not	don't
8	me	it	my
9	many	any	a lot
10	it	they	them
11	look for	looking for	looks for
12	are you finding	do you find	you find

6 How can we be athletic?

VOCABULARY
Sports

1 ☆ **Complete the word puzzle. Use the pictures (1–12). What is the mystery word in gray?**

2 ☆☆ **Complete the rules with *play*, *do*, or *go*.**

We usually use [1] ________ with sports that end in *-ing*.

We usually use [2] ________ with sports with balls and other objects.

We usually use [3] ________ with other sports.

3 ☆☆ **Circle the correct options.**

I like playing sports. At school, we do [1]*running* / *track and field* and I like that. Sometimes on the weekend I go [2]*swimming* / *yoga* with my brother. He does [3]*gymnastics* / *football* at an after-school gym and goes [4]*running* / *table tennis* twice a week. I don't really like team sports, but in the summer, I sometimes play [5]*sailing* / *volleyball* with my friends on the beach. And I love going [6]*yoga* / *rock climbing* with my dad in the mountains.

4 ☆☆☆ **Answer the questions.**

1 What are your favorite sports?

____

2 Do you play sports at school? Which sports?

____

Explore It!

Guess the correct answer.

Which sport comes from Canada?

a hockey b table tennis c football

Find another interesting fact about sports in your country. Write a question and send it to a classmate in an email, or ask them in the the next class.

READING
Online FAQs

1 Read the article. What sport is it about? Mark (✓) the correct photo (1–3).

1 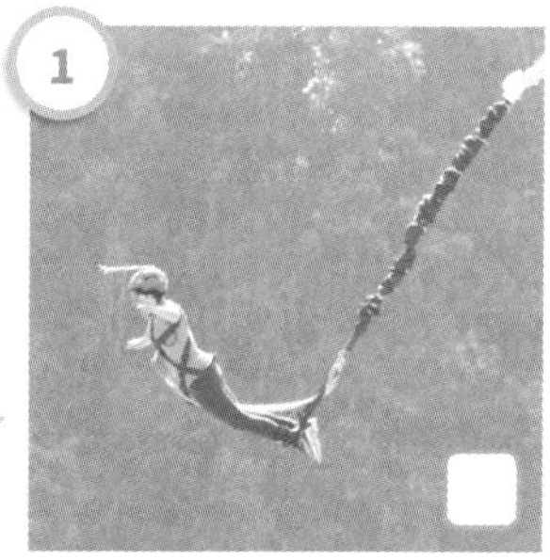

2 

3 

FUN IN THE SUN!

Are you looking for a new sport? Do you want to try something more exciting? In New Zealand, we have the answer – try zorbing! It's new and it's different!

FAQs

Q1: What is Zorbing?

Zorbing is a fun outdoor sport. It's more popular here in New Zealand than in other countries.

Q2: ______

You need a large plastic ball. This is called a zorb. You get inside the ball and run or walk. When you move, the ball moves, too! You know where you're going and how you're moving because you can see through the ball. A lot of people love going down a hill in their zorb. It's exciting!

Q3: ______

No, it's an individual sport. You get inside the zorb on your own, but it's really fun to go with family or friends because you can have races – sometimes children are faster than their parents!

Q4: ______

Yes, it is, but always do it in a zorbing center and follow the rules. Have fun, but be careful – don't get hurt!

Q5: ______

Yes. To go zorbing, you usually need to be six years old or older.

Q6: ______

There are zorbing centers in many places on the South Island. Click here for a list of centers.

Q7: ______

Yes, it's more expensive than other traditional sports, but it's a great activity for special days. So, are you ready for zorbing? What are you waiting for!

2 Read the article again. Complete it with the missing questions.

a Is there an age limit?
b Is it a team sport?
c What do you do?
d ~~What is zorbing~~?
e Where can I do it?
f Is it expensive?
g Is it safe?

3 Read the article again and <u>underline</u> these words. Then check their meaning in a dictionary and complete the sentences.

get hurt hill race ~~safe~~ try

1 Be careful! Going out alone at night isn't safe.
2 The Spartathlon is a ______ in Greece. People run 246 kilometers!
3 I live at the top of a ______. Walking down to school is easy!
4 I love tennis, but this year I want to ______ a new sport.
5 Careful there! You can fall and ______!

4 Answer the questions.

1 Do you want to try zorbing? Why / Why not?

______

2 What fun outdoor sports are popular in your country?

______

GRAMMAR IN ACTION

Comparatives

1 ☆ Write the comparative forms.

1 small ___smaller___
2 big ______
3 good ______
4 happy ______
5 interesting ______
6 bad ______

2 ☆ Complete the rules with the adjectives from Exercise 1.

1 For one-syllable adjectives, add *-er*: ___smaller___.
2 For two-syllable adjectives ending in *-y*, remove the *-y* and add *-ier*: ______.
3 For long adjectives, add *more* before the adjective: ______.
4 For one-syllable adjectives ending in a vowel and a consonant, double the consonant and add *-er*: ______.
5 For irregular adjectives, use a different word: ______ and ______.

3 ☆☆ Underline and correct one mistake in each sentence.

1 Windsurfing is more expensive that running. ___than___
2 Basketball is more fast than football. ______
3 Runners are usually thiner than swimmers. ______
4 Which sport is noisyer, volleyball, or yoga? ______
5 She's badder at gymastics than at hockey. ______
6 Playing sports is more better than watching it. ______

4 ☆☆ Complete the sentences with the comparative form of the adjectives in parentheses.

1 A hockey match is ___longer___ than a basketball game. (long)
2 I think rock climbing is ______ than yoga. (exciting)
3 Lola's ______ at tennis than her dad. (good)
4 Our school hockey team is ______ than the football team. (bad)
5 We think soccer is a ______ game than football. (difficult)
6 Playing sports is ______ than watching TV. (healthy)

5 ☆☆ Complete the questions with a comparative adjective. Then check the answers at the bottom of the page.

DANIEL Let's do this quiz! First question: Which ball is [1] ___faster___, a table tennis or a tennis ball?
ANIYAH A table tennis ball?
DANIEL Next question: Which is [2] ______, a basketball game or a hockey match?
ANIYAH I don't know. Hockey?
DANIEL Number three: Which country is [3] ______ at table tennis, China or South Korea?
ANIYAH South Korea, I think.
DANIEL And the last question: Which sport is [4] ______ in schools here in New Zealand, hockey or track and field?
ANIYAH Oh, no! I don't know. Track and field maybe. What are the answers?

6 ☆☆☆ Write three sentences comparing sports. Look at Exercise 4 to help you.

I think soccer is more entertaining than football.

______

______

______

Answers

1 table tennis ball: 116 km/h; tennis ball: 263 km/h
2 hockey match: 60 minutes; basketball game: 48 minutes
3 China (1); South Korea (2)
4 number of people playing in schools in New Zealand: hockey: 13,967, track and field: 12,713

VOCABULARY AND LISTENING

Sports Verbs

1 ☆ **Match photos 1–6 with six of the sports verbs a–l.**

a ~~bounce~~ b catch c climb d dive e hit f jump g kick h lift i pass j run k score l throw

1  a

2 

3 

4 

5 

6 

2 ☆☆ **Circle the correct verbs.**

I don't understand rugby! OK, the players [1]*pass* / *score* the ball to each other. Then they [2]*catch* / *run* up the field and put the ball over a line to [3]*score* / *hit* points. They also [4]*kick* / *jump* the ball over a big goalpost. But sometimes the teams make a circle and push each other. Then one player [5]*scores* / *throws* the ball into the circle and another player from the same team gets it. And sometimes some players [6]*lift* / *jump* on top of other players!

3 ☆☆☆ **Write two sentences describing what players can and can't do in a sport. Use the sports verbs from Exercise 1.**

In soccer, the players can kick the ball, but they can't score goals with their hands.

____

____

____

A Conversation

6.01 **4** ☆ **Look at the photo and listen to a conversation about goalball, a sport for people who are visually impaired. Circle the correct answers.**

1 Goalball players use a special ball with *lights* / *sound*.
2 Goalball is *a team* / *an individual* sport.

6.01 **5** ☆☆☆ **Listen again. Complete the sentences with one word.**

1 The goalball ball is like a basketball, but heavier.
2 A goalball team has _______ players on it.
3 Players try to _______ the ball to score a goal.
4 They use their _______ to stop the ball.
5 Some players throw the ball _______ kilometers per hour.
6 Jon plays goalball on a _______ court.
7 The boy wants to watch Jon's match on _______.

6 ☆☆☆ **Watch part of a Paralympics goalball match on the Internet. Then write three things you like about it.**

I like how the players throw the ball.

____

____

____

GRAMMAR IN ACTION

Superlatives

1 ☆ **Complete the chart with the superlative form of the adjectives in the box.**

bad ~~entertaining~~ fit healthy old

The most + adjective	*The* + double the final consonant + *-est*	*The* + change *y* to *i* + *-est*	*The* + adjective + *-est*	*The* + irregular form
the most popular	2 ______	the easiest	4 ______	the best
1 the most entertaining	the biggest	3 ______	the fastest	5 ______

2 ☆☆ **Complete the text with the superlative form of the adjectives in parentheses.**

My cousin Nick is the 1 most popular (popular) person in my family. He's the 2 ______ (tall) of my cousins and also the 3 ______ (fit) – on the weekend, he does yoga and plays hockey! Everybody loves Nick.

He's the 4 ______ (happy) person I know! I'm the 5 ______ (young) person in my family and the 6 ______ (bad) at sports! But that's OK because we're all different. I love reading and writing stories. Nick says I write the 7 ______ (interesting) stories in the world.

3 ☆☆ **Write the questions in the quiz using the superlative form of the adjectives. Then circle the correct answers. Check your answers at the bottom of the quiz!**

SPORTS QUESTION TIME!

1 Which is / popular / sport in Brazil?
Which is the most popular sport in Brazil?
a basketball (**b**) soccer

2 Which is one of the / old / ball sports?
______
a Ulama from Mexico
b Alama from Ecuador

3 Which is one of the / new / sports?
______
a table tennis
b 360Ball

4 Which is one of the / difficult / sports for many people?
______
a rock climbing **b** running

5 Which is one of the / expensive / sports in the world?
______
a tennis **b** swimming

ANSWERS
1 b 2 a 3 b 4 a 5 a

4 ☆☆☆ **Complete the questions with the superlative form of the adjectives. Then answer them for you.**

1 Who is the youngest (young) person in your family?
______

2 Which is ______ (popular) sport at your school?
______

3 Which is ______ (difficult) school subject?
______

4 Which is ______ (entertaining) movie you know?
______

WRITING

A Profile of an Athlete

1 ☆ **Look at the photos and read the profile. Then complete the sentence.**

For Ivan, Natalia Partyka is an ______________ athlete because she plays table tennis with ______________.

A Popular Athlete from My Country

By Ivan Nowak

1 I'm from Poland, and I think one of the [1]*more / most* popular athletes from my country is Natalia Partyka. She's a table tennis player. She's 1.73 m tall and weighs 64 kg. She only has one hand and part of her right arm.

2 Natalia trains for about six hours a day. She often plays with her [2]*older / more older* sister, Sandra. Sometimes she practices bouncing the ball on the top part of her arm to begin the game. In her free time, Natalia loves reading the letters from her fans. She also likes going to the beach with her friends.

3 I think Natalia is the [3]*more / most* amazing athlete from my country because she plays with one hand. She's also an excellent athlete – she's part of the Paralympic team and the Olympic Games team, too. She has more gold medals than any other table tennis player in Poland, and she's one of the [4]*most / more* successful players in the world, too.

2 ☆☆ **Circle the correct options (1–4) in the profile.**

3 ☆☆ **Read the profile again. Underline two sentences with *also* and two sentences with *too*. Then complete the rules with *also* or *too*.**

We use *too* and *also* to give extra information. We use [1] ______________ at the end of a sentence. We use [2] ______________ after the verb *to be* and before other verbs.

4 ☆☆ **Read the profile again. Match topics a–c with paragraphs 1–3.**

a training and other interests ☐
b achievements ☐
c basic information and description ☐

PLAN

5 ☆☆ **Write a profile of a popular athlete from your country. Make notes about the athlete. Decide what information to include in each paragraph. Use the information in Exercise 4 to help you.**

WRITE

6 ☆☆☆ **Write your profile. Remember to include three paragraphs, comparatives and superlatives, and expressions from the *Useful Language* box (see Student's Book, p77).**

CHECK

7 **Do you ...**

- give basic information and a description of your athlete?
- describe their sport using sports verbs?
- talk about their achievements and why you like them?

6 REVIEW

VOCABULARY

1 Complete the chart with the sports in the box.

football running sailing
swimming tennis track and field
volleyball windsurfing yoga

Water Sports	Ball Sports	Other Sports

2 Find 12 sports verbs in the word search.

B	D	I	B	T	D	I	V	E	H
U	I	C	S	D	Q	H	G	R	I
V	O	L	I	F	T	A	H	B	T
Y	K	I	C	K	R	Z	O	S	P
E	C	M	W	Q	M	N	S	C	A
N	P	B	O	U	N	C	E	O	L
L	Y	K	J	C	J	A	T	R	U
T	H	R	O	W	V	T	G	E	R
H	J	U	M	P	W	C	E	F	U
F	P	A	S	S	K	H	X	G	N

3 Complete the sentences with the correct form of the verbs from Exercise 2.

1 A basketball player b__________ the ball on the court.

2 My brother loves j__________ on the bed!

3 Mount Everest, the highest mountain in the world, is very difficult to c__________.

4 We never s__________ many goals in soccer.

5 Tennis players can't h__________ the ball with their hands. They use a racket.

6 In gymnastics, we sometimes l__________ heavy boxes to make our arms strong.

GRAMMAR IN ACTION

4 Write sentences using the comparative form of the adjectives in parentheses.

1 zorbing / running (exciting)

____

2 water / soda (healthy)

____

3 sweatpants / jeans (comfortable)

____

4 a table tennis ball / a tennis ball (small)

____

5 jumping / rock climbing (easy)

____

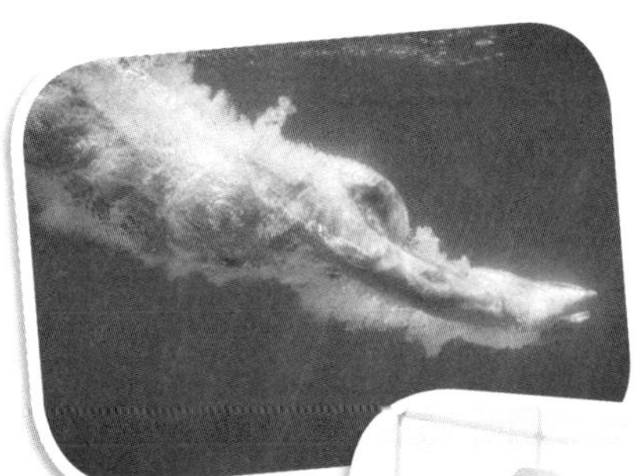

5 Complete the text with the superlative form of the adjectives in parentheses.

I think tennis is the [1] ________ (boring) sport, but my dad loves it! At the moment, he's in London at the All England Club. This club is the [2] ________ (old) in the world. Every year, there are different tennis tournaments there. The [3] ________ (popular) one is called Wimbledon. My dad says all the [4] ________ (good) players want to win there. People watching tennis at Wimbledon don't usually speak to each other a lot. The [5] ________ (bad) thing you can do at Wimbledon is talk! The players don't like noise. I think the [6] ________ (easy) thing is to watch Wimbledon on TV, but not for me – I prefer a good movie!

CUMULATIVE GRAMMAR

6 Complete the conversation with the missing words. Circle the correct options.

ESMA Which sports [1] ________ you like, Rafael?

RAFAEL I like [2] ________ track and field and playing baseball.

ESMA I think baseball is the [3] ________ sport in the world.

RAFAEL Me, too! Today, I [4] ________ baseball practice and then yoga.

ESMA Yoga! I think it's [5] ________ than track and field!

RAFAEL Then try it with me! I can teach you the [6] ________ exercises.

ESMA Sounds great, but I'm the [7] ________ student in the world!

RAFAEL Ah! But I'm a [8] ________ teacher!

ESMA OK! I [9] ________ try.

RAFAEL [10] ________ your sweatpants in your bag?

ESMA No, but I can [11] ________ home and get them now.

RAFAEL Perfect. Run home and bring [12] ________ sweatpants!

	a	b	c
1	does	are	do
2	does	do	doing
3	best	better	good
4	has	have	having
5	most interesting	more interesting	interesting
6	more easy	most easy	easiest
7	bad	worse	worst
8	good	the better	best
9	can	have	do
10	Do you have	Do have	You have
11	go to	go	come
12	yours	you	your

7 Why are animals important?

VOCABULARY

Animals

1 ☆ **Find 13 more words for animals in the word search.**

C	R	O	C	O	D	I	L	E	D	E	Y
H	I	P	P	O	B	D	O	N	K	E	Y
J	L	S	I	S	W	A	Y	U	K	A	G
P	H	W	B	C	N	G	D	N	T	G	I
A	M	H	E	K	M	A	N	I	J	L	R
R	Q	O	A	V	I	D	K	T	H	E	A
R	K	R	R	P	L	U	Z	E	B	C	F
O	R	S	O	E	N	C	D	W	V	E	F
T	X	E	G	T	W	K	M	O	U	S	E
Z	F	W	H	A	L	E	G	K	S	B	A
A	N	F	M	P	B	M	O	N	K	E	Y
L	I	O	N	V	T	C	N	U	I	J	X

2 ☆ **Circle the animal in each category which is not correct. Then add a different animal to each category in the list.**

1 **Birds**	2 **Mammals**	3 **Reptiles**
duck	eagle	snake
hippo	giraffe	bear
parrot	lion	crocodile
______	______	______

3 ☆☆ **Read the descriptions and write the names of the animals from Exercise 1.**

1 This animal is a mammal. It usually lives in forests and cold places. It's very big and has a lot of hair. bear

2 This animal lives in water in hot countries. It's a reptile with a big mouth and a lot of big teeth. ______

3 This is a bird. It eats plants and it can swim and fly. It usually lives near water. ______

4 This animal likes cheese, but it doesn't like cats! It's usually gray and has a lot of babies. ______

5 This animal eats meat. It doesn't have any legs. Some of them can kill other animals and sometimes people, too. ______

6 This is a very large sea mammal. It has a hole on the top of its head. ______

4 ☆☆ **Choose another animal from Exercise 1 and write a definition.**

This animal is ______

______

______

______

Explore It!

Guess the correct answer.

Which bird sometimes sleeps with an eye open?

a duck   b parrot   c eagle

Find another interesting fact about birds. Write a question and send it to a classmate in an email, or ask them it in the next class.

READING
Fact Files

1 ☆ **Read the fact file below and circle the correct answers.**

1 Polar bears weigh …
 a about 360 kg. b about 560 kg.
2 Polar bears live in …
 a the Arctic. b the Antarctic.
3 Polar bears eat … of seal in a week.
 a about 35 kg b about 55 kg

POLAR BEAR

Weight: about 360 kg
Habitat: the Arctic
Food: seals
Fact: Polar bears can smell a seal 32 km away! They can eat 55 kg of seal in a week.

2 ☆ **Read the article. What's special about the town of Churchill?** ____________

3 ☆☆ **Read the article again and underline these words. Then check their meaning in a dictionary and complete the sentences.**

attack	escape	hunt	~~ice~~	male	prison

1 In winter, there is *ice* on the river.
2 A female animal is a girl and a ____________ is a boy.
3 People can go to ____________ for killing an elephant.
4 Hungry lions are dangerous, and they sometimes ____________ people.
5 Killer whales often ____________ other mammals, like seals, at night.
6 The man saw the polar bear in the street and ran into a store to ____________ .

Polar Bears Are in Town!

Churchill is a small town on the Hudson Bay in Canada. Every October, November, and December, it has some special visitors: polar bears! They can't hunt seals until it is colder and there is more ice, so they visit the town looking for food.

From October to December in 2016, there were 800 people living in Churchill and 10,000 tourists. The tourists were there to see the polar bears – there were more than 1,000 bears.

Some bears attack people, so the police ask people to be careful and to leave their cars open in town. Then people can jump inside if they need to escape an angry bear! To keep people safe, the police sometimes put angry bears in prison for a few days. Then they take them out of the town.

People in the town say the worst year was 1983. On November 29, a young male bear killed a man downtown. This was the first attack for many years. In 2013, a large bear attacked a man in the street. The bear was put in prison and the man went to the doctor, but he was fine after a few days.

4 ☆☆ **Read the article again. Are the sentences *T* (true) or *F* (false)? Correct the false sentences.**

1 Polar bears visit the town every August.
 F. Polar bears visit the town from October to December.
2 The polar bears go to the town because it's colder there.
 ____
3 When the polar bears are angry, people can hide in cars.
 ____
4 The polar bears that attack people go to prison.
 ____

5 ☆☆☆ **Answer the questions with your own ideas.**

1 What do you think the polar bears eat in Churchill?
 ____
2 Do you think the food they eat in Churchill is good for them? Why / Why not?
 ____

GRAMMAR IN ACTION

Simple Past: *To Be, There Was/Were*

1 ☆ Circle the correct options.

1 The polar bears *was* / *were* in Churchill in November because *there wasn't* / *there weren't* enough food for them to eat in the river.

2 In the past, the weather *was* / *were* always cold in November, and *there was* / *there were* a lot of ice on the river.

3 When it *was* / *were* colder, *there was* / *there were* seals for the polar bears to eat in the river.

4 In the past, *there was* / *there were* more ice because the temperatures *wasn't* / *weren't* as high.

2 ☆ Match the questions with the answers.

1 Was it hotter in the past? ☐ a Yes, there were.
2 Were they wild animals? ☐ b No, there wasn't.
3 Was there ice in summer? ☐ c Yes, they were.
4 Were there seals? ☐ d No, it wasn't.

3 ☆☆ Complete the text with *was(n't)/were(n't)*.

Thousands of years ago, there were mammoths in Europe. They [1] *were* large mammals with very big tusks. They [2] ______ very strong. They [3] ______ like the elephants we see today because they [4] ______ much bigger and had fur. The saber-toothed tiger also lived in Europe at the same time. It [5] ______ really a tiger. It [6] ______ a big cat. Its teeth [7] ______ very long, and it [8] ______ a very dangerous animal.

4 ☆☆ Complete the text with the correct form of *there was* or *there were*.

When I was a girl, I lived in South Africa. Around my house, [1] *there wasn't* a lot to do, but [2] ______ a lot of animals to see because we lived next to a wildlife park. In my bedroom, [3] ______ a big window, and in the mornings, I could see a lot of animals. [4] ______ hippos in the water, and [5] ______ enormous elephants sleeping. [6] ______ always a big giraffe next to a tree and a strange bird sitting on the tree that looked angry! My favorite animals are tigers, but [7] ______ any tigers in the wildlife park. That's because there aren't any tigers in South Africa. [8] ______ a lot of time to see the animals because I was at school all day, but I remember all of them.

5 ☆☆ Put the words in the correct order to complete the questions. Then write answers for you in your notebook.

1 were / Where / on Saturday / you / ?
Where were you on Saturday?

2 your / favorite / six / animal / when / you / were / ?
What was ______

3 people / were / there / last year / your / class / in / ?
How many ______

4 in / 2011 / were / you / ?
How old ______

5 your town / in / were / you / when / young / a zoo / ?
Was there ______

6 ☆☆☆ Find out about an animal from the past, like mammoths or saber-toothed tigers. Write three sentences about them. Use *was* and *were*.

______

______

______

VOCABULARY AND LISTENING

Adjectives

1 ☆ **Choose the correct letters to complete the adjectives.**

a c d f g i l m n r u y

1 beauti *f* ul	5 heav __	9 ti __ y
2 s __ art	6 l __ zy	10 la __ ge
3 __ ute	7 wil __	11 q __ iet
4 dan __ erous	8 no __ sy	12 __ ong

2 ☆☆ **Complete the text with adjectives from Exercise 1.**

I have a [1] *beautiful* little cat. He has a pretty face, and I think he's really [2] ________. He's [3] ________, too, and can do a lot of tricks. My mom likes him because he doesn't make a lot of noise like some pets. She says he's very [4] ________. He can't run fast because his legs aren't very [5] ________! I prefer small pets because some of my friends' big pets are [6] ________, and they make me nervous.

3 ☆☆☆ **Which pets do your family or friends have? Use the adjectives and your own ideas to write four sentences.**

My best friend has a tiny mouse.

A Class Discussion

🎧 7.01 4 ☆ **Listen to a teacher talking about wolves with her class. Circle the correct answers.**

1 The teacher is talking about wolves that live in an *American park* / *English zoo*.

2 There weren't any wolves there for *50* / *100* years.

3 There were about *6* / *100* wolves there last year.

🎧 7.01 5 ☆☆ **Listen again and answer the questions. Remember the *Learn to Learn* tip: look for the question words and think about the answers before you listen.**

1 How does one student describe wolves?
They are fast, dangerous, and smart.

2 Why weren't there any wolves in Yellowstone Park for 100 years?

3 How many wolves were in the park about 25 years ago?

4 Why was it difficult for the wolves at first?

5 Why is it difficult to see wolves in the park?

6 ☆☆☆ **Which other wild animals do you think live in Yellowstone Park? Write some ideas below.**

GRAMMAR IN ACTION

Simple Past: Regular and Irregular Verbs

1 ☆ **Write the infinitive of these past tense verbs.**

1 had *have*	5 heard ______	9 shared ______
2 slept ______	6 saw ______	10 wanted ______
3 took ______	7 became ______	11 found ______
4 looked ______	8 gave ______	12 went ______

2 ☆☆ **Complete the sentences with the correct simple past form of the verbs in the box.**

look ~~not give~~ have not want
sleep not find see not go

1 You *didn't give* the donkey its food.
2 We ______ a lot of snakes at the wildlife park.
3 The horse ______ to eat my apple. It wasn't hungry.
4 They ______ for the cat in the yard, but they ______ him.
5 My dad ______ a parrot as a pet when he was a child.
6 The cat ______ out. She ______ on my bed all day.

3 ☆☆ **Write the words in the correct order to make sentences.**

1 park / years / The / 20 / safari / opened / ago
The safari park opened 20 years ago.
2 Crocodiles / killed / year / 1,000 / people / last
______
3 bears / days / in town / ago, / Two / three / were / there
______
4 blue / last / saw / whales / summer / They
______
5 an / The / home / hour / cat / came / ago
______

4 ☆☆☆ **Complete the text with the simple past form of the verbs in parentheses.**

Flo, a dog from Northern Ireland, disappeared in October 2011. The Gallaghers, Flo's family, [1] *looked* (look) for her, but they [2] ______ (not find) her. They were very sad. Then in 2014, a volunteer at the local animal hospital [3] ______ (hear) about a dog with no home. The dog [4] ______ (sleep) in an old building about ten miles from the Gallaghers' house. The volunteers at the hospital [5] ______ (not want) the dog to stay there. They [6] ______ (go) to find her. Soon the dog [7] ______ (have) a new home at the animal hospital, and they [8] ______ (share) photos of her on Facebook. The Gallagher family [9] ______ (see) the photos and [10] ______ (become) very excited – it was Flo! The next day they [11] ______ (take) her home. They [12] ______ (give) her a big dinner.

WRITING

A Biography

1 Look at the photos and read the biography. Which animals did Jack help?

Jack Oliver

1 Jack Oliver was born in Australia [1]in / on 1978. His family started an animal sanctuary to give animals a safe place to live. [2]*When / At* Jack was five, he found a three-meter snake in his yard! It was injured! Jack and his parents decided to take care of it. Jack helped at the sanctuary, and he became an animal expert.

2 Jack met his wife Alison [3]*on / in* 2003. They had a daughter named Ava. [4]*In / On* 2005, Jack started to make TV shows with a local TV channel. He filmed several series at his family's sanctuary. He also went to other countries to find and help injured animals. He helped to make them better and find a safe place for them to live. [5]*In / On* September 25, 2012, Jack had an accident with a crocodile, but he survived.

3 Jack's wife and daughter help with his work. A few weeks [6]*when / ago*, Ava found an injured duck and decided to take it to her father's sanctuary. She helped her father to take care of it. Ava wants to be an animal expert one day, just like her father!

2 Circle the correct prepositions (1–6) in the biography.

3 Read the biography again and write the events in the box in the timeline below.

~~born~~ crocodile attack found a snake met Alison TV shows

1978 1983 2003 2005 2012

1 born 3 ______ 5 ______

2 ______ 4 ______

4 Match headings a–c with paragraphs 1–3.

a Now ☐

b Early life ☐

c Main events ☐

PLAN

5 Write a biography about a famous person who works with animals. Look for information on the Internet and create a timeline about his or her life. Use Exercise 3 to help you.

6 Decide what information to include in each paragraph. Use Exercise 4 to help you.

WRITE

7 Write your biography. Remember to include three paragraphs, the simple past, and time expressions, and the *Useful Language* expressions (see Student's Book, p89).

CHECK

8 Do you ...

- give information from the timeline of your famous person?
- write about the events in their life in the correct order?

VOCABULARY

1 Complete the crossword. Use the pictures.

ACROSS →

DOWN ↓

2 Complete the sentences with an adjective from the box.

beautiful	cute	dangerous	heavy	large	lazy	noisy	quiet	smart	tiny	wild

1 Kodiak brown bears are very ________ animals, but their babies are ________ – they are only about 23 cm long, and they weigh only 450 g.

2 Hippos are very ________ animals. They kill a lot of people.

3 My snake doesn't make much noise. He is very ________.

4 When blue whales are born, they weigh about 2,700 kg. That's ________!

5 Male lions are ________. They sleep, and the female lions hunt.

6 African gray parrots can learn 1,000 words. They are really ________.

7 Howler monkeys are very ________. You can hear them from 4 km away!

8 Baby lions look ________, but be careful! They are ________ animals, not pets, and can attack you.

9 Oh, I love looking at photos of tigers! I think tigers are really ________ animals.

GRAMMAR IN ACTION

3 Circle the correct options in the conversation.

A [1]*Was / Were* you at school yesterday?

B No, I [2]*wasn't / weren't*. [3]*There were / I was* on a school field trip to an aquarium.

A [4]*Was it / Was there* good?

B It was fantastic! There [5]*was / were* hundreds of different fish. My favorites [6]*were / was* the parrot fish and the clown fish. [7]*There was / It was* a dolphin area, too.

A [8]*Were there / There was* any sharks?

B Yes, [9]*they were / there were*, but there [10]*wasn't / weren't* time to go and see them. The aquarium's really big!

4 Complete the text with the simple past form of the verbs in parentheses.

Last year, I [1] ________ (want) a pet, but I [2] ________ (not have) a lot of money, so I [3] ________ (go) to an animal rescue center. At the center, I [4] ________ (see) a lot of animals, but I [5] ________ (not know) which one I [6] ________ (like) best. Then I [7] ________ (hear) a noise in a corner. A tiny white cat [8] ________ (look) up at me with his big blue eyes. He was really cute. I [9] ________ (take) him home, and he [10] ________ (become) my best friend.

CUMULATIVE GRAMMAR

5 Complete the conversation with the missing words. Circle the correct options.

ISA Hi, Adela! How [1] ________ your weekend?

ADELA [2] ________ really nice, thanks! On Saturday morning I [3] ________ basketball with my team – we [4] ________ our game.

ISA No way! Your team always wins!

ADELA I know, but it [5] ________ fun to play, and we are still at the top of the league table. Anyway, on Saturday afternoon I [6] ________ to a soccer match with my cousins and my uncle – my team [7] ________ so I [8] ________ really happy!

ISA Wow! Lucky you!

ADELA Yes, then on Sunday afternoon, I [9] ________ my friends, and we went to the movies. [10] ________ a great movie! The best part was the burger we [11] ________ in a restaurant near the theater after the movie. It was delicious!

ISA Really? Where's the restaurant?

ADELA On George Street. Let's go there now!

1 a was b are c were
2 a There was b There were c It was
3 a plays b did play c played
4 a lost b losed c loses
5 a were b weren't c was
6 a was b go c went
7 a wins b won c win
8 a wasn't b aren't c was
9 a meet b meeted c met
10 a It was b It weren't c It wasn't
11 a eat b eated c ate

8 What did you find?

VOCABULARY

Places in Town

1 ☆ **Look at the photos and complete the words for places.**

1 swimming pool
2 b______ a______
3 p____ o______
4 g____
5 a__________
6 h__________
7 s__________ m____
8 p__________ l____
9 m______ t__________
10 i____ r______
11 s______ p____

2 ☆ **Look at the words in Exercise 1. How many are compound nouns?** ______

3 ☆ **Write a place from Exercise 1.**

1 I went there when I fell off my bike. hospital
2 It was cold in there, but we wore gloves and it was fun! ______
3 We went there to buy some clothes and gifts. ______
4 I went there to send a letter. ______

4 ☆☆ **Complete the text with the places from Exercise 1.**

My friend Edie lives in a small town. She always goes to the city to buy her clothes because there isn't a [1] shopping mall in her town. There's a library with a lot of good books, and a [2] ______ to send letters, but nothing else. There isn't a [3] ______ to watch movies! I live in a big town, and there's everything we need. I go to the [4] ______ to play tennis and take swimming classes at the [5] ______. In December, I love ice skating at the [6] ______ and going bowling at the [7] ______. My town also has a [8] ______ – I was there last year when I broke my arm! But my favorite place is downtown – it's an [9] ______ with a lot of fish. My dad takes me there sometimes and leaves the car in a big [10] ______. After that, I usually go skateboarding in a cool [11] ______ nearby.

Explore It!

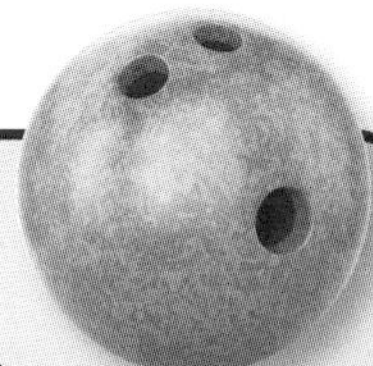

Guess the correct answer.

The first bowling alley opened in …

a London in 1889. b New York in 1840.

Find another interesting fact about a place from Exercise 1 in your country. Write a question and send it to a classmate in an email, or ask them in the next class.

READING

An Online Travel Article

1 ☆ **Look at the photos and read the article. Which photo (1–3) is the article not about?** ______

2 ☆☆ **Read the article and underline these words. Check their meaning in a dictionary and then complete the sentences.**

believe belong case ~~scuba diving~~ social media

1 I love swimming, but I prefer *scuba diving* underwater.
2 Matt has a blog and shares his videos on ______ .
3 I can't ______ it! Our birthdays are on the same day!
4 Keep the camera safe. Put it in its ______ .
5 This cap isn't mine. Does it ______ to you?

3 ☆☆ **Read the article again. Put the events in the correct order (1–8).**

a Serina saw the photos on social media. ☐
b Serina went scuba diving. 1
c The teacher put a message on social media. ☐
d The teacher looked at the photos on the camera. ☐
e Some children found a camera on the beach. ☐
f Serina lost her camera. ☐
g The children and their teacher took the camera back to school. ☐
h Thousands of people shared the message. ☐

4 ☆☆☆ **Imagine you are Serina. Write a thank-you note to Mr. Park Lee and his class. Write at least four sentences.**

Dear Mr. Park Lee and students: … ______

Lost Under the Ocean

In March 2018, a class from Mount Elementary School in Su'ao, Taiwan, went to clean the beach. They found a camera in an underwater case. They didn't know it was a camera at first because the case had things from the ocean all over it. They showed their teacher, Mr. Park Lee. He opened the case. Inside was a digital camera, and no sea water!

The class took the camera back to school. Everyone had questions: Did it work? Were there any photos in it? Did it belong to someone from Su'ao? Could they find him or her? The camera worked! Mr. Park Lee looked at the photos. They showed fish and people underwater, and streets in Japan. Mr. Lee put some photos with a message in Chinese and Japanese on social media. He asked people to share the message with their friends. In the next 24 hours, thousands of people saw the message. One of them was Serina Tsubakihara, a Japanese student. She couldn't believe it – they were her photos!

Serina went scuba diving near Okinawa, in Japan, in September 2015. She lost her camera there. It was in the ocean for more than two years and traveled 250 kilometers to Taiwan!

GRAMMAR IN ACTION

Simple Past: Questions

1 ☆ **Match questions 1–5 with answers a–e.**

1 Did Sam find his hat? [c]
2 Did the students go to the bowling alley? [ ]
3 Did you and Dana finish your project? [ ]
4 Did the ice rink close at six o'clock? [ ]
5 Did Rosa go to the movies? [ ]

a Yes, we did.
b No, she didn't.
c Yes, he did.
d Yes, it did.
e No, they didn't.

2 ☆ **Answer the questions for you. Mark (✓) the correct column.**

Yesterday, did you …	**Yes, I did.**	**No, I didn't.**
… have a big breakfast?		
… play any sports?		
… go to the movies?		
… visit a family member?		
… hang out with friends after school?		

3 ☆☆ **Write the words in the correct order to make simple past questions.**

1 Alex / to / post office / Did / go / the / ?
Did Alex go to the post office?
2 buy / a / Clara / bag / new / Did / ?
____
3 Did / time / they / good / have / a / ?
____
4 aquarium / the / Did / enjoy / you / ?
____
5 your / Did / to / parents / walk / restaurant / the / ?
____

4 ☆☆ **Write simple past questions. Do you know the answers?**

1 Shakespeare / write *Romeo and Juliet* / ?
Did Shakespeare write Romeo and Juliet?
2 Marie Curie / win a Nobel Prize / ?
____
3 Picasso / paint the *Mona Lisa* / ?
____
4 Columbus / discover Australia / ?
____
5 Emma Watson / work in the movie *Frozen* / ?
____

5 ☆☆☆ **Complete the conversation with simple past questions. Use the words in parentheses and the underlined verbs.**

MOM Hi! [1]*Did you have a good match*? (you / good match)
RYAN No, we <u>had</u> a terrible match.
MOM Oh, no! [2] ________________? (your team)
RYAN Yes. We <u>lost</u> 5–3.
MOM [3] ________________ (you / a goal)
RYAN No, I didn't <u>score</u> this time.
MOM What about Henry? [4] ________________? (he)
RYAN No, he didn't <u>play</u>. He fell off his skateboard the other day.
MOM Oh, no. [5] ________________? (he / anything)
RYAN Luckily, he didn't <u>break</u> his leg. He just hurt it.
MOM Good! [6] ________________ after the match? (you / a snack)
RYAN Yes, I <u>had</u> some chocolate. That was the best part!

VOCABULARY AND LISTENING

Personal Possessions

1 ☆ **Complete the definitions with the words in the box.**

bus pass	camera	~~headphones~~	ID card	keys	money	passport	phone	portable charger

We use …

1 *headphones* to listen to music.
2 our ________ and ________ to show who we are.
3 ________ to buy things.
4 ________ to open a door.
5 a ________ to travel on public transportation.
6 a ________ to text or talk to someone.
7 a ________ to take photos or make videos.
8 a ________ to keep our phone, tablet, or laptop working.

2 ☆☆ **Complete the text with words from Exercise 1.**

Home News **Blog** Lifestyle

I had a bad day on Tuesday. I couldn't take the bus home because I couldn't find my [1] *bus pass*. Then I couldn't get into our apartment because I didn't have my [2] ________. I used my [3] ________ to text my mom, but she was at the doctor's! I went to the library to do some homework on my laptop, but it had no battery power and the [4] ________ was at home. I had some [5] ________ in my pocket, so I bought a drink at the café.

My sister loses things, too. Last July, she lost her [6] ________ on vacation and couldn't take any photos. Then she left her [7] ________ on a bus, so she couldn't listen to music on her phone. What a family!

A Radio Interview

8.01 **3** ☆ **Look at the photos and answer the questions with your own ideas. Then listen and check your answers.**

1 What did Sabina lose? ________
2 Where did she find it/them? ________

8.01 **4** ☆☆ **Listen again. Underline and correct one mistake in each sentence.**

1 The tickets <u>weren't</u> Sabina's birthday present. *were*
2 Sabina asked her mom for help. ________
3 Sabina's friend put the envelope in the trash can. ________
4 Sabina's CD wasn't in her room. ________
5 She didn't go to the concert. ________

8.01 **5** ☆☆ **Listen again and complete the sentences.**

1 The radio show today is about ________.
2 Sabina's best friend never ________.
3 The questions helped Sabina ________.

GRAMMAR IN ACTION

Simple Past: *Wh-* Questions

1 ☆ **Complete the questions with the question words in the box.**

How much	What	When	~~Where~~	Who

1 A: *Where* did you buy your new headphones? B: Around the corner.
2 A: ______ did they cost? B: About $20.
3 A: ______ did you do last weekend? B: I went to the movies.
4 A: ______ did you go with? B: My cousin.
5 A: ______ did you get that camera? B: Last week, for my birthday.

2 ☆☆ **Write simple past questions. Then match them with answers a–e.**

1 What / you / do / last night? *e*
What did you do last night?
2 How / you / get / to school / today? ☐
______
3 Who / you / sit / with in class / yesterday? ☐
______
4 Where / you / go / last weekend? ☐
______
5 What time / get up / on Sunday? ☐
______

a My best friend.
b Really late! At 11 o'clock!
c I caught the bus.
d I went to the aquarium with my friends.
e ~~I watched TV and read a book.~~

3 ☆☆☆ **Complete questions in the conversation with the simple past. Use the answers to help you.**

ANA Hey! I went to a baseball game in Chicago.
ROB Wow! When [1] *did you go* ?
ANA I went last weekend, on Saturday.
ROB Who [2] ______ ?
ANA I went with my family and my American cousin, Martin.
ROB Who [3] ______ ?
ANA I sat with Martin. He told me everything about the game.

ROB What [4] ______ ?
ANA I ate a big burger!
ROB How [5] ______ ?
ANA We went home by bus.
ROB What time [6] ______ ?
ANA I can't remember, but I know we got home really late!

4 ☆☆☆ **Think about an interesting event you went to. Write the questions. Then answer them.**

1 where / go? *Where did you go?*
2 when / go? ______
3 who / go with? ______
4 how / feel? ______

I went ... ______

WRITING

A Blog Post

1 ☆ **Read the blog post. What problem started Bruno's bad day? (Circle) the correct answer.**

a His camera didn't work.

b His sister's camera didn't work.

c His parents' car didn't work.

HOME ABOUT ME ARCHIVE FOLLOW

BRUNO'S BIG BLOG

A Bad Day on the Weekend

1 Last Saturday, it was my sister's birthday. We gave her a camera, but it didn't work. My mom and dad decided to go to the shopping mall to exchange it, so we all got ready.

2 When we got into the car, it didn't work, so we decided to take the bus. But it got worse! It started raining, so we arrived wet and cold at the store. Awful. 😱

3 At the store, the sales assistant asked for the receipt to exchange the camera, and guess what? My parents didn't have it … so my dad went back home to get it. After an hour, he came back, and my sister got her new camera.

4 It was lunchtime, and we were really hungry, so we had lunch in the shopping mall. But when my parents wanted to pay, they couldn't find their wallets … they were at home! 😩

5 When did you have a bad day on a weekend? What happened? Tell me!

2 ☆☆ **Read the blog again. Put the events in the correct order (1–5).**

a Bruno's dad went back home. ☐

b They needed a receipt for the camera. ☐

c They took the bus to the shopping mall. ☐

d The family car didn't work. [1]

e Bruno's parents couldn't pay for lunch. ☐

3 ☆☆ **Join the sentences with *so*.**

1 It was my sister's birthday. We bought her a phone.

It was my sister's birthday, so we bought her a phone.

2 The phone didn't work. We decided to exchange it.

____

3 My dad showed the receipt. My sister got her new phone.

____

4 My parents couldn't find their wallets. They couldn't pay for lunch.

____

4 **Read the blog post again. Match topics a–e with paragraphs 1–5.**

a what happened next ☐

b what day it was and how it started [1]

c what happened later ☐

d sign off and ask questions ☐

e the end of the bad day ☐

PLAN

5 ☆☆ **Write a blog post about a bad day on the weekend. Make notes about your bad day. Think about the answers to these questions.**

When did the bad day start?
What problems did you and your family/friends have?
When and where did each problem happen?
What did you do? What did the other people do?
How did you feel?

6 **Decide what information to include in each paragraph. Use the information in Exercise 4 to help you.**

WRITE

7 ☆☆☆ **Write your blog post. Remember to include four paragraphs, the simple past for the questions at the end, and the expressions from the *Useful Language* box (see Student's Book, p101).**

CHECK

8 **Do you …**

- use a title for your blog post?
- use *so* to join ideas and explain the results?
- say how you felt on your bad day?

8 REVIEW

VOCABULARY

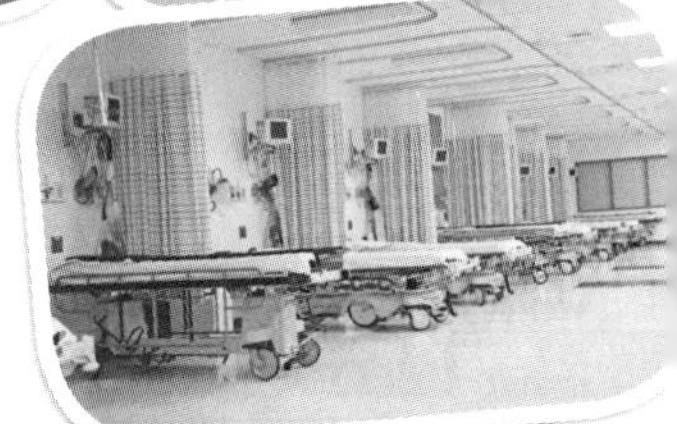

1 Where did Tim go last week? Match the sentences with the words in the box. Circle the four extra words.

aquarium	bowling alley	gym	hospital	ice rink	movie theater	parking lot	post office	shopping mall	skate park	swimming pool

1 He mailed a letter to Ben. ______
2 He saw a basketball game. ______
3 He visited his sick uncle. ______
4 He saw an amazing movie. ______
5 He bought a new pair of jeans. ______
6 He saw a lot of dolphins! ______
7 He dived into the water. ______

2 Which four places from Exercise 1 didn't Tim go to?

______ ______
______ ______

3 Complete the sentences with the words in the box.

camera	concert tickets	headphones	keys	money	passport	phone	tablet

1 I don't have any ______ to buy a drink.
2 You need your ______ to travel to a different country.
3 These ______ don't work. I can't hear anything!
4 These days, everyone has a ______ to text and call people.
5 It's easy to use a ______. You just touch the screen and it works!
6 Let's buy ______ to see Katy Perry.
7 Henry doesn't use his phone to take photos. He uses his ______.
8 Where are the ______ to open the door?

GRAMMAR IN ACTION

4 Complete the questions and short answers with the simple past. Use the verbs in parentheses.

ASHLEY [1] ______ you ______ (go) to the bowling alley yesterday, Max?
MAX Yes, I [2] ______.
ASHLEY [3] ______ you ______ (meet) Maddie there?
MAX No, I [4] ______. I was with Alex and Elena.
ASHLEY Cool! And [5] ______ you ______ (have) a good time?
MAX No, we [6] ______. Alex dropped the bowling ball on his foot!
ASHLEY Oh, no! Poor Alex! [7] ______ his parents ______ (take) him to the hospital?
MAX Yes, they [8] ______.
ASHLEY Was his foot OK? [9] ______ he ______ (break) it?
MAX No, he [10] ______. He was very lucky!

5 Write simple past questions.

1 What / you / do / last night? ____________________
2 How / your dad / get to work / this morning? ____________________
3 What time / you / get home / after school? ____________________
4 Who / you / see / yesterday? ____________________
5 Where / you / go / last weekend? ____________________
6 How / you / feel / after the exam? ____________________

CUMULATIVE GRAMMAR

6 Complete the conversation with the missing words. Circle the correct options.

BRENDA Hi, Theo. Where [1] ____________ go yesterday?

THEO I [2] ____________ to the ice rink to watch my brother.

BRENDA [3] ____________ go ice skating, too?

THEO No! I don't [4] ____________ ice skating. I think it's dangerous!

BRENDA Yes, me too! The first time I [5] ____________ it, I nearly [6] ____________ my leg!

THEO The other problem is that [7] ____________ usually a lot of people on the ice.

BRENDA Yes, you're right! [8] ____________ does your brother go?

THEO He [9] ____________ every week for about three hours. He says he wants to be the [10] ____________ ice skater in town!

BRENDA [11] ____________ you at the ice rink all day yesterday?

THEO Yes, but he [12] ____________ me out for dinner afterward!

	a	b	c
1	do you	did you	you did
2	go	went	goes
3	Did you	You	Were you
4	like	likes	liked
5	try	tries	tried
6	broke	break	breaks
7	there is	there are	there were
8	How often	How many	How
9	practice	practices	practiced
10	good	better	best
11	Did	Was	Were
12	take	took	takes

9 What makes a great vacation?

VOCABULARY

Outdoor Life

1 ☆ Look at the pictures. Complete the activities with the words and phrases in the box.

a compass a fire a map a shelter fish ~~food and water~~ fruit over a campfire plants wood

1 find *food and water*

2 pick ______

3 light ______

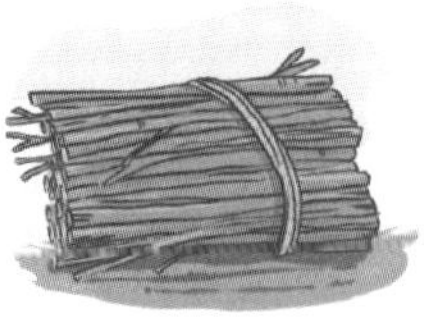

4 collect ______

5 use ______

6 cook ______

7 identify ______

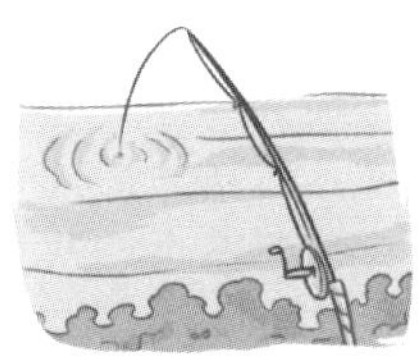

8 catch ______

9 build ______

10 read ______

2 ☆☆ Match the sentences with activities from Exercise 1.

a You do this before nighttime. You sleep there. [9]
b You need to do this before you light a fire. [ ]
c You need to find trees with apples, pears, etc. to do this. [ ]
d You use this to see where places are. [ ]
e You use this to know which way to go. [ ]
f You do this to keep warm and to cook. [ ]
g You do this when you are hungry or thirsty. [ ]

3 ☆☆ Complete the text with the correct form of the verbs from Exercise 1.

I often go to the mountains with my family. When we get there, some of us [1] *collect* wood for the fire and others [2] ______ a shelter. Next, we all go to [3] ______ water and [4] ______ fish for lunch. My dad always [5] ______ the fish over a campfire. It can take a long time to [6] ______ the fire if the wood is wet. In the afternoon, we go for a walk to [7] ______ plants. I write their names in my notebook. We sometimes [8] ______ fruit, too. We [9] ______ a compass in the mountains because it's easy to get lost!

4 ☆☆☆ Write about one or more outdoor activities that you do on vacation. Look at Exercise 3 to help you.

______

______

______

______

Explore It!

Guess the correct answer.

In this country, students have the longest summer break from school in Europe. They get 13 weeks! Which country is it?

a Italy b Germany c Portugal

Find another interesting fact about how people spend their free time in your country. Write a question and send it to a classmate in an email, or ask them it in the next class.

READING

A Pamphlet

ADVENTURE TRIPS

FIND AN ADVENTURE TRIP FOR YOU THIS SUMMER!

You'll learn new things and have a lot of fun! Join us on one of our three Adventure Trips. Read and choose the best one for you!

1. WHITE WATER KAYAKING TRIP (THREE DAYS)

Day 1: Meet your instructors and practice on white water.

Day 2: Learn how to use a compass and choose the best part of the river for your kayak.

Day 3: Follow the fast water and show your instructors how good you are!

We'll also teach you to build a shelter and help you collect wood for a campfire.

2. MOUNTAIN CLIMBING TRIP (FIVE DAYS)

Days 1–2: Walk five kilometers in the mountains each day with your guide. Learn how to identify plants and pick the right fruit to eat!

Days 3–5: Spend three days mountain climbing. Learn how to read a map and help each other.

You won't get much time to sit down! But you'll become the best mountain climber!

3. WATER AND COUNTRY TRIP (SIX DAYS)

Day 1: Learn how to catch fish in the river and then cook them over a campfire!

Days 2–3: Travel along the river in a kayak and work as a team.

Days 4–6: Leave the water to go horseback riding in the country with your guides!

You won't be bored on this trip. We'll play fun games, and you'll make good friends!

WHAT ARE YOU WAITING FOR?

CHOOSE THE BEST ADVENTURE TRIP FOR YOU!

You'll learn new sports and skills, meet new people, and have a great time!

For more information and booking details, visit our website.

We'll give you breakfast and lunch, but sometimes … you'll need to find your own dinner!

1 ★ **Read the pamphlet. Then complete the sentences with the phrases in the box.**

mountain climbing	water and country	white water kayaking

1 You can learn how to read a map and identify plants on the ________ trip.
2 You can learn how to cook your own food over a campfire on the ________ trip.
3 You can learn how to use a compass on the ________ trip.

2 ★★ **Read the pamphlet again and underline these words. Then check their meaning in a dictionary and complete the sentences.**

white water	~~river~~	follow	guides	spend

1 There are a lot of fish in that *river* .
2 The water in a river that moves very quickly is called ________ .
3 Our mountain ________ showed us some good places to climb.
4 Don't walk alone in the forest. Always ________ the instructor.
5 I need to ________ more time learning how to build a shelter!

3 ★★★ **Answer the questions.**

1 On Trip 1, who do you meet on Day 1?
your instructors
2 On which day do you use a compass?
3 On Trip 2, how far do you walk on Day 1?
4 What things can you learn on Trip 2?
5 On Trip 3, when do you do water activities?

4 ★★★ **Answer the questions with your own ideas.**

1 Which trip is the most exciting? Why?
2 Which trip is the most difficult? Why?

GRAMMAR IN ACTION
Future with *Will/Won't*

1 ☆ **Circle the correct options.**

1 The climbing trip *be* / *will be* a lot of fun. It *not will* / *won't* be boring.
2 We *won't* / *not will* make our own lunch. The instructors *make will* / *will make* it.
3 **A:** *Will you* / *You will* go on the kayaking trip?
B: Yes, *I'll* / *I will*.
4 **A:** *Will* / *Will not* the instructors make dinner for you?
B: No, they *not will* / *won't*.

2 ☆☆ **Write sentences with *I'll* or *I won't*.**

1 (✓) learn how to catch fish
I'll learn how to catch fish.
2 (✗) get bored
______
3 (✓) go in a kayak
______
4 (✗) stay for two weeks
______
5 (✓) walk six kilometers
______
6 (✓) cook food over a campfire
______

3 ☆☆ **Complete the email with the correct form of *will* and the verbs in parentheses.**

Hi Victoria,

I got back a few hours ago from my family camping trip. It was OK, but my sister says she [1] *won't go* (not go) again. She also [2] ______ (not sleep) in a shelter again! She says she [3] ______ (go) with her friends on a beach vacation because it [4] ______ (be) sunny and they [5] ______ (not do) anything all day – just sleep and swim! She's 18 now, so I guess we [6] ______ (not be) together next summer. I [7] ______ (miss) her! How was your vacation?

4 ☆☆ **Write the words in the correct order to make questions. Then answer the questions for you in your notebook.**

1 with your family / Will / this year / you / go on vacation / ?
Will you go on vacation with your family this year?
2 you / Will / see / on the weekend / your best friend / ?
______
3 tomorrow / will / you / do / What / ?
______
4 this summer / go / you / Where / will / ?
______
5 will / you / Who / next week / see / ?
______
6 go shopping / you / Will / tomorrow / ?
______

5 ☆☆☆ **You are going on one of the adventure trips from the pamphlet on p73. Make four predictions about it with *will/won't*.**

1 *I'll make new friends.*
2 ______
3 ______
4 ______
5 ______

VOCABULARY AND LISTENING

Vacations

1 ☆ Complete the accommodation words in the spidergram with the missing vowels.

VACATIONS

1 apartment
2 b__d & br__kf__st
3 c__mp__r
4 r__s__rt
5 r__cr__t__n__l v__h__cl__
6 c__b__n
7 h__t__l
8 t__nt
9 y__th h__st__l

2 ☆☆ Complete the text with words from Exercise 1.

My family and I want to go on vacation, but everyone wants to stay in a different place! My dad wants to stay in a [1]hotel ______, but my mom prefers a [2]b______ & b______. My brother loves moving from place to place, so he thinks a [3]r______ v______ is perfect! My grandma wants a little house like a [4]c______, but my dad says that's very small. My aunt showed me a picture of an amazing city [5]a______. It looks great, but I want to stay in a [6]y______ h______ – it's the best place to make friends!

A Conversation

3 ☆ Listen to the conversation. Where will the girls spend their summer vacations? Circle the correct answer. (9.01)

a in a cabin b at home c in Canada

4 ☆☆ Listen again. Match the phrases with the people in the box. (9.01)

aunt and uncle Camila ~~parents~~ Tara

1 on vacation in another country ___parents___
2 a lot of fun ______
3 at home with her parents in the summer ______
4 invites her friend to do an outdoor activity ______

5 ☆☆ Listen again and answer the questions. (9.01)

1 How will Camila's parents travel around Canada?
in an RV
2 Who will be with Camila for two weeks?
______
3 Whose parents have a vacation cabin?
______
4 What will Tara's parents do in July and August?
______
5 Why does Camila ask Tara to stay with her?
______
6 Why doesn't Tara like camping?
______

6 ☆☆☆ Your parents are going on vacation, and you will stay at home with someone else from your family. Make a spidergram with positive/negative things about this.

GRAMMAR IN ACTION

Present Continuous for Future

1 ☆ **Match 1–6 with a–f.**

1 My mom's working on Saturday. [c]
2 Are you watching the match tomorrow? [ ]
3 Mario isn't playing tennis after school. [ ]
4 Are your cousins arriving soon? [ ]
5 We're going on a field trip tomorrow. [ ]
6 How are you getting to the gym? [ ]

a We're visiting a museum.
b My dad's driving me.
c ~~She's going to a meeting~~.
d He's going to the dentist.
e No, I'm not. I'm studying.
f Yes, they are. On Sunday.

2 ☆☆ **Write sentences with the present continuous.**

1 We / go / to the beach / on the weekend
We're going to the beach on the weekend.
2 Debra / not have / a birthday party / this year
______
3 My grandparents / fly / to Italy / in August
______
4 you / have / lunch / at a restaurant / on Sunday / ?
______
5 We / not do / anything special / this weekend
______
6 How / she / get / to work / today / ?
______

3 ☆☆ **Complete the conversation with the present continuous form of the verbs in parentheses.**

CARLA What [1] *are you doing* (you / do) in the summer?
NICO In July, I [2] ______ (go) to a summer camp in the mountains.
CARLA That sounds fun! [3] ______ (you / sleep) in a tent?
NICO No, I [4] ______ (not camp). We [5] ______ (stay) in cabins.
CARLA What [6] ______ (your parents / do)?
NICO They [7] ______ (start) their vacation in August. They [8] ______ (meet) me at the summer camp, and we [9] ______ (drive) across the country in an RV.

Be Going To

4 ☆ **Underline and correct one mistake in each sentence.**

1 <u>We going</u> to visit the water park. *We're going*
2 Are you going see the new movie? ______
3 I'm not go to buy a camera. ______
4 They're going living in the country. ______
5 Mia isn't to go swimming after school. ______
6 Leo going to learn to skateboard. ______

5 ☆☆☆ **Write questions with the present continuous or *be going to*. Then answer the questions for you.**

1 What / do / this weekend? (present continuous)
What are you doing this weekend?
______
2 What / do / tonight? (present continuous)
______
______
3 What TV shows / watch / this week? (*be going to*)
______
______
4 How / celebrate / your birthday / this year? (*be going to*)
______
______

WRITING

An Email

1 ☆ **Read the email. How does Paige know Ava?**

____

2 ☆☆ **Circle the correct prepositions (1–10) in the email.**

Hi Ava,

1 Thanks for your email. I'm really excited you're coming to stay with us in New Zealand [1]*on* / (*in*) January! We'll have a great time! You'll enjoy Mission Bay and seeing our friends from elementary school again.

2 Here are the arrangements. [2]*On* / *In* Friday, Mom and I are meeting you [3]*at* / *on* the airport in Auckland. Then we're going to have a night [4]*in* / *at* home, and my dad's cooking. You're sleeping with me [5]*in* / *at* my room. We can talk about your new life in Australia and compare our schools!

3 [6]*In* / *On* Saturday, we're going to the beach. It'll be hot, so we'll go swimming. Hayley, Lily, and Ryan from our elementary school are coming, too! [7]*In* / *On* the evening, we're going to have dinner [8]*on* / *at* my favorite restaurant. Then [9]*on* / *at* Sunday, we're going to Te Urewera National Park for four days. We're staying [10]*in* / *on* a nice cabin. There are beautiful lakes and birds. What do you think?

4 It'll be great to see you again! Is there anything you would like to do? Let me know!

See you soon,

Paige XX

3 **Match topics a–d with paragraphs 1–4.**

a end the email [4]
b respond to your friend's last email [ ]
c describe the first day [ ]
d describe the weekend [ ]

4 ☆☆ **Read the email again. Are the sentences *T* (true) or *F* (false)?**

1 Ava is traveling to Auckland by car. F
2 Ava and Paige are sleeping in the same room. ____
3 They're spending one day at the beach. ____
4 They're having dinner at home on Saturday evening. ____
5 At Te Urewera National Park, they're not staying in a hotel. ____

PLAN

5 ☆☆ **Write an email to a friend from elementary school about plans for their visit. Your friend now lives in another place and is coming to stay with you. Make notes about these things for your email:**

your arrangements
things you intend to do
predictions about what will happen
the place where you are meeting them

6 ☆☆ **Decide what information to include in each paragraph. Use the information in Exercise 3 to help you.**

WRITE

7 ☆☆☆ **Write your email. Remember to include four paragraphs, *will*, *be going to*, and the present continuous for future, and expressions from the *Useful Language* box (see Student's Book, p113).**

CHECK

8 **Do you ...**

- include an arrangement and a prediction for the weekend and the week ahead?
- make predictions about what will or won't happen?
- tell your friend where you are going to meet them?

9 REVIEW

VOCABULARY

1 Circle the correct verb.

1 *catch* / *build* a shelter
2 *light* / *cook* a fire
3 *build* / *pick* fruit
4 *catch* / *light* fish
5 *use* / *cook* over a campfire
6 *collect* / *build* wood
7 *read* / *collect* a map
8 *build* / *identify* plants

2 Find nine words for accommodation in the word search. Then match them with sentences 1–9 below.

C	T	E	N	T	Y	B	E	G	F	B
A	B	R	L	H	O	C	I	J	N	E
M	C	E	O	I	U	E	O	G	C	D
P	A	S	M	K	T	G	U	B	T	&
E	I	O	E	M	H	O	T	E	L	B
R	T	R	Y	R	H	M	E	V	L	R
V	F	T	X	C	O	X	T	G	A	E
K	A	Z	C	W	S	N	A	S	A	A
N	A	P	A	R	T	M	E	N	T	K
J	O	G	B	X	E	Q	M	R	B	F
K	P	E	I	O	L	T	X	S	C	A
R	M	V	N	A	A	R	V	N	A	S
O	U	H	O	H	I	D	G	Y	S	T

1 This can be a problem in the rain. ______
2 A place where young people normally stay. ______
3 You can drive with your bed in this! ______
4 A small country house. ______
5 You can drive this. ______
6 You only stay here to sleep and eat in the morning. ______
7 This is in a building, often in a city. ______
8 An expensive one has five stars. ______
9 A ski or beach vacation destination. ______

GRAMMAR IN ACTION

3 Complete the conversation with the correct form of *will* or *won't*. Use the verbs in parentheses.

Wall | Find friends | Chat

IAN 1h ago
1 ______ (we / sleep) in tents?

GUIDE 1h ago
No, you 2 ______ (not sleep) in a tent. You 3 ______ (stay) in a resort. Every night, we 4 ______ (cook) dinner over a campfire.

IAN 1h ago
Sounds fun. What activities 5 ______ (we / do)?

GUIDE 1h ago
You 6 ______ (go) walking and climbing in the mountains. We 7 ______ (teach) you how to read a map, so you 8 ______ (not get) lost. It 9 ______ (be) fantastic. You 10 ______ (not forget) the experience, I'm sure!

4 Complete the email with the present continuous form of the verbs in parentheses.

Hi Sonia,

What 1 ______ (you / do) this summer? In July, my parents 2 ______ (work), so Paul and I 3 ______ (not plan) anything special. He 4 ______ (go) to a soccer camp, and I 5 ______ (stay) with my grandparents. Then in August we 6 ______ (fly) to Mexico for a family vacation. My parents 7 ______ (rent) an apartment at the beach, and then we 8 ______ (drive) up to the mountains in a camper. I'm very excited!

5 Write sentences about the pictures. Use the correct form of *be going to* and the phrases in the box.

climb a mountain	get on a plane	go horseback riding
play volleyball	sleep in a tent	walk in the forest

1 He ______

2 She ______

3 He ______

4 She ______

5 They ______

6 They ______

CUMULATIVE GRAMMAR

6 Complete the text with the missing words. (Circle) the correct options.

I had [1] ______ amazing vacation of my life last year. [2] ______ go? I went to Peru on [3] ______ adventure vacation! We built a shelter to sleep in and learned [4] ______ new things, like how to catch fish and find fruit to eat in the forest. We played [5] ______ sports, too. They were fun! I loved [6] ______ kayaking, but I [7] ______ horseback riding. It was frightening! I have a lot of photos. Would you like to see [8] ______?

This vacation was [9] ______ than my vacation two years ago. Now I [10] ______ a lot of new friends. At the moment, we [11] ______ emails to each other to get together this year. I can't [12] ______!

	a	b	c
1	the more	most	the most
2	Where did I	What I did	When did I
3	some	a	an
4	much	a lot	a lot of
5	an	any	some
6	going	go	do
7	wasn't enjoy	didn't enjoy	not enjoy
8	them	they	it
9	better	the best	good
10	has	had	have
11	writing	're writing	write
12	to wait	wait	waiting

EXAM TIPS: Reading Skills

Reading: Multiple Matching

You will read three short texts about three different people.
They are all about the same topic. The title tells you what the topic is. There are seven questions.
To answer the question, you need to choose the correct answer, A, B, or C.

Example:

	Tim	*Tom*	*Ted*
Which person did a lot of sports at school?	*A*	*B*	*C*

Exam Guide: Multiple Matching

- Start by reading the title of the text so you know what the topic is.
- Read all the questions carefully and underline the important words. This helps when you look for the same information in the texts.

  Example:

  Which person did a lot of sports at school?
- Now read the three texts for the first time without stopping. Maybe you see information similar to the questions, but read to the end.
- Now read the first question again. Then look at the texts to find which person says this. Maybe you remember something from one of the texts, so go to that text first to check. If not, just read from the beginning until you find what you need.
- When you find the correct answer, underline the words in the text with the same meaning as the question. Write the number of the question next to the part you underlined. Then choose your answer, A, B, or C.

  Example:

  When I was a teenager, I was on the school hockey, track and field, and swimming teams.
- Then read the next question and do the same until you finish.
- You don't lose points for a wrong answer, so always choose a letter, even if you're not sure.

REMEMBER!

When you look for the answer, remember that the words in the question are probably different from the words in the text, but the meaning is the same. So if you see a word in the text that is the same as a word in the question, it is not automatically the correct answer.

Example:

I played a lot of sports after school when I was younger.

This is **NOT** the correct answer to the example question because the meaning is different from the question.

Reading Practice: Multiple Matching

1 Underline the most important words in these questions.

1 Which person does a lot of sports on the weekend?

Which person …

2 loves trying new activities after school?

3 has a lot of online friends?

4 reads science and nature magazines on the Internet?

5 wants to study art or drama at school next year?

6 doesn't have any aunts, uncles, or cousins?

7 doesn't like living in a big city?

Tip! Underlining the most important words in the questions helps you to remember the information you need to find in the text.

2 Match words 1–10 with their opposites in the box.

after	boring	difficult	evening	finish	good	hate	late	short	~~small~~

1 big *small*

2 easy ______ 5 long ______ 8 morning ______

3 early ______ 6 start ______ 9 fun ______

4 love ______ 7 before ______ 10 bad ______

Tip! When reading the text, look for words or phrases that are opposites (often with a negative verb), or synonyms of the words in the question.

3 Read the text and match the words in bold with the synonyms (1–9).

One place on my **road** that's very popular with **young people** is the skate park. Some of my friends spend all their free time there. There is also a **big** gym near me, with some good **courses**, like swimming and dancing. **Many** of my friends **tell me** they would like to go there, too, but the **price** is too high. I **travel** to a cheaper gym, but it's not very near my house and so it's **difficult** to get to.

1 street *road* 3 large ______ 5 teenagers ______ 7 go ______ 9 classes ______

2 a lot ______ 4 say ______ 6 hard ______ 8 cost ______

4 Choose the option, A or B, that has the same meaning as the question.

0 Which person has a lot of homework to do?

(A) I spend about two hours every night on school work.

B In my school, the teachers don't usually give us much homework.

1 Which person isn't happy about their hair color?

A I have red hair, but I don't mind. It's the same as Ed Sheeran's!

B Everyone in my family has blond hair. It's boring. I want to be different.

2 Which person reads information about science on the Internet?

A There is so much interesting stuff to read online these days, especially science articles.

B I love reading my dad's science magazines. He buys them every month.

3 Which person doesn't mind getting up early in the morning?

A I have to get up at seven so I'm not late for school, but that isn't a problem.

B I'm glad when it's Saturday and I can get up late.

4 Which person thinks living in the country is boring?

A People say that the country is boring, but I think there's a lot to do.

B I'm happy I live in the city. I'm sure it's more exciting than being in a small town.

EXAM TIPS: Writing Skills

Writing: A Short Email or Note

You will write a short email or note of 25 words or more. The instructions in the test tell you exactly what you need to do.

Example:

You want to ***go to the movies*** *with* ***your friend*** *Jan on* ***Saturday****. Write an email to Jan.*

The instructions also explain three things you need to include in the text. For example:

In the email:

- **ask** Jan to **go to the movies** with you
- say **what movie** you want to see
- say **where** you can **meet**.

Exam Guide: Writing a Short Email or Note

- Read the instructions carefully and decide what kind of message is required.
- It is important to include all the points from the instructions in the text. It is also better to keep them in the same order as in the instructions.
- The text needs
  - an opening sentence
  - three sentences, one for each point
  - a sentence to close (for example a question asking your friend's opinion)
  - (in an email) your name at the end.
- When you finish, read the text again and count the number of words. If you have included all the information from the plan above, the text should be at least 25 words. If it's more, that's OK. If you haven't written 25 words, go back and check that you have included all the points and the opening and the closing sentences.

Writing: A Short Story

You will write a short story of 35 words or more. To help you there are three pictures. You write the story they show.

Exam Guide: Writing a Short Story

- Don't start writing immediately. Look at the pictures for a minute and decide what the story is about. A good way to plan a story is to think about *Who? Where? When?* and *What?*
- Give any people in the picture a name. Then write any useful vocabulary you want to use (nouns, verbs, adjectives, etc.) next to each picture.
- Decide how to start (e.g., *One day/Yesterday*). Use the past tense when you write your story.
- When you finish writing, count the words. You need to write at least 35 words.

REMEMBER!

You will receive a piece of paper to write notes or a draft. Use it to plan your writing.

Writing Practice: An Email or Note; a Short Story

1 Match the phrases from a text message with the right category A–C.

> **Tip!** Try to use different phrases for inviting and suggesting ideas.

A opening B inviting or suggesting C closing phrase

1 I'd like to see the new X-Men movie. B
2 What do you think? ____
3 Do you want to go swimming this afternoon? ____
4 Let me know soon. ____
5 Hey ____
6 Can we meet at the bus stop at seven? ____
7 Hi, Jan ____
8 We can try the new pool. ____
9 How about going to the movies on Saturday? ____

2 Order the words to make sentences from an email.

1 cheap / to / a / go / restaurant / Let's / . Let's go to a cheap restaurant.
2 want / during / Do / break / to / you / meet / the / ?
____
3 for / Why / days / we / don't / go / a few / camping / ?
____
4 what / know / Let / you / me / think / .
____
5 Tania / Hi / ,
____
6 climbing / I'd / go / again / to / like / .
____
7 my / can / tent / take / We / brother's / .
____

3 Separate the text into words and sentences. Then rewrite the email with the correct format and punctuation in your notebook.

> **Tip!** Always check your writing for spelling or punctuation.

heyjosedoyouwanttohangouttogetheronsaturdaywecangotothe newshoppingmallcanicometoyourhouseatfourletmeknowsooncarlos

Hey José,

4 Correct the spelling of these words.

1 swiming swimming
2 shoping ____
3 wich ____
4 tenis ____
5 Wenesday ____
6 tomorow ____
7 bycicle ____
8 diferent ____
9 scool ____
10 begining ____

5 Put the words in the box in the correct place in the story.

> **Tip!** Use time words like *yesterday*, *after*, and *then* to make the order of events clear. Use words like *but* and *so* to show how the events connect.

After but so Then ~~Yesterday~~

0 Yesterday Annie had a technology presentation at school, 1 ____ she got up late. 2 ____ she got to school, she saw her notes weren't in her bag. They were important, 3 ____ she called her dad and asked him to look for them. He found them in her room. 4 ____ he brought her notes to school. She was very happy.

EXAM TIPS: Listening Skills

Listening: Three-Option Multiple Choice

You will listen to five short texts. You will hear the text twice. Each text is about something different, and the question usually explains who is speaking, who they are speaking to, and what they are talking about.

Example:

You will hear ***two friends*** *talking about* ***their plans for the weekend.***

You then have to answer a question about each text, with three options, A, B, and C.

Example:

You will hear two friends talking about their plans for the weekend. ***What do they both plan to do?***

A They are ***both going*** *to a* ***basketball game.***

B They are ***both visiting*** *their* ***grandparents.***

C They are ***both going shopping*** *with* ***friends.***

You can write your answers on the question paper.

Exam Guide: Three-Option Multiple Choice

- Read the questions before you listen. Read the questions carefully because they tell you what to listen for.
- Underline the important words in the question. In the example, the most important word in the question is **both**.

  Example:

  What do they both plan to do?

  A They are both going to a basketball game.

  B They are both visiting their grandparents.

  C They are both going shopping with friends.

- When you listen the first time, try to decide what the correct answer is and circle A, B, or C. If you're not sure, don't worry. The second time you listen, you can check your first answer or decide for the first time.
- Sometimes the first time you listen, you hear that one answer is definitely wrong. Cross it out. Then the second time you listen, just focus on the other two possible answers.
- Always give an answer, even if you don't know which one is correct. You don't lose points for a wrong answer.
- When you have heard one text twice, don't spend a lot of time thinking about it. Focus on the next listening text when it starts.

REMEMBER!

You will usually hear the people talk about all the possible answers in some way, but this is a "trap." Only one answer is correct.

To avoid traps, listen carefully to every word. You will hear negative verbs (for example: *I'm not visiting my grandparents this weekend*) or things which are similar but not the same as the correct answer (for example: *I'm going shopping with my sister on Saturday*).

Listening Practice: Three-Option Multiple Choice

E.01 **1 Listen to the sentences. Mark (✓) if they are affirmative or (✗) if they are negative.**

1 ______ 2 ______ 3 ______ 4 ______ 5 ______ 6 ______

E.02 **2 Is the meaning of the sentences you hear the same as sentences 1–6? Write *Y* (yes) or *N* (no).**

1 I decided not to buy the shirt because I didn't like the color. ______
2 It takes Martin a quarter of an hour to walk home. ______
3 It was sunny yesterday. ______
4 Martin is flying to Spain on vacation. ______
5 Paula's sister has dark hair. ______
6 The teacher tells Eric to do his homework again. ______

E.03 **3 Read sentences 1–6. Then listen and correct the information that is different.**

1 Alex went to Scotland by bus last year. ______
2 Laia is going to stay in a hotel with her grandparents. ______
3 Donna usually goes to the bowling alley on the weekend. ______
4 Harry's mom lost her bus pass yesterday. ______
5 Last week, Megan saw a show about bears on TV. ______
6 Tom has a basketball game on Saturday morning. ______

E.04 **4 Listen and choose the correct option, A or B. You will hear each text twice.**

1 The teacher has a problem with Sarah's homework because …
A she made a lot of mistakes.
B she did the wrong page.

2 What's the weather like today?
A It's cold and wet.
B It's cloudy and warm.

3 What did Corrin and Vanessa do today?
A They went out for a meal.
B They went out with school friends.

4 How did Nico get home after the concert?
A He caught the last bus.
B His friend's dad gave him a ride.

5 What did Ollie buy at the shopping mall?
A a new gym bag
B some new sweatpants

6 What does Chloe's mother want her to do?
A go shopping
B clean her room

GRAMMAR REFERENCE

STARTER

Subject Pronouns

Singul	Plural
I	we
you	you
he / she / it	they

- We use a subject pronoun before a verb.
  She is Brazilian. (NOT ~~*Is Brazilian*~~.)
- The singular and plural form of ***you*** is the same.

Possessive Adjectives

Singular	Plural
my	our
your	your
his / her / its	their

- We use possessive adjectives to show that something belongs to somebody. We always use possessive adjectives with a noun.
  Our house is big. *Their school is fun.*

Verb *To Be*

Affirmative	Negative
I'm Mexican.	I'm not Mexican.
You're Mexican.	You aren't Mexican.
He's / She's / It's Mexican.	He / She / It isn't Mexican.
We're Mexican.	We aren't Mexican.
You're Mexican.	You aren't Mexican.
They're Mexican.	They aren't Mexican.

Questions	Short Answers	
	Affirmative	Negative
Am I Mexican?	Yes, I am.	No, I'm not.
Are you Mexican?	Yes, you are.	No, you aren't.
Is he / she / it Mexican?	Yes, he / she / it is.	No, he / she / it isn't.
Are we Mexican?	Yes, we are.	No we aren't.
Are you Mexican?	Yes, you are.	No, you aren't.
Are they Mexican?	Yes, they are.	No, they aren't.

- We use **verb *to be*** to identify or describe something.
  They're red. *He's Spanish.* *It's good.*
- We usually use contractions in conversation.
  We're from Canada. *She's ten.*
- We change the word order in questions; we put ***to be*** before the subject.
  Is David OK? *Are you from London?*
  (NOT ~~*You are from London*~~*?*)
- We usually reply with short answers.
  A: *Is it blue?* ***B:*** *Yes, it is.* ***A:*** *Is it red?* ***B:*** *No, it isn't.*

Question Words

- We use ***what*** to ask for information.
  What is your favorite color?
- We use ***where*** to ask about places.
  Where are you from?
- We use ***when*** to ask about time.
  When is your birthday?
- We use ***how old*** to ask about age.
  How old is your father?
- We use ***who*** to ask about people.
  Who is your best friend?

Whose + Possessive Pronouns

	Singular	Plural
Whose book is this?	It's mine.	It's ours.
	It's yours.	It's yours.
	It's his / hers.	It's theirs.

- ***Whose*** asks about possession or ownership.
- We often use possessive pronouns to answer ***whose*** questions. They help us to avoid repeating information.
  Whose pencil is this? It's mine. (instead of *It's my pencil.*)
  We don't use ***its*** as a possessive pronoun.
  Whose book is this? (NOT ~~*It's its*~~.)
- We use ***this*** (singular) and ***these*** (plural) to talk about things that are near.
  This is my pencil. *These are my books.*
- We use ***that*** (singular) and ***those*** (plural) to talk about things that are not near.
  That is my bag. *Those are my pens.*

Imperatives

Affirmative	Negative
Stand up!	Don't stand up!
Open the book!	Don't open the book!

- We use the imperative to give orders or instructions.
  Come here, please.
- We use ***don't*** to form the negative.
  Don't write in your textbook.

Subject Pronouns and Possessive Adjectives

1 Complete the sentences with the correct subject pronouns and possessive adjectives.

1 My best friend Maria is from Paris. _She_ 's French. _Her_ house is very big!

2 My name's Pablo. ______ 'm from Ecuador. I'm in ______ classroom.

3 Berat and Ahmet are Turkish. ______ 're from Istanbul. These are ______ books.

4 My English teacher is Mr. Jones. ______ 's from New York. ______ classes are fun!

5 Susie, ______ 're my friend! Today is ______ birthday! Happy birthday!

Verb *To Be*

2 Circle the correct form of the verb *to be*.

Hi, my name [1] (is) / *are* Alicia. My favorite color [2] *is* / *are* blue. I [3] *are* / *am* 12 years old. My best friends [4] *is* / *are* Laura and Eva. They [5] *isn't* / *aren't* from Mexico like me. They are from China. We [6] *is* / *are* in school today.

3 Match questions 1–6 with answers a–f.

1 Are you hungry?	d	a Yes, we are.
2 Is your school big?		b No, she isn't.
3 Is he in the room?		c No, it isn't.
4 Is she from China?		d ~~Yes, I am!~~
5 Are we 12 years old?		e No, they aren't.
6 Are they Canadian?		f Yes, he is.

Question Words

4 Complete the conversation with the words in the box.

How old When ~~Where~~ Who

A: Hi, Mateo. [1] _Where_ are you from?
B: I'm from Argentina.
A: [2] ______ are you?
B: I'm 13.
A: [3] ______ 's your birthday?
B: It's in February.
A: [4] ______ 's your favorite singer?
B: Taylor Swift. She's great!

Whose + Possessive Pronouns

5 Write the words in the correct order to make questions. Then complete the answers with the correct possessive pronouns.

1 book / is / Whose / this /?
Whose book is this?
It's my book. It's _mine._.

2 is / this / Whose / dictionary / ?
______
It's your dictionary. It's ______.

3 calculator / is / Whose / that / ?
______
It's his calculator. It's ______.

4 these / pens / Whose / are / ?
______
They're her pens. They're ______.

5 notebooks / those / are / Whose / ?
______
They're our notebooks. They're ______.

6 desks / are / Whose / those / ?
______
They're their desks. They're ______.

Imperatives

6 Write the affirmative or the negative.

1 Write on the paper.
Don't write on the paper.

2 ______
Don't use your calculator.

3 Use your dictionary.
______

4 ______
Don't listen to your teacher.

5 Close the door.
______

6 ______
Don't do your homework.

GRAMMAR REFERENCE

UNIT 1

To Have: Affirmative and Negative

Affirmative		Negative	
I have	short hair.	I don't have	brown eyes.
You have		You don't have	
He / She / It has		He / She / It doesn't have	
We have		We don't have	
You have		You don't have	
They have		They don't have	

- We use ***have*** to talk about possession.
  I have five cousins. *She has 12 grandchildren.*
- To make the negative, we put ***don't / doesn't*** before ***have***.
  We don't have a big house.
  She doesn't have a sister.

Possessive *'s*

Singular Nouns	Plural Nouns	Irregular Plural Nouns
Beth's computer	His parents' house	The women's soccer team
Carlos's bike	The students' books	The children's favorite toy

- We use **apostrophe + *s*** to indicate possession.
  This is Andrea's notebook.
- We put ***'s*** after a singular name or noun and ***s'*** after a plural name or noun.
  Carla's phone (NOT ~~*The phone of Carla*~~)
  His grandparents' house (NOT ~~*The house of his grandparents*~~)
- Some plural nouns are irregular. To show possession, we add ***'s***.
  men's, people's, children's
- When two people possess something, we use ***'s*** after the second noun.
  Paul and Amy's family
  Mom and Dad's computer

To Have: Questions

Question		Short Answers	
		Affirmative	Negative
Do	I have a blue book? you have a blue book? we have a blue book? you have a blue book? they have a blue book?	Yes, I do. Yes, you do. Yes, we do. Yes, you do. Yes, they do.	No, I don't. No, you don't. No, we don't. No, you don't. No, they don't.
Does	he / she / it have a blue book?	Yes, he / she / it does.	No, he / she / it doesn't.

- We use ***do*** + **subject** + ***have*** + **object** in questions.
  Do you have a bike? *Does your mom have a cousin?*
- In spoken English, we reply to questions with short answers.
  A: *Do you have a brother?*
  B: *Yes, I do.* (NOT *Yes, I do* ~~*have*~~.) / *No, I don't.* (NOT *No, I don't* ~~*have*~~.)

How Many … Do You Have?

- We use ***how many*** + **object** + ***do*** + **subject** + ***have*** in questions to ask about the number of things.
  A: *How many cousins does he have?* ***B:*** *He has 30.*
  A: *How many brothers and sisters do you have?* ***B:*** *I have two sisters. I don't have a brother.*

GRAMMAR PRACTICE

To Have: Affirmative and Negative

1 Complete the sentences with the correct affirmative form of *to have*.

1 I ___have___ a dictionary.
2 We ______ six red pens.
3 My aunt ______ three sisters.
4 Mom and Dad ______ a mobile home.
5 You ______ 12 cousins.
6 Our house ______ five bedrooms.

2 Write the sentences in the negative.

1 I have two brothers.
I don't have two brothers.
2 We have a new teacher at school.
______
3 My grandma has ten grandchildren.
______
4 My best friends have green uniforms.
______
5 He has a bike.
______
6 We have a big house.
______

3 Look at the chart and complete the text with the correct form of *to have*.

	Javier	Rosa
sisters	1	2
brothers	0	1
cousins	2	2
bike	1	0
computer	0	0

Javier [1] ___has___ one sister; her name is Cecilia. He [2] ______ any brothers. He [3] ______ a blue bike. Rosa [4] ______ two sisters and one brother. She [5] ______ a bike. Javier and Rosa [6] ______ two cousins. They [7] ______ a computer.

Possessive *'s*

4 Write *s'* or *'s* in the correct places in the sentences.

1 My ~~dad~~ bike is gray and my ~~uncle~~ bike is black.
dad's and my uncle's
2 Natalia favorite color is green and her sister is blue.
______
3 His grandparent house is big, but his parent house is small.
______
4 Myra family are from India, and Diego family are from Spain.
______
5 Vero and Isaac English books are red. Their mom book is yellow.
______

To Have: Questions

5 Write the words in the correct order to make questions. Then match them with answers a–e.

1 have / I / Do / book / an / English / ?
Do I have an English book? ___d___
2 bike / a / Do / blue / have / you / ?
______ ___
3 pets / Alex / Does / two / have / ?
______ ___
4 Catalina / brother / have / a / Does / ?
______ ___
5 big / have / house / Do / they / a / ?
______ ___

a Yes, he does. He has two cats.
b No, she doesn't. She has a sister.
c Yes, they do.
~~d Yes, you do.~~
e No, I don't. It's green.

How Many ... Do You Have?

6 Write questions with *How many* for the answers.

1 How many cousins do you have?
I have three cousins.
2 ______
My mom has two nephews.
3 ______
We have 20 teachers at our school.
4 ______
My best friend has two sisters.
5 ______
We have four subjects on Friday.

GRAMMAR REFERENCE UNIT 2

Simple Present: Affirmative and Negative

Affirmative	
I live	in Lima.
You live	
He / She / It lives	
We / You / They live	
Negative	
I don't live	in Lima.
You don't live	
He / She / It doesn't live	
We / You / They don't live	

- We use the simple present to talk about facts, habits, and routines.
  I speak Chinese. He goes to school.
  They study English.
- We form the negative of the simple present with the **subject** + ***don't*** / ***doesn't*** + **infinitive**.
  They don't speak English.
- We use ***doesn't*** in the third person (*he* / *she* / *it*).
  He doesn't do his homework.

Spelling: Third Person

- The third person form (*he* / *she* / *it*) of the simple present ends in ***-s***.
  eat – he eats read – she reads
- With verbs ending in **consonant** + ***y***, we replace the ***y*** with ***-ies*** for the *he* / *she* / *it* forms.
  study – she studies
- The *he* / *she* / *it* form of verbs ending in ***-ss***, ***-sh***, ***-ch***, ***-x***, and ***-o*** is ***-es***.
  kiss – she kisses relax – he relaxes
  finish – he finishes go – she goes
  teach – she teaches
- Some verbs have an irregular spelling in the third person.
  have – she has be – he is

Adverbs of Frequency

never sometimes often usually always

0% ⟵⟶ 100%

- Adverbs of frequency say how often we do something. They go after the verb *to be* but before all other verbs.
  She's always happy. He sometimes checks his phone in the afternoons.
  We usually do homework after school.
- With ***never***, we always use an affirmative verb.
  I never go out with my friends on Monday.
- In questions, adverbs of frequency always come after the subject.
  Do you always have English class on Wednesday?

Simple Present: Questions

Questions		Short Answers	
		Affirmative	**Negative**
Do	I like oranges? you like oranges?	Yes, I do. Yes, you do.	No, I don't. No, you don't.
Does	he / she / it like oranges?	Yes, he / she / it does.	No, he / she / it doesn't.
Do	we like oranges? you like oranges? they like oranges?	Yes, we do. Yes, you do. Yes, they do.	No, we don't. No, you don't. No, they don't.

- We form simple present ***Yes/No*** questions with ***do/does*** + **subject** + **infinitive**.
  Do you brush your teeth in the morning? Does she go to bed at 9 p.m.?
- We use short answers with ***do/does***. We don't repeat the main verb.
  A: *Do you often go to school by car?* ***B:*** *Yes, I do.*
  A: *Does he live in London?* ***B:*** *No, he doesn't.*

Wh- Questions

Question Word	*Do/Does*	Subject	Verb
Who	do	you	live (with)?
What time	does	the party	start?
Where	does	she	live?
What	does	his dad	do?
When	do	they	play?

- We form ***Wh-*** questions with a **question word** + ***do/does*** + **subject** + **verb**.
  What time do you go to bed? (NOT ~~*What time you go to bed*~~?)
  Where does he go to school?
- We also use the question ***How often … ?*** to ask about frequency.
  How often do you play video games?

GRAMMAR PRACTICE

Simple Present: Affirmative and Negative

1 Write the words in the correct order to make sentences.

1 I / every / day / wake / up / at / 7 p.m.
I wake up at 7 p.m. every day.
2 gets / up / takes / a / Antonio / shower / when / he
____
3 have / homework / Isa / Mondays / doesn't / on
____
4 don't / brothers / My / at / 8:30 p.m. / to / bed / go
____
5 lunch / school / We / have / at
____
6 my / with / homework / helps / My / dad / me
____

2 Complete the text with the simple present form of the verbs in parentheses.

On Saturday mornings, Chloe [1] gets up (get up) at 9 a.m. She [2] _______ (take) a shower and [3] _______ (brush) her teeth. Then she [4] _______ (get dressed) and [5] _______ (have) her favorite breakfast: toast and fruit juice. She [6] _______ (not see) her dad on Saturday mornings because he [7] _______ (go) to work.

At 10 a.m., she [8] _______ (go) to see her best friends, Grace and Ella. They [9] _______ (not live) near Chloe. She [10] _______ (go) on the bus to see them. Chloe [11] _______ (stay) at their house for about two hours. Then she [12] _______ (get) the bus to her grandma's house. She [13] _______ (visit) her grandma on Saturdays because she [14] _______ (not see) her during the week.

Adverbs of Frequency

3 Circle the correct options.

1 I _____ early in the morning.
(a) usually get up b get up usually
2 I _____ sports on the weekend.
a play often b often play
3 I _____ lunch with my sister at school.
a sometimes have b have sometimes
4 I _____ my homework in the evening.
a do always b always do
5 I _____ burgers for dinner.
a never eat b eat never

Simple Present: Questions

4 Complete the questions and answers. Use the verbs in parentheses.

1 Do you play tennis on the weekend? (play)
No, I don't.
2 _______ your cousin _______ to your school? (go)
Yes, he _______! He's in my class.
3 _______ your parents _______ Spanish? (speak)
No, they _______.
4 _______ you often _______ your phone? (check)
Yes, I _______.
5 _______ your aunt _______ in the United States? (live)
No, she _______.
6 _______ your sister _______ her school uniform? (like)
Yes, she _______.

Wh- Questions

5 Complete the questions with the words in the box.

How often	What	What time	~~When~~	Where	Who

1 When do you go to school?
2 _______ do your aunt and uncle live?
3 _______ does your dad do?
4 _______ do you walk to school with?
5 _______ do you have exams at school?
6 _______ does your mom get up?

6 Match the answers (a–f) with the questions in Exercise 5.

a My best friend. 4
b From Monday to Friday. ___
c In front of my house! ___
d Every month! ___
e He's an English teacher! ___
f At seven o'clock during the week and eight o'clock on the weekend. ___

GRAMMAR REFERENCE

UNIT 3

Can for Ability and Permission

Affirmative		Negative	
I	can play the piano.	I	can't play the piano.
You		You	
He / She / It		He / She / It	
We		We	
You		You	
They		They	

- We use ***can*** to express ability or permission.
  He can play the guitar. (ability)
  Dad says we can play video games tonight. (permission)
- ***Can*** is the same in all forms. The *he/she/it* form doesn't end in ***-s***.
  She can speak Portuguese.
- We always use the infinitive without ***to*** after ***can***.
  They can go to school.
  (NOT *~~They can to go to school~~.*)

Can: Questions

Yes/No Questions	Short Answers	
	Affirmative	Negative
Can I go?	Yes, I can.	No, I can't.
Can you go?	Yes, you can.	No, you can't.
Can he / she / it go?	Yes, he / she / it can.	No, he / she / it can't.
Can we go?	Yes, we can.	No, we can't.
Can you go?	Yes, you can.	No, you can't.
Can they go?	Yes, they can.	No, they can't.

- We change the word order when we form questions. We don't use ***do/does***.
  Can you use your dictionary at school?
  (NOT *~~Do you can use your dictionary at school~~?*)
- We use the adverbs ***very well***, ***well***, ***quite well***, ***not very well***, ***badly***, or ***not at all*** to describe how we are able to do things.
  A: *Can you play the guitar?* **B:** *Yes, but not very well.*

Verb Forms: *(Don't) Like, Don't Mind, Love, Hate + -ing*

- We use the ***-ing*** form of the verb after ***like***, ***don't like***, ***don't mind***, ***love***, and ***hate***.
  She loves reading books. (NOT *She loves ~~read~~ books.*)
  I don't mind going to school. (NOT *I don't mind ~~go~~ to school.*)
- We can also use nouns after these verbs.
  They don't mind geography, but they love history.

Object Pronouns

Subject Pronoun	I	you	he	she	it	we	you	they
Object Pronoun	me	you	him	her	it	us	you	them

- We use object pronouns after some verbs and prepositions.
  She meets my sister and me after school every day. – She meets us after school every day.
  I usually have lunch with my friends. – I usually have lunch with them.
- For animals and things, we use ***it*** (singular) and ***them*** (plural).
  Don't feed the bird! – Don't feed it!
  Do you read books? – Do you read them?
- We can also put an object pronoun after ***like***, ***don't like***, ***don't mind***, ***love***, and ***hate***.
  This is my new book. Do you like it? (NOT *~~Do you like~~?*)
  I don't like Mondays. I hate them.

Can for Ability and Permission

1 Write sentences with *can*. Then write *A* (ability) or *P* (permission).

1 Daniel / sing / very well
Daniel can sing very well. *A*

2 My dad / speak / French

3 I / use / my dad's / computer / in the evening

4 My brother / dance / well

5 Harry / play / the guitar well

6 You / use my / phone

2 Change the sentences in Exercise 1 to the negative.

1 *Daniel can't sing very well.*
2
3
4
5
6

Can: Questions

3 Look at the chart and write questions and answers about Alberto and Sara.

	Alberto	Sara
take good photos	✔	✘
paint well	✘	✔
dance salsa	✔	✘

1 *Can Alberto take good photos?* *Yes, he can.*
2
3
4
5
6

Verb Forms: (*Don't*) *Like*, *Don't Mind*, *Love*, *Hate* + *-ing*

4 Complete the text with the words in parentheses.

My sister [1] *loves going* (love / go) to school.
She [2] ___ (like / study). I'm different!
I [3] ___ (love / see) my friends at school.
I [4] ___ (not mind / learn) new things,
but I [5] ___ (not like / take) exams and
I [6] ___ (hate / get up) early every day!

Object Pronouns

5 Match questions 1–5 with answers a–e. Then circle the correct object pronouns.

1 Do you like listening to your teacher? *b*
2 Does your brother talk a lot?
3 Do you love hanging out with your friends?
4 Can your friends help you and your sister?
5 Do you always go to judo classes?

a Yes, he does, but I don't listen to *it* / *him*.
b Yes, I love listening to *me* / (*her*).
c Yes, and my cousin comes to classes with *him* / *me*.
d Yes, I do. I meet *them* / *it* every day.
e No, they can't help *us* / *you*.

6 Rewrite the sentences with the object pronouns in the box.

her him it them ~~them~~ us

1 I like hanging out with my friends.
I like hanging out with them.

2 I can't find my pen.

3 I like my aunt.

4 They can't see you or me.

5 I love chatting online with my cousin, David!

6 I visit my grandparents on Sundays.

GRAMMAR REFERENCE UNIT 4

Countable and Uncountable Nouns

- Countable nouns can be counted individually. They have a singular and a plural form.
  one apple – two apples   *one book – three books*
- Uncountable nouns can't be counted individually. They don't have a plural and are always singular.
  bread (NOT ~~*a bread*~~)   *milk* (NOT ~~*a milk*~~)   *homework* (NOT ~~*a homework*~~)   *music* (NOT ~~*a music*~~)

A/An, Some/Any

	Singular Countable	Plural Countable	Uncountable
Affirmative	I have an orange.	I have some tomatoes.	I have some chocolate.
Negative	I don't have an orange.	I don't have any tomatoes.	I don't have any chocolate.
Question	Do you have an orange?	Do you have any tomatoes?	Do you have any chocolate?

- We use ***a*** with singular countable nouns.
  a banana   *a cat*   *a snack*
- We use ***an*** with singular countable nouns when the noun starts with a vowel sound.
  an orange   *an uncle*
- We use ***some*** and ***any*** when we don't know a quantity or it's not important.
- We use ***some*** and ***any*** with plural countable nouns. ***Some*** is usually used in affirmative sentences and ***any*** in negative sentences and questions.
  We need some apples.   *He doesn't have any tomatoes.*   *Do we have any carrots?*
- We also use ***some*** and ***any*** with uncountable nouns. ***Some*** is usually used in affirmative sentences, and ***any*** in negative sentences and questions.
  We need some juice.   *Marta doesn't have any water.*   *Do we have any rice?*

There Is/Isn't, There Are/Aren't

	Singular	Plural
Affirmative	There's a quiz today.	There are some eggs on the table.
Negative	There isn't a quiz today.	There aren't any eggs on the table.
Questions	Is there a quiz today?	Are there any eggs on the table?
Short Answers	Yes, there is. No, there isn't.	Yes, there are. No, there aren't.

- We use ***there is*** with singular countable and uncountable nouns.
  There is a school.
  There is some cheese. (NOT *There ~~are~~ some cheese.*)
- We use ***there are*** with plural countable nouns.
  There are some potatoes.   *There are four pizzas.*
- In questions and negatives we usually use ***any*** with plural countable and uncountable nouns.
  Are there any bananas?   *Is there any milk?*
  There aren't any burgers.   *There isn't any bread.*
- In informal English we can use the contraction ***there's***, but we don't use a contraction for ***there are***.

Much/Many, A Lot Of

	Countable Plural	Uncountable
Affirmative	There are a lot of eggs.	There's a lot of cheese.
Negative	There aren't many eggs.	There isn't much cheese.
Questions	How many eggs are there?	How much cheese is there?

- We use ***much***, ***many***, and ***a lot of*** to express quantity.
- We use ***much*** in negative sentences with uncountable nouns.
  There isn't much water.
- We use ***many*** in negative sentences with countable nouns.
  There aren't many tomatoes.
- We use ***a lot of*** in affirmative sentences with plural countable and uncountable nouns to describe a big quantity of something.
  There are a lot of vegetables.   *We have a lot of rice.*
- We use ***how many*** with plural countable nouns and ***how much*** with uncountable nouns to ask about quantity.
  How many carrots are there?   *How much juice do you have?*

GRAMMAR PRACTICE

Countable and Uncountable Nouns

1 Circle the correct options.

1 I have an *apple* / *oranges* in my bag.
2 Alba has some *potato* / *meat* for lunch.
3 I have a *banana* / *bread*.
4 He doesn't have an *cheese* / *egg* for breakfast.
5 We don't have any *chocolate* / *carrot*.
6 They have some *pear* / *milk*.

A/An, Some/Any

2 Complete the sentences with *a*, *an*, *some*, or *any*.

1 We need _some_ milk and _some_ eggs.
2 I have ______ apple and ______ cheese for lunch.
3 Do you have ______ oranges, Mom? I want to make ______ orange juice.
4 We can't make a cake! We don't have ______ eggs!
5 I want to make a sandwich. I need ______ tomato and ______ egg.
6 Let's buy ______ bottle of soda and ______ fruit at the supermarket.

There Is/Isn't, There Are/Aren't

3 Complete the conversation with the correct form of *there is* / *there are*.

A: Let's make a salad!
B: [1] _Are there_ any tomatoes?
A: Yes, [2] ______, but [3] ______ any onions.
B: OK, that's not a problem. [4] ______ some cheese, and [5] ______ ten carrots.
A: I don't want ten carrots in my salad! Let's make spaghetti!
B: Sorry! [6] ______ any pasta!

4 Write sentences about the food and drink words in the box. Use the correct form of *there is* / *there are* and *some* or *any*.

apples ✔ bread ✘ carrots ✔ eggs ✘ water ✔ bananas ✘

1 _There are some apples._
2 ______
3 ______
4 ______
5 ______
6 ______

Much/Many, A Lot Of

5 Circle the correct options. Then match questions 1–5 with answers a–f.

1 How *much* / *many* fruit do you eat every day? [e]
2 How *much* / *many* people are there in your family? [ ]
3 Do you spend *much* / *many* time checking your phone? [ ]
4 How *many* / *much* snacks do you have every day? [ ]
5 How *much* / *many* water do you drink at home? [ ]
6 Are there *much* / *many* bottles of soda in your fridge? [ ]

a There are seven: I have a lot of brothers and sisters!
b About two liters a day – more if I play tennis.
c There aren't any. We only drink water and milk at home.
d No! I don't have much time to look at it!
e ~~I eat an apple every morning.~~
f I don't eat any! I'm too busy.

GRAMMAR REFERENCE

Present Continuous: Affirmative and Negative

Affirmative		Negative	
I'm	eating dinner.	I'm not	eating dinner.
You're		You're not	
He's / She's / It's		He's / She's / It's not	
We're		We're not	
You're		You're not	
They're		They're not	

- We use the present continuous to talk about actions in progress at the time of speaking.
  You are reading this sentence.
- For the affirmative, we use **subject** + ***to be*** + **verb** + ***-ing***.
  The dog is sleeping. *The children are playing.*
- For the negative, we put ***not*** after ***to be***.
  She is not (isn't) downloading songs.

Present Continuous: Questions

(Question Word)	*To Be*	Subject	Verb + *-ing*
-	Am	I	reading?
-	Are	you	thinking?
-	Is	he / she / it	sleeping?
-	Are	we / you / they	learning?
What	are	you	doing?
Where	is	she	going?

Short Answers	
Affirmative	**Negative**
Yes, I am.	No, I'm not.
Yes, you are.	No, you aren't.
Yes, he / she / it is.	No, he / she / it isn't.
Yes, we / you / they are.	No, we / you / they aren't.

- To form questions, we use ***to be*** + **subject** + **verb** + ***-ing***.
  Are you listening?
- We don't use the **verb** + ***-ing*** in short answers.
  Yes, I am. (NOT *Yes, I am ~~listening~~.*)
- We form information questions with the ***Wh-*** question word before *be*.
  Who are you talking to? *What are they doing?*

Spelling: *-ing* Form

- With most verbs, we add ***-ing*** to the infinitive.
  eat – eating *read – reading* *think – thinking*
- For verbs ending in ***-e***, we remove the ***-e*** and add ***-ing***.
  write – writing *have – having* *give – giving*
- For verbs ending in a vowel and a consonant, we double the final consonant and add ***-ing***.
  stop – stopping *shop – shopping*
  plan – planning

Simple Present and Present Continuous

- We use the simple present to talk about facts, habits, and routines.
  Red and yellow make orange.
  I read a lot of books.
  He usually wears boots.
- We use the present continuous to talk about actions in progress at the time of speaking.
  I read a lot of books. At the moment, I'm reading a really good one.
  He usually wears boots, but he's wearing sneakers today.
- Some verbs are not usually used in the continuous form: ***hate***, ***know***, ***like***, ***love***, ***need***, ***remember***, ***think***, ***understand***, ***want***.
  I like that song. (NOT *I'm ~~liking~~ that song.*)
- We use expressions like ***at the moment*** and ***right now*** with the present continuous.
  He's playing video games at the moment.

GRAMMAR PRACTICE

UNIT 5

Present Continuous: Affirmative and Negative

1 Write the *-ing* form of the verbs.

1 eat ______ eating ______
2 write ______
3 chat ______
4 play ______
5 swim ______
6 have ______

2 Complete the sentences with the present continuous form of the verbs in the box.

chat	get dressed	have	listen	~~read~~	use

1 Luis ______ is reading ______ a book.
2 My grandparents ______ their dinner.
3 The teacher ______ to our stories.
4 My mom ______ to go to a party this evening.
5 You ______ my computer in school today.
6 I ______ with my friends online.

3 Rewrite the sentences in Exercise 2 in the negative form of the present continuous. Use contractions.

1 Luis isn't reading a book. ______
2 ______
3 ______
4 ______
5 ______
6 ______

Present Continuous: Questions

4 Complete the questions with the present continuous form of the verbs in parentheses. Then write the short answers.

1 ______ Are ______ you ______ doing ______ (do) your homework?
Yes, ______ I am ______.
2 ______ your sister ______ (read) a book?
No, ______.
3 ______ your uncle ______ (make) dinner?
Yes, ______.
4 ______ we ______ (have) sandwiches for lunch?
No, ______.
5 ______ my grandparents ______ (watch) TV?
No, ______.
6 ______ the cat ______ (sleep) on my bed?
Yes, ______.

Simple Present and Present Continuous

5 Complete the rules. Write *present continuous* or *simple present*.

1 To talk about facts, routines, and habits, we use the ______.
2 To talk about an action in progress at the time of speaking, we use the ______.
3 We use *always*, *often*, *usually*, *sometimes,* and *never* with the ______.
4 We use *right now* and *at the moment* with the ______.

6 Circle the correct options.

My name is Carolina. At the moment, I'm on vacation and I [1]*help* / *'m helping* my dad. We have a big yard, and he usually [2]*works* / *is working* all the time, so he's tired on the weekend. Now he is on vacation, too. I [3]*like* / *'m liking* flowers, and we usually [4]*collect* / *are collecting* some to put in the house. Right now, my dad [5]*paints* / *is painting* the fence and, of course, my brother [6]*watches* / *is watching* us do all the work!

Comparatives

Comparatives	
Short Adjectives *smart*	add *-er*: *smarter*
Short Adjectives Ending in Vowel + Consonant *big*	double the final consonant and add *-er*: *bigger*
Adjectives Ending in *-e* *safe*	add *-r*: *safer*
Adjectives Ending in *-y* *easy*	remove the *-y* and add *-ier*: *easier*
Long Adjectives *interesting*	put ***more*** before the adjective: *more interesting*
Irregular Adjectives *good* *bad*	 *better* *worse*

- We use comparative adjectives to compare one thing with another. We use the **verb *to be*** + **a comparative adjective** + ***than***.
  Daniel is taller than his father.

Superlatives

Superlatives	
Short Adjectives *smart*	add *-est* *smartest*
Short Adjectives Ending in Vowel + Consonant *big*	double the final consonant and add *-est*: *biggest*
Adjectives Ending in *-e* *safe*	add *-est*: *safest*
Adjectives Ending in *-y* *easy*	remove the *-y* and add *-iest*: *easiest*
Long Adjectives *interesting*	put ***most*** before the adjective: *most interesting*
Irregular Adjectives *good* *bad*	 *best* *worst*

- We use superlative adjectives to say a thing or person has the most of a particular quality. We use ***the*** with a **superlative adjective**.
  Daniel is the tallest person in his family.

GRAMMAR PRACTICE

UNIT 6

Comparatives

1 Match the adjectives with their opposites.

1 big	d	a	unhealthy
2 boring		b	short
3 easy		c	new
4 tall		d	~~small~~
5 old		e	difficult
6 healthy		f	interesting

2 Write the comparative form of the adjectives in the box next to the comparative with the same spelling rule.

bad comfortable heavy nice ~~old~~ thin

1 smarter _older_
2 bigger ______
3 safer ______
4 easier ______
5 more interesting ______
6 better ______

3 Write sentences with comparatives about Amy's family.

1 my sister / short / me
My sister is shorter than me.
2 my brother / young / me
______
3 my sister / funny / my brother
______
4 my mom / thin / my dad
______
5 my brother / old / my sister
______
6 my / cousin / intelligent / me
______

Superlatives

4 Complete the chart with the superlative.

Adjective	Comparative	Superlative
high	higher	1 _the highest_
amazing	more amazing	2
easy	easier	3
bad	worse	4
popular	more popular	5
big	bigger	6

5 Complete the sentences with the superlative form of the adjectives in parentheses.

1 I think my dad is the _best_ (good) dad in the world.
2 Many soccer players are the ______ (rich) people in sports.
3 My mom says Formula 1 racing is the ______ (fast) sport.
4 This is the ______ (heavy) bag in the world! What do you have in it?
5 I think hockey is one of the ______ (dangerous) sports.
6 Which is the ______ (easy) sport to learn?

6 Complete the text with the comparative or superlative form of the adjectives in parentheses.

On Saturdays, I usually go and see my cousin play soccer. She's [1] _the best_ (good) player on the team. She always scores [2] ______ (amazing) goals! She's [3] ______ (tall) player on the team, and she's [4] ______ (fast) than the others. I think she's also [5] ______ (intelligent) than her teammates because she watches what is happening all the time! She's also [6] ______ (popular) player on the team!

Simple Past: *To Be*

Affirmative		Negative	
I / He / She / It	was good.	I / He / She / It	wasn't good.
You / We / They	were good.	You / We / They	weren't good.

Questions	Short Answers	
	Affirmative	Negative
Was I / he / she / it good?	Yes, I / he / she / it was.	No, I / he / she / it wasn't.
Were you / we / they good?	Yes, you / we / they were.	No, you / we / they weren't.

- ***Was*** and ***were*** are the simple past forms of ***to be***.
  There was a special gorilla in the Barcelona zoo.
  The elephants were born without tusks.
- To form questions, we use ***was/were***. We don't use ***do***.
  Was he a white tiger? (NOT ~~*Does he was a white tiger?*~~)
  Were the elephants enormous?
- We form information questions with the ***Wh-*** question before ***was/were***.
  What was it? *Where were you last night?*

There Was/Were

	Affirmative	Negative
Singular	There was a gorilla at the zoo.	There wasn't a gorilla at the zoo.
Plural	There were three lions.	There weren't three lions.

Questions	Short Answers	
	Affirmative	Negative
Was there a gorilla at the zoo?	Yes, there was.	No, there wasn't.
Were there three lions?	Yes, there were.	No, there weren't.

- ***There was/were*** are the simple past forms of ***there is/are***.
  There was a park here. *There were two cars.*
- We use ***there was*** with singular countable nouns and uncountable nouns.
  There was a pen here. *There was some milk in the fridge.*
- We use ***there were*** with plural countable nouns.
  There were a lot of tourists in our town last weekend.
- In questions and negatives, we usually use ***any*** with plural countable and uncountable nouns
  Were there any interesting animals at the zoo?
  Was there any bread at home?
  There weren't any cats. *There wasn't any rice.*

Simple Past: Regular and Irregular Verbs

- We use the simple past to talk about completed events and actions in the past.
  I played basketball yesterday.
  He lived in Boston last year.

Spelling

Most Verbs	add ***-ed***: *show – showed*
Verbs Ending in *-e*	add ***-d***: *live – lived*
Verbs Ending in Consonant + *-y*	remove the ***-y*** and add ***-ied***: *study – studied*
Verbs Ending in Consonant + Vowel + Consonant	double the final consonant and add ***-ed***: *shop – shopped* *stop – stopped*

Irregular Verbs

- Irregular simple past verbs don't follow any pattern.
  get – got *do – did* *see – saw* *have – had*

Simple Past: Negative

	Didn't	Infinitive	Other Words
I / You / He / She / It / You / We / They	didn't	play	soccer yesterday.
		go	to the movies.

- To form the simple past negative, we use **subject + *didn't* + infinitive**.
  Javier didn't watch TV last night.
  They didn't have lunch at home today.
- We can use time expressions such as ***yesterday***, ***last night***, ***last weekend***, and ***last summer*** with the simple past. We usually put them at the end of a sentence.
  We went to a safari park last weekend.
- We use ***ago*** with the simple past to talk about when something happened. We usually put it at the end of a sentence.
  Alex arrived home two hours ago.

Simple Past: *To Be*

1 Circle the correct options.

1 The monkey *was* / *were* in a tree at the zoo.
2 The baby elephant *was* / *were* beautiful!
3 The bears *wasn't* / *weren't* very big, but the lions *was* / *were* enormous!
4 It *wasn't* / *weren't* a very interesting documentary – it *was* / *were* very boring!
5 We *was* / *were* at the zoo for hours!
6 Lalo *was* / *were* happy, but Emilia *wasn't* / *weren't*!

2 Put the words in the correct order to make questions. Then complete the answers with *was* or *were*.

1 happy / Lisa / was / ?
A: Was Lisa happy?
B: Yes, she was .
2 yesterday / were / Where / you / ?
A: ______
B: I ______ at home.
3 were / Who / with / you / ?
A: ______
B: My friend ______ at home with me.
4 the / zoo / Was / big / ?
A: ______
B: Yes, it ______ enormous!
5 most / What / animal / was / the / interesting / ?
A: ______
B: The tigers! They ______ beautiful.

There Was/Were

3 Circle the correct options.

For many years, [1]*there wasn't* / *there weren't* many people in my town, and [2]*there wasn't* / *there weren't* a place to see animals, but in 2015, everything changed – [3]*there was* / *there were* houses, people, children, and stores, and [4]*there was* / *there were* a new animal park! [5]*There wasn't* / *There weren't* any big animals, like elephants, but [6]*there was* / *there were* cute little animals, like rabbits and a lot of different birds. Now, it's my favorite place!

Simple Past: Regular and Irregular Verbs

4 Write the simple past form of the verbs in the chart.

Regular	watch	live	hate
	1 watched	5	9
	plan	stop	study
	2	6	10
Irregular	do	eat	get
	3	7	11
	go	have	see
	4	8	12

5 Complete the text with the simple past form of the verbs in parentheses.

We [1] arrived (arrive) at the animal park in the morning. My little sister [2] ______ (want) to see the birds, but they were at the other end of the park. She [3] ______ (cry) for a few minutes. Then I [4] ______ (show) her the rabbits. She [5] ______ (love) them! She [6] ______ (play) with them for hours!

6 Write the words in the correct order to make sentences.

1 week / my / went / to / dad / mountains / Last / I / the / with
Last week, I went to the mountains with my dad.
2 brown / bears / saw / big / We / two
______
3 so / we / had / My / dad / a sandwich / was / hungry,
______
4 behind / I / bear / me / heard / a
______
5 up / a / tree, / I / went / bear / ate / my / sandwich / and / the
______
6 My / the / ran / to / car / eat / his / sandwich, but / dad / didn't
______

Simple Past: Questions

Did	Subject	Infinitive	Short Answers	
			Affirmative	Negative
Did	I / you / he / she / it / we / you / they	play?	Yes, I / you / he / she / it / we / you / they did.	No, I / you / he / she / it / we / you / they didn't.

- We make simple past questions with ***Did*** + **subject** + **the infinitive**.
  Did she enjoy the yoga class?

Simple Past: *Wh-* Questions

Question Word	*Did*	Subject	Verb	Other Words
Who	did	I / you / he / she / it / we / you / they	go	with?
What time				?
Where				?
What				for?
When				?
How				?

- We form ***Wh-*** questions in the simple past with a **question word** + ***did*** + **subject** + **the infinitive**.
  What time did you go to bed?
  Where did they go on vacation?
  What did you do on the weekend?
  Who did she see there?
  How did he feel?
  When did you arrive?

Simple Past: Questions

1 Match questions 1–5 with answers a–e.

1 Did you go to the post office this morning? d
2 Did you and Antonia watch TV last night? ☐
3 Did the store close early yesterday? ☐
4 Did your friends go to the bowling alley with you? ☐
5 Did our English teacher correct our homework? ☐

a No, she didn't.
b Yes, we did.
c Yes, they did.
d ~~Yes, I did~~.
e No, it didn't.

2 Look at the information about the activities Sergio and Andrea did on the weekend. Write short answers.

	Go Bowling	Clean Bedroom	Visit Grandparents	Go Swimming
Sergio	✓	✗	✓	✗
Andrea	✗	✓	✓	✗

1 Did Sergio go bowling? Yes, he did.
2 Did Sergio clean his bedroom? ______
3 Did Andrea clean her bedroom? ______
4 Did Sergio visit his grandparents? ______
5 Did Andrea go swimming? ______
6 Did Sergio go swimming? ______

3 Write questions and short answers.

1 your cousins / see / the fish / at the / aquarium ✓
A: Did your cousins see the fish at the aquarium?
B: Yes, they did.

2 Daniel / go to / the skate park / yesterday ✗
A: ______
B: ______

3 you and Melody / meet / at the movies / today ✓
A: ______
B: ______

4 Olga / do / judo / last year ✗
A: ______
B: ______

5 you / stay / at the hospital / for a long time ✓
A: ______
B: ______

Simple Past: *Wh-* Questions

4 Circle the correct options.

1 A: *What* / *Where* did you do on the weekend?
B: I stayed at home.

2 A: *Where* / *When* did they play handball on Sunday?
B: At the gym.

3 A: *What* / *Who* did he see at the ice rink?
B: Nobody he knew.

4 A: *How* / *When* did he feel?
B: Not very well.

5 A: *How* / *What* time did they leave?
B: About 5 p.m.

6 A: *When* / *Who* did they catch the train?
B: Early this morning.

5 Complete the conversation with *Wh-* question words from Exercise 4.

Eduardo: I like your phone. [1] Where did you get it?
Ali: It's from the new shopping mall.
Eduardo: Was it expensive?
Ali: I don't know! It was a present.
Eduardo: [2] ______ bought it for you?
Ali: My mom. She got it for my birthday!
Eduardo: Wow, that's a fantastic present! [3] ______ did she get it?
Ali: She got it last week when we went shopping, but I didn't see her buy it!
Eduardo: [4] ______ did you feel when you got it?
Ali: Surprised and happy!
Eduardo: [5] ______ did I get you? I can't remember!
Ali: Nothing, you forgot!
Eduardo: Sorry!

Future with *Will/Won't*

Affirmative		Negative		Questions		Short Answers	
						Affirmative	Negative
I/You/He/ She/It/We / You/They	will pass the exam.	I/You/He/ She/It/We / You/They	won't pass the exam.	Will I/you/ he/she/it/ we/you/they	pass the exam?	Yes, I/you/ he/she/it/ we/you/they will.	No, I/you/ he/she/it/ we/you/they won't.

- We use ***will*** and ***won't*** to make predictions about the future.
  Computers will control our lives in the future.
- ***Will/Won't*** doesn't change in the third person.
- We change the word order when we form questions. We don't use ***do/does***.
  Will we travel in cars in the future?
- In informal English, we use the contraction ***'ll***.
  They'll sleep in a camper on vacation.

Present Continuous for Future

- We can use the present continuous to talk about fixed arrangements in the future.
  I'm meeting my friend Maite at 6:30.
  My sister's traveling to Brazil in October.
- We often use future time expressions such as ***tonight***, ***tomorrow***, ***this weekend***, ***this summer***, ***next week***, ***next month***, and ***after class/school***.
  What are you doing tonight?
  We're traveling to Paris this summer.
  Is he coming to the party on Saturday?

Be Going To

Affirmative		Negative	
I'm	going to run.	I'm not	going to run.
You're		You aren't	
He's		He isn't	
She's		She isn't	
It's		It isn't	
We're		We aren't	
You're		You aren't	
They're		They aren't	

- We use ***to be going to*** to talk about future plans and intentions.
  She's going to take her camera on vacation.
  I'm going to wear my new sneakers.
- To form the affirmative, we use **verb *to be*** + ***going to*** + **infinitive**.
  We're going to have dinner in a restaurant.
- To form the negative, we use **verb *to be*** + ***not*** + ***going to*** + **verb infinitive**. ***Not*** is usually contracted.
  They aren't going to go on vacation this summer.

Questions	Short Answers	
	Affirmative	Negative
Am I going to be there?	Yes, I am.	No, I'm not.
Are you going to be there?	Yes, you are.	No, you aren't.
Is he going to be there?	Yes, he is.	No, he isn't.
Is she going to be there?	Yes, she is.	No, she isn't.
Is it going to be there?	Yes, it is.	No, it isn't.
Are we going to be there?	Yes, we are.	No, we aren't.
Are you going to be there?	Yes, you are.	No, you aren't.
Are they going to be there?	Yes, they are.	No, they aren't.

- We form questions with **verb *to be*** before the subject.
  Is he going to tell us the answers to the homework?
- We form information questions with a ***Wh-*** question word before **verb *to be***.
  Who is he going to ask?
  What are you going to wear to the party?
  Why is Susana going to be late?

GRAMMAR PRACTICE

UNIT 9

Future with *Will/Won't*

1 Complete the sentences about a camping trip. Write *'ll* or *won't*.

1 Don't sit at the bottom of the boat. You *'ll* ______ get wet.
2 Don't make the shelter. You ______ know how to do it.
3 Don't swim in the river. It's dangerous, so you ______ be safe!
4 Don't eat and then swim. You ______ feel sick!
5 Don't walk alone at night because you ______ get lost!
6 Don't lose your compass. You ______ know how to get back to the camp.

2 Write sentences with *will* or *won't* about the things you can do on vacation.

1 have a good time ✓ *I will have a good time.*
2 get bored ✗ ______
3 go to the beach every day ✓ ______
4 stay in a tent ✗ ______
5 eat good food ✓ ______
6 do any homework ✗ ______

Present Continuous for Future

3 Complete the email with the present continuous form of the verbs in parentheses.

Hi Sandra,

How are you? It's summer break next week! I [1] *'m going* (go) on an adventure trip, and my sister [2] ______ (come), too! In August, my dad [3] ______ (take) me on a boat trip! My mom [4] ______ (not go) because she doesn't like boats! She [5] ______ (visit) my grandparents. I think you [6] ______ (fly) to England for a week. Is that right? What are you doing after that?

Jorge

4 Complete the sentences with the present continuous form of the verbs in the box.

come	go	have	~~meet~~	not visit	play

1 I'm *meeting* my friends tomorrow morning.
2 When ______ you ______ basketball?
3 ______ grandpa ______ to visit on Sunday?
4 ______ Ben and Sam ______ a party next week?
5 We ______ my aunt and uncle this weekend.
6 Where ______ you ______ shopping on Friday?

Be Going To

5 Rewrite the sentences in the negative.

1 I'm going to see my grandma next week.
I'm not going to see my grandma next week.
2 You are going to make new friends.
______
3 Marina is going to visit the wildlife park next month.
______
4 Sam is going to go to a summer camp next year.
______
5 We are going to learn how to make a shelter.
______
6 They are going to climb the mountain.
______

6 Complete the conversations with the correct form of *be going to*. Use the verbs in parentheses.

1 **A:** *What are you going to do* (do) on summer break?
B: I ______ (visit) my aunt in Chicago.
2 **A:** ______ (he / stay) in a hotel?
B: No, he ______.
3 **A:** ______ (Gabriel and Ana / go) rock climbing in the mountains?
B: Yes, they ______.
4 **A:** We ______ (not go) on vacation this year.
B: ______ (you / stay) at home?

LANGUAGE BANK

STARTER

Vocabulary

Months

January February March April May
June July August September
October November December

Cardinal Numbers

one two three four five
six seven eight nine ten

Ordinal Numbers

first second third fourth fifth sixth
seventh eighth ninth tenth

Colors

black blue green orange pink
red yellow white

Classroom Objects

board calculator chair dictionary
door notebook pen pencil poster
ruler table window

Grammar in Action

Subject Pronouns and
Possessive Adjectives
Verb *To Be*
Question Words
Whose + Possessive Pronouns
Imperatives

Writing

Useful Language

An Informal Letter

To start: Dear + Mr. (*man*) or Mrs./Ms. (*woman*) + person's surname
To end: Best wishes, Sincerely
To join two ideas in one sentence: and

UNIT 1

Vocabulary

Family Members

aunt brother cousin dad daughter
granddaughter grandma
grandpa grandson husband mom
nephew niece sister son uncle wife

Describing People

Eyes: brown, gray
Hairstyle: long, short, wavy
Hair Color: blond, brown, gray, red
Height: short, tall
Other features: beard, freckles, glasses, mustache

Grammar in Action

To Have: Affirmative and Negative
how many … ?
Possessive *'s*

Speaking

Everyday English

Are you alright?
Cool!
Gotta go!
That's funny!
That's so not funny!

Useful Language

Bye!
Hey, (Evan).
How's it going?
OK/Fine, thanks. You?
See you later.

Writing

Useful Language

An Informal Email

At the beginning: Hi, Hey, Hello
At the end: Email me soon, That's all for now, Write soon!
Contractions: I'm, He's, She's, We're, Here's, Who's
Symbols: use emojis to help express your feelings

LANGUAGE BANK

UNIT 2

Vocabulary

Daily Routines

brush your teeth   check your phone
do your homework   get dressed   get up
go home   go to bed   go to school
have breakfast   pack your bag
take a shower   wake up

Free-Time Activities

chat online   download songs   go for a bike ride
go shopping   hang out with friends
listen to music   make videos
play an instrument   play video games
read a book/magazine   take photos   watch TV

Grammar in Action

Simple Present: Affirmative and Negative
Adverbs of Frequency
Simple Present: Questions
Wh- Questions

Speaking

Everyday English

Go ahead.
It depends.
No problem.
Sure.
That's easy!

Useful Language

Is that OK?
Thank you very much for your time.
I just have some questions to ask you.
I just have one more question.
That's interesting.

Writing

Useful Language

An article

apostrophe **'**	exclamation point **!**
comma **,**	period **.**
capital letter **A**, **B**, **C**	question mark **?**

UNIT 3

Vocabulary

School Subjects

art   drama   English   geography
information technology (IT)   math   music
nutrition   physical education (PE)   science
Spanish   vocational education

Places in a School

athletic field   auditorium   cafeteria
classroom   computer lab   gymnasium
library   locker room   office   restrooms
science lab   teacher's lounge

Grammar in Action

Can for Ability and Permission
Verb Forms: (*Don't*) *Like*, *Don't Mind*, *Love*, *Hate* + *-ing*
Object Pronouns

Speaking

Everyday English

Don't be silly!
I'm stuck.
Not again!
Not great.
Oh, dear!

Useful Language

Are you sure?
Can you do me a favor?
Can you help me, please?
Do you need a hand with … ?

Writing

Useful Language

A Description

for example
like
such as

LANGUAGE BANK

UNIT 4

Vocabulary

Food and Drink

apples bananas beans carrots cheese
chicken chocolate eggs fish
juice meat rice soda water

Adjectives

cold delicious disgusting fresh healthy
hot salty spicy sweet unhealthy

Grammar in Action

Countable and Uncountable Nouns
A/An, Some/Any
There Is/Isn't, There Are/Aren't
Much, Many, A Lot Of

Speaking

Everyday English

Enjoy!
Here you go.
No problem.
No worries.

Useful Language

Can I have … ?
Can I help you?
How much is that?
I'd like a/an/some …
Is that everything?
That's … , please.
What kind?
What's in the … ?

Writing

Useful Language

A Description

We use *and* to add similar information.
We use *but* to contrast different information.
We use *or* when there is a choice (usually between two things).

UNIT 5

Vocabulary

Clothes

boots cap flip-flops hoodie jacket
jeans shirt shorts
skirt sneakers sweatpants T-shirt

Accessories

belt bracelet earrings gloves necklace
purse ring scarf sunglasses umbrella
wallet watch

Grammar in Action

Present Continuous
Simple Present and Present Continuous

Speaking

Everyday English

It's a bargain.
It's perfect.
No, honestly.
You're in luck!

Useful Language

Can I help you?
Can I see the … one, please?
Do you have it in a different (size/color/style)?
How about this one / these?
I'm looking for …
It comes in …

Writing

Useful Language

A Description of a Photo

in the back
in the middle
on the left/right
next to (someone)

LANGUAGE BANK

UNIT 6

Vocabulary

Sports

basketball football gymnastics
hockey rock climbing rugby running
sailing swimming table tennis
track and field volleyball windsurfing yoga

Sports Verbs

bounce catch climb dive hit jump
kick lift pass run score throw

Grammar in Action

Comparatives
Superlatives

Speaking

Everyday English

Got them!
Look!
That's crazy!
What are we waiting for?
Why not?

Useful Language

Do you want to go?
How much are the tickets?
Let's buy them.
Let's go.
They're ($145).
What's the (quickest/best/cheapest) way to get there?

Writing

Useful Language

A Profile of an Athlete

We use *also* and *too* to give extra information.
We use *also* after the verb *to be*.
We use *also* before other verbs.
We use *too* at the end of a sentence.
We use a comma before *too*.

UNIT 7

Vocabulary

Animals

Birds:
duck eagle parrot
Mammals:
bear donkey giraffe hippo horse
lion monkey mouse whale
Reptiles:
crocodile snake

Adjectives

beautiful cute dangerous heavy
huge large lazy light long noisy
quiet safe short smart tiny wild

Grammar in Action

Simple Past: *To Be, There Was/Were*
Simple Past: Regular and Irregular Verbs

Speaking

Everyday English

No way!
Really?
Wow!
You're joking!

Useful Language

How was (the field trip)?
It was (really cool).
What about (lions)?
What was (it) like?

Writing

Useful Language

An Article

In 2017
On October 10, 2015
Several years ago

LANGUAGE BANK

UNIT 8

Vocabulary

Places in Town

aquarium | bowling alley | gym | hospital | ice rink | movie theater | parking lot | post office | shopping mall | skate park | swimming pool

Personal Possessions

bus pass | camera | concert ticket | headphones | ID card | keys | laptop | money | passport | phone | portable charger | tablet

Grammar in Action

Simple Past: Questions
Simple Past: *Wh-* Questions

Speaking

Everyday English

Calm down.
Don't panic!
Gross!
Let's think.

Useful Language

Did you have it when you (got to school)?
Did you put it (in your bag)?
What did you do with it after that?
When did you last (have/use/see) it?

Writing

Useful Language

A Blog Post

I didn't hear my alarm, **so** I got up late.

UNIT 9

Vocabulary

Outdoor Life

build a shelter | catch fish | collect wood | cook over a campfire | find food and water | identify plants | light a fire | pick fruit | read a map | use a compass

Vacations

apartment | (beach/ski) resort | B&B (bed & breakfast) | cabin | camper | hotel | RV (recreational vehicle) | tent | youth hostel

Grammar in Action

Future with *Will/Won't*
Present Continuous for Future
Be Going To

Speaking

Everyday English

Easy!
Forget that.
I'm on it!
You're unbelievable!

Useful Language

How about a (movie night)?
I'm not sure about that.
I'd rather not do that.
Let's do that!
What are we going to do?
Why don't we (have a picnic)?

Writing

Useful Language

An Email

at home
in August
in the morning
on Monday
on August 3
at the airport